$22.00

THE AFRICAN MEMORY OF MARK

REASSESSING EARLY CHURCH TRADITION

THOMAS C. ODEN

An imprint of InterVarsity Press
Downers Grove, Illinois

InterVarsity Press
P.O. Box 1400, Downers Grove, IL 60515-1426
World Wide Web: www.ivpress.com
E-mail: email@ivpress.com

InterVarsity Press® is the book-publishing division of InterVarsity Christian Fellowship/USA®, a movement of students and faculty active on campus at hundreds of universities, colleges and schools of nursing in the United States of America, and a member movement of the International Fellowship of Evangelical Students. For information about local and regional activities, write Public Relations Dept., InterVarsity Christian Fellowship/USA, 6400 Schroeder Rd., P.O. Box 7895, Madison, WI 53707-7895, or visit the IVCF website at <www.intervarsity.org>.

Design: Cindy Kiple
Images: African hand-woven tapestry: Brock Meeler/iStockphoto
Mosaic of Mark: A mosaic on the walls of St. Mark's Coptic Orthodox cathedral, Alexandria, Egypt - © Ariadne van Zandbergen / Afripics.com

ISBN 978-0-8308-3933-9

Printed in the United States of America ∞

InterVarsity Press is committed to protecting the environment and to the responsible use of natural resources. As a member of Green Press Initiative we use recycled paper whenever possible. To learn more about the Green Press Initiative, visit <www.greenpressinitiative.org>.

Library of Congress Cataloging-in-Publication Data

Oden, Thomas C.
The African memory of mark: reassessing early church tradition / Thomas C. Oden.
p. cm.
Includes bibliographical references and index.
ISBN 978-0-8308-3933-9 (pbk.: alk. paper)
1. Mark, Saint. 2. Theology—Africa. I. Title.
BS2475.O34 2011
226.3'092—dc22

2011006819

P 20 19 18 17 16 15 14 13 12 11 10 9 8 7 6 5 4 3 2 1
Y 28 27 26 25 24 23 22 21 20 19 18 17 16 15 14 13 12 11

CONTENTS

PART FOUR: MARK IN THE HISTORICAL RECORD

PART FIVE: THE UBIQUITY OF MARK

ILLUSTRATIONS

MAPS

TABLES

FIGURES

ABBREVIATIONS

ACCS	Ancient Christian Commentary on Scripture. 15 OT vols., 14 NT vols.
ANF	Ante-Nicene Fathers
Bapt.	Tertullian, *On Baptism [De baptismo]*
BHG	*Bibliotheca hagiographica Graeca,* 3 vols.
BST	Bible Speaks Today
CH	Eusebius, *Church History [Historia ecclesiastica]*
Comm. Matt.	Jerome, *Commentary on Matthew [Commentoriarum in Matthaeum].* Also, Origen, *Commentary on Matthew [Commentarium in evangelium Matthaei]*
CSCO	Corpus scriptorum christianorum orientalium
Dial.	Justin Martyr, *Dialogue with Trypho [Dialogus cum Tryphone]*
DJG	Joel B. Green, Scot McKnight and I. Howard Marshall, eds. *Dictionary of Jesus and the Gospels.* Downers Grove, Ill.: InterVarsity Press, 1992.
Girgis	Samir Fawzy Girgis. *A Chronology of Saint Mark.* Cairo: St. John the Beloved Publishing House, 2002.
Hom. Matt.	John Chrysostom, *Homilies on Matthew [Homiliae in Matthaeum]*
HP	Sawirus, *History of the Patriarchs of the Coptic Church of Alexandria* 1.1, Engl. trans. B. Evetts, PO 1.2. Paris, 1904.
Lives	Jerome, *Lives of Illustrious Men [De viris inlustribus]*
Marc.	Tertullian, *Against Marcion [Adversus Marcionem]*
NBD^3	I. Howard Marshall et al., eds. *New Bible Dictionary.* 3rd ed. Downers Grove, Ill.: InterVarsity Press, 1996.
OF	John of Damascus, *Exposition of the Orthodox Faith*
PL	Patrologia Latina
PO	Patrologia Orientalis

Praescr.	Tertullian, *Prescription Against Heresies [De praescriptione haereticorum]*
REC	Birger A. Pearson and James E. Goehring, eds. *The Roots of Egyptian Christianity.* Philadelphia: Fortress Press, 1986.
Shenouda III	H. H. Pope Shenouda III. *Beholder of God: Mark the Evangelist: Saint and Martyr,* trans. Samir F. Mikhail and Maged S. Mikhail from the 4th ed. Santa Monica, Calif.: St. Peter and St. Paul Coptic Orthodox Church, 1995.
TNTC	Tyndale New Testament Commentaries
TUGAL	Texte und Untersuchungen zur Geschichte der altchristlichen Literatur
Weymouth	*The New Testament in Modern Speech.* 6th ed. 1952.

PREFACE

NOT FOR AFRICANS ALONE

The African memory of Mark is not for Africans alone. It is a story of heroism, leadership, strategic vision and sacrifice. It is a story long known by parents of little ones, and by pastors and teachers. It has been learned by heart and celebrated by millions of Africans over two thousand years. For many Africans, it has long been a moving epic for grandmothers to tell granddaughters and fathers to tell sons. For others in the modern world, it is a bold story of a saint whose history is mixed with legend. After two thousand years, the traditional African narrative of Mark still calls young Africans to a world vision and to risk-laden commitment. Young people instantly bond with its prophetic hopes.

It is first of all an African story. But the world is watching. This is not just a story for one continent but for all. Whoever values courage in telling the truth will be inspired by it. All continents have been affected by the resilience and resourcefulness of the African followers of Mark. Today they number over four hundred million believers—Catholic, Orthodox, Protestant and Pentecostal. By 2025 all of these are projected to exceed a half billion people on that great continent alone. More Anglicans live in Africa than in England. To anyone who has a heart for Africa, this story begs to be told accurately. For Westerners it supplies a missing chapter that helps to resolve many of the mysteries otherwise dangling in the biblical references to John Mark.

Today it may seem to be a superficial academic debate. But for many it probes a deep well of faith, hope and love that reaches into the heart of world Christianity. Christians today around the world have been interceding and caring for Africa amid its ongoing tribulations. They have been providing food relief and economic assistance; built hospitals and supplied medicines for HIV-AIDS and malaria. It is time now for world Christians to benefit from African Christianity, as they once did in ancient times. The roots of African Christianity lie in Mark. His story is waiting to be told to those who have not heard it. This story illumines Africa's venerated intellectual traditions. It introduces us to brilliant texts from ancient times. It encourages freedom from the syndrome of diminished self-esteem in Africa that followed on the harsh heels of colonialism.

TO THOSE WHO ARE LISTENING

New discoveries about this history are finding a ready audience among a wide variety of people. Among them:

- parents of children who have never heard the stories of African Christianity
- African Americans who yearn to discover more about their premodern, precolonial African Christian ancestors
- those who have not grasped how profoundly the early African exegetes became a seedbed for Western Christianity
- students of the Bible who have studied Mark without ever hearing of the African memory of him
- young African scholars and their teachers in the many cultures of the great African continent
- travelers who visit the ancient cities of Africa that had five hundred years of Christian teaching and life (Carthage, Alexandria, Tripoli, Luxor), hoping to find something of their own Christian roots buried in the sands and portrayed on stones
- Western historians sincerely seeking to reexamine neglected African voices still buried in the archives of libraries
- lay and professional readers of the Lives of the Saints, and the Desert

Fathers and Mothers, and of the ancient ecumenical Christian minds

- peace and justice advocates who wonder about the African roots of the modern quest for justice, especially racial and gender fairness

As director of the Center for Early African Christianity housed at Eastern University in the Philadelphia area at St. Davids, Pennsylvania, I have been charged with a unique vocation uncommon in Western academic circles: to develop a team of international scholars, analogous to the team that produced the Ancient Christian Commentary on Scripture, whose primary interest is in the texts and teachings of early African Christianity. For those who wish to learn more of this project, all are invited to seek out the Center's website: earlyafricanchristianity.com. It will enlarge this discussion, which is introductory. It will provide many useful follow-up sources, descriptions and reflections for those who want to go deeper. This is the exciting mission to which a growing number understand themselves to be called. Our goal has been to grasp the wisdom of ancient Christian texts written on the continent of Africa and to communicate them to modern readers.

Professional scholars are not the primary audience of this study. They remain an influential group, but the discussion here is primarily for ordinary believers who enjoy the special pleasures of Scripture study. We do not expect to achieve unanimous agreement among scholars concerning the true identity of Mark. It is beyond our expectation to try to convince everyone in the professional communities of distinguished New Testament scholars. We ask only for an open hearing for some neglected texts, sources and ideas that echo out of Africa—particularly those about Mark. The African story of Mark deserves retelling in a way that young people can understand and appropriate. This is the first full-length book in recent decades, as far as I can find, to make a reasoned case for the African memory of Mark.

THE CLASH OF ASSUMPTIONS

The African memory has been largely ignored in the West, first in the universities, then among biblical scholars, and hence among those whose views have been informed by them. But many fresh voices within the academic community are reevaluating their attitude to tradition. This book reassesses the value of tradition with respect to Mark as Gospel writer, interpreter of Peter and evangelist to Africa.

Useful investigative journalism includes both news reporting (including current research) and editorial writing (including advocacy and opinion) in the same publication. These pages embrace both interests. Indicators will be clear when I toggle from one to the other. Due to its subject matter focused on ancient African narratives, we will not be bound to some narrow empirical standards common in the West. This exercise requires more: courage and imagination. My intent is not to add courage and imagination to the interpretation of the events, but to convey accurately the courage and imagination that the events required.

THE DECISION MAKERS WILL BE YOUNG AFRICANS

These pages are primarily addressed to youthful Christian believers on the African continent. Western intellectual dominance is waning. The future lies in the minds and hearts of the up-and-coming leaders of the Global South. The largest numbers of them are emerging in Africa. The rapid growth of Christian believers in Africa has made them a formidable force in the vision of the Christian future. Yet the distribution of books, journals, texts and translations faces many obstacles on the multiethnic African continent. The obstacles include linguistic, political, and economic impediments. Dozens of regional languages compete. Distribution channels are not yet as highly developed as they someday will be.

This is why the unifying, consensual, ecumenical work to be done on Mark will rely heavily on internet and digital technology in its early phases. The first phase is to nurture an international conversation whose vital center is young African scholars. The focus is not on North America or Europe or the Western academic world. Young men and women on the continent of Africa will provide the leadership for the later phases of scholarship, curricular development, text translation and social implications. Those from other continents who have a heart for Africa, including many global Christians of African descent, will be probing the implications of early African Christianity for societies today. Only then will the African memory of Mark be better understood with respect to its importance for the worshiping communities.

Why does the decisive arena lie not in Euro-American academic circles but on the African continent? Why will the decisive participants be young Africans? Why will so much of the destiny of Christianity in our time be decided in Africa? Why will young Africans take the lead? They have the most at stake and the greatest human resources for accomplishing the tasks.

These pages intend to strike at the heart of the issue of what Africa has to offer world Christianity. Its future contribution will be built on a better understanding of its neglected past.[1]

We will begin with Mark. Here we can show how the forgetfulness of Western Christianity has worked mischievously in one neglected but important arena of early Christian history. I am speaking of the brilliant intellectual history of ancient African Christianity.

---

[1]For recent African discussions of the African future, see works in the bibliography by Tokunboh Adeyemo, Bénézet Bujo, Byang H. Kato, Kä Mana and J. N. K. Mugambi.

1

A BOY NAMED JOHN MARK

Over two thousand years ago a great African city overlooked a blue sea. Behind it to the south were the Green Mountains and vast stretches of the plains and deserts of the great continent of Africa. The sea is the Mediterranean. This famous city was called Cyrene, whose ancient ruins are still found in the mountain clefts of Libya.[1]

From the outset Cyrene was a city of refugees who took root in this advantageous mountain slope near the sea. The Greeks under conditions of starvation had long been migrating to the African continent—from the sixth century B.C., hundreds of years before the story of Mark begins. More pertinently, refugees of Jewish descent had lived in this African city as permanent residents for three centuries before Christianity appeared. They lived in Africa long enough to consider themselves as a people belonging to the African continent and lodged within its cultures. They considered Africa their home. They, like all Cyrenians, traded and interacted with the surrounding native tribes of the Maghreb (Guarantians, Libyans, Berbers, Taureg and others).

These Diaspora Jewish traders and farmers had lived in Africa for over a millennium before the Arab conquest. That time frame stretches from the third century B.C. to the seventh century A.D. They were as

[1]For recent background discussions of Egyptian, Maghreb and North African history, see the works in the bibliography by Jamil M. Abun-Nasr and Roger S. Bagnall.

indigenous to Africa as other great African refugee cities to the south (Axoume, Mogadishu, Oran, and later Nairobi and Dakar). No one would ever think of Casablanca as anything other than an African city—so it was with Cyrene, both on the maps and in the world of commerce and intellectual life. With centuries of sustained African presence, the Jews of Cyrene had become permanent residents of the African continent. By definition, those who had been living for centuries on the African continent are rightly called Africans.

Cyrene did not live as if detached from the rest of its home continent. The city was not, like Alexandria and Carthage, clustered on the protected seacoast cove as basically a port city. Rather, Cyrene was an inland city. It had an agricultural base high up in the Green Mountains. But like Alexandria, it became an African asylum city accessible to refugees fleeing from other countries. As Geneva would later become a sixteenth-century refugee city for Protestants, so did Cyrene become, long before the Christians arrived.

WHAT WERE JEWS DOING IN AFRICA?

In the times of the Maccabees, the Jews of Palestine were suffering through harsh wars, population displacement and foreign occupation. Many Jews had fled to the safety of Africa during the years from the third century B.C. to the first century. Most went to either of two cities of refuge: Cyrene or Alexandria. Especially when trouble arose in Cyprus, many Jews migrated to these cities. They remained religiously observant Jews while living, trading and thriving in Africa. They plowed the soil of Africa. Their livestock fed on African seeds and leaves. In this way Jews came to dwell as permanent residents for many generations in Cyrene and around Alexandria. These were among the most crosscultural cities of the continent.

Many resident Jews, after a long struggle with economic hardship, became prosperous citizens of Africa. The African Jews adapted their ways to the way of life of their continent, while remaining faithful to the Mosaic covenant. This covenant called for seasonal visits back to the sacred temple and city of Jerusalem. Their religious leaders were called Levites, well learned in Hebrew Scriptures. They had highly developed religious and moral sensibilities.

Many Jews spoke Berber. Berber Jews were called Maghrebim. Their garb was similar to the Berbers. Their religion was embraced by some Berbers, at times including whole tribes. The Judaization of some Berber tribes from northern Libya toward the Saharan oases took place before the end of the first century.[2] Judeo-Berber as a language was not only used in commerce, but for explaining religious texts, and it was sometimes written using Hebrew characters. Along with Hausa and Somali, the Berber language is of Afroasiatic origin. It is considered an aboriginal language of North Africa.

THE DIASPORA JEWS OF CYRENE (200 B.C.–A.D. 120)

Cyrene and its surrounding territory, Cyrenaica, is found on the map in the northernmost part of the continent of Africa, in modern-day Libya (see map 1). Cyrene was on the northern slope of the great Green Mountains, only a short sea distance due south from Greek Peloponnesus and the Greek island of Thera, from which its founding inhabitants came. Any well-traveled first-century Jew from African Cyrenaica would have little difficulty speaking Greek. Cyrene had been Greek speaking for six centuries before Mark was born.

Cyrene was an international trading city, but located inland and upland in the mountains where it enjoyed a favorable climate. It was sufficiently near the port of Apollonia to be active in international commerce, particularly in the therapeutic and mysterious medicine called Silphium, over which it had a monopoly. Being an inland city it was more indigenized to inland African ways than most other African port cities located directly on the coast.

Cyrene of the first century had a sizeable Jewish population. Some of its Jewish citizens were known to be actively messianic in their hopes and historical perspective. Messianic Jewish enclaves had already been actively present in Cyrenaica long before Mark arrived. This long-

---

[2]Eugène Albertini, *L'Afrique romaine: notes prises aux conférences faites par m. Albertini . . . février-mars 1922* (Algiers: Fontana, 1922); ET *Roman Africa, a Series of Lectures Delivered in February and March 1922,* trans. G. P. Chruchill (Algiers: Impr. administrative et commerciale É. Pfister, 1927); cf. Marcel Simon and André Benoit, *Le judaïsme et le christianisme antique: d'Antiochus Epiphane à Constantin,* 3rd ed. (Paris: Presses universitaires de France, 1991).

standing Diaspora Jewish population lived amid the thriving multiethnic inland city of Cyrene, a city of sufficient size to have Greek, Roman, Punic, Berber and Nilotic speaking peoples in the mix. Prosperous Cyrenian Jews were internationally well connected. They depended on multilingual communication skills, similar to those in Carthage, Pelusium, Tyre and Cyprus.

The early Christians of Libya emerged out of these Jewish communities, just as they did in Alexandria. Many African Jewish communities had congregants who were messianic, expecting the coming Messiah to fulfill the purpose of God in history. The Christians were those who thought that the Messiah had come and his name was Jesus. They differed from other Jews chiefly in one obvious dissimilarity—orthodox Jews thought that the Messiah was still to be expected.

WHAT WERE CYRENIANS DOING IN JERUSALEM?

However different these messianic Jews and new proto-Christians were, they were deeply engaged in a debate about the meaning of universal human history and providence. They sought through Scripture to discern how the God of Israel was fulfilling his promises even within the catastrophic circumstances of the Diaspora. We see this debate beginning in the second century B.C. and later continuing through the fifth century A.D. in the writings of leading Jews and Christians on the African continent. After Philo came Clement, Origen, Athanasius, and later Cyril. The emerging communities of Christian believers regarded their mobility and cosmopolitan culture and worldwide interconnectedness as a providential act for which God's grace and providence had long been preparing them.[3]

There were tribal conflicts and civil disturbances in Cyrenaica in the times immediately before the New Testament. It would hardly have been surprising if a crosscultural Levitical family like the family of John Mark would flee temporarily to visit Palestine for ceremonial purposes and then immigrate permanently to Jerusalem. Following civil disturbances in Cyrene (A.D. 5–20), according to African memory (sy-

[3]Eusebius, *Preparation of the Gospel* 1-4.

naxaries, Shenouda III and Sawirus, *HP*), the family of Mark left Cyrenaica for Palestine where Mark and his mother became engaged in the company of Jesus of Nazareth. The traditional African narrative of Mark begins with his birth in Cyrene (ca. A.D. 5–15), and from there tracks him to Jerusalem, to Rome, back to Cyrene in Africa and finally to his death in Egypt. But where is the corroborating evidence? Our task begins by setting forth the scattered pieces of circumstantial evidence that show that the African narrative of Mark is in many ways more plausible than we may have imagined.

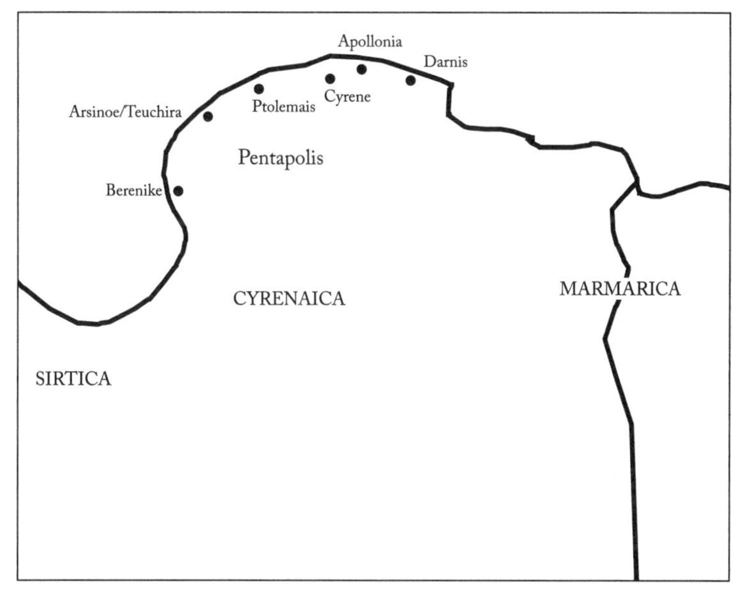

Map 1. Cities of the Pentapolis in Cyrenaica, Libya

A BOY IS BORN NAMED JOHN MARK

Around the beginning of the new millennium (early first century A.D.) a boy was born to a Jewish family of Cyrene. His father's name was Aristopolus (or variously Aristobulus, Aristobolus, Aristo-Paulus), and his mother's name was Mary. They were of the tribe of Levi. Closely adherent to Jewish customs, they returned to Jerusalem, if possible, several times a year for seasonal feasts. The boy's name signaled his multicultural family background. It was John Mark. That name brought together a Hebrew name (John) with a Latin name (Mark, variously

Marcus, Marcos). When wars, pillaging and civil disturbances came to Cyrene early in the first century, this boy's family was forced by encroaching marauders to move from Africa to Palestine.

We hear of Mark next in Jerusalem, where his mother had access to a spacious place of residence (Acts 12:12), possibly with an upper room as African memory understands, the same upper room as noted in Mark 14:15 and Acts 1:13. As a young man, Mark and his mother joined the followers of Jesus. They became a part of a culture-transforming movement within Judaism. Later Mark would be the first among the disciples to write the good news of the coming of this incomparable person who changed his life entirely. Mark's story about Jesus became the oldest of all the surviving written efforts to tell non-Jews of the good news of the beginning of Christianity. Mark became the pattern for all subsequent reports of the history of Jesus.[4]

This boy who grew up in Africa was also remembered as the first one to take the good news of Jesus, Son of God, back to Africa. This is why he is so much loved and honored by Christians in Africa today. I want to retell this story just as it has been told over centuries on the African continent—how John Mark, according to these traditions, came from and returned to Africa to become the first person sent by Jesus' followers to teach firsthand of Christianity on the African continent. This story will clarify how and why this boy became proficient in several languages, and how those gifts and cultural experiences shaped his calling to return to Africa. John Mark's mother would be chosen by Jesus himself to offer hospitality to the earliest disciples. Mark's life would end in the most populous city of Africa: Alexandria on the coast of the Nile delta. Out of this city, the most influential intellectual center of the whole Mediterranean world, came the first Christian school. It was a catechetical school, designed to communicate the gospel to the world. Its distinctive learning process, from apostolic texts and in dia-

[4]For recent discussions of technical issues on Mark's Gospel, see Ernest E. Best, *The Gospel as Story* (Edinburgh: T & T Clark, 1983); John R. Donahue and Daniel J. Harrington, *The Gospel of Mark* (Collegeville, Minn.: Liturgical, 2002); W. R. Telford, *The Theology of the Gospel of Mark,* New Testament Theology (Cambridge: Cambridge University Press, 1999); Ben Witherington III, *The Gospel of Mark: A Socio-Rhetorical Commentary* (Grand Rapids: Eerdmans, 2001).

logue with culture, was born in Africa. Out of Mark's life and death came an enduring gift to all early Christians: the emergence of African Christianity.

SOME DIFFERENCES BETWEEN AFRICAN AND WESTERN PERCEPTIONS OF MARK

While the African memory, as we will see, holds that Mark was born in Cyrene and died in Alexandria, the rest of the world has seldom listened. Despite the neglect, African memory is beginning to be reread and reconsidered. Meanwhile ordinary African Christians hold Mark close to their hearts as one of their very own—as the first witness to Christian faith in Africa. Western scholars have tended to treat Mark as one who shows up frequently throughout the New Testament but is probably Palestinian in origin, and almost never regarded as African. The problem: African popular memory of Mark is very different from the Western memory. The African narrative is often pigeonholed as unsupported by reliable textual evidence and thought to be naive, since accompanied by miracles, dreams and visions.

It deserves to be read as what it is: the story of a saint.[5] It asks to be read through the eyes of those who conveyed it, not through modern eyes alone. This is a different genre than that of much modern historical inquiry. The reading of this genre of literature requires what Paul Ricoeur calls a "second naiveté"[6]—second in the sense that the reader has been disillusioned by modernity from the first stage of naiveté where belief was the source of immense energy. Having been obscured through empirical criticism, it is being rediscovered.

The birthplace and martyrdom of Mark the apostle provides a stun-

[5]For discussions of Egyptian and other African martyrs and saints, see Theofried Baumeister, *Martyr invictus* (Münster: Regensberg, 1972); Hippolyte Delehaye, "Les martyrs d'Égypte," *Analecta Bollandiana* 40 (1922): 5-154, 299-364; De Lacy O'Leary, *The Saints of Egypt* (1937; repr., Whitefish, Mont.: Kessinger, 2005); Tito Orlandi, "Hagiography," in *The Coptic Encyclopedia*, ed. Aziz S. Atiya, 8 vols. (New York: Maxwell Macmillan International, 1991), 4:1191-97; idem, "La patrologia copta," in *Complementi interdisciplinari di patrologia*, ed. Antonio Quacquarelli (Rome: Città Nuova, 1989), pp. 457-502; idem, *Storia della Chiesa di Alessandria*, 2 vols. (Milan-Varese: Istituto editoriale Cisalpino, 1968–70); C. Wilfred Griggs, *Early Egyptian Christianity from Its Origins to 451 C.E.* (Leiden: Brill, 1993).

[6]Paul Ricoeur, *The Symbolism of Evil* (Boston: Beacon Press, 1967); cf. Mark I. Wallace, *The Second Naiveté: Barth, Ricoeur, and the New Yale Theology* (Macon, Ga.: Mercer, 1990).

ning case in point where there are stark differences between European and African perceptions of both the data and the interpretation of the documents. If the outcome of this inquiry turns out to be a bit contentious at points, it hopes to be stimulating for the right reasons and with guarded positive results.

My first task is to clarify specifically what I mean by *African memory*.

PART ONE

The African Memory of St. Mark

2

DEFINING AFRICAN MEMORY

What do I mean by the term *African memory?* The African memory is the characteristic way of looking at history from within the special experience and outlook of the continent of Africa. *Memory* does not here refer to the *contemporary* African memory alone, but to a two-thousand-year-long *history* of a way of remembering. It is memorable because it embraces a long-shared tradition of intellectual vitality. This tradition has borne extensive literary fruits over many centuries. It has produced an astonishing history of textual output. It has a literary history that has had decisive effects upon subsequent human history. It is how Africans, taken as a whole, have historically viewed events and persons, and how they still characteristically remember them.[1] To qualify under the rubric of "African memory" an alleged event must have these characteristics:

- the event has been commonly remembered on the continent of Africa
- the event is remembered in the same or very similar ways
- consent to the event is uncoerced
- the event has been remembered over many generations of Africans

[1]For recent discussions of a characteristic African memory/story/imagination, see works in the bibliography by Ernest Best, Bénézet Bujo, Ogbu Kalu, Lamin Sanneh and David E. Wilhite.

- the narratives of the event have been told in many of the indigenous languages of the African continent

In the case of the African identity of Mark, his birth, life and death in Africa have been:

- well known and the story retold in every part of the African continent
- remembered in a similar way with similar root sources
- with full and free voluntary consent
- for nearly two thousand years, six centuries prior to Islam
- in virtually all of the major indigenous languages of Africa[2]

It takes both space and time to make a memory. This memory is identified in a succession of revered sacred and secular texts stretching out over many centuries, cultures and languages. Continent-wide African Christianity is best understood through this textual history that begins with Mark.

The characteristic African memory of Mark is not vague or indefinite. It is concretized in known texts, long subject to critical examination and passionate expression: philosophical, liturgical, musical and moral. The chief sources of all these narratives of Mark, of course, are those texts of the New Testament that were written by or about Mark. The African narrative of Mark conforms to this canonical base text without overt revisions but with amplifications and applications. When I speak of "the African narrative of Mark," I am referring compositely to the melded picture of Mark derived from early African sources of the earliest Christian centuries.

It includes the ancient liturgy of St. Mark and the primitive editions of the Synaxary, a calendar of recollections of saints. The African memory of Mark is found not only in the Gospel According to St. Mark and the Acts of the Apostles, but also in the anonymous primitive Urtext of the third century, *Martyrium Marci,* and the writings of Clement of Alexandria, Origen, Athanasius and Cyril—all to be later investigated. These and other documents, and many others now unher-

[2]For recent African discussion of African identity and culture, see works in the bibliography by Bénézet Bujo, Kwame Bediako, James L. Cox and Gerrie ter Haar, Lamin Sanneh and Tite Tiénou.

alded, fed into the history of Sawirus ibn al-Muqaffa, bishop of al-Ashmunein, sometimes referred to as Severus.

Similarly, we might speak of the characteristic American memory of Thomas Jefferson as writer of the Declaration of Independence. The Jeffersonian memory is concretized in texts which can be examined, pondered and grasped. The African memory, as I use the term, takes into account the full weight of cumulative evidences coming out of the African continent over the length of centuries, including evidences from archaeology, epigraphic and literary sources, as well as oral traditions and stories of the saints.[3]

Much divides Christians in Africa, but the memory of Mark unites them. They are divided by (1) Protestant suspicions and stereotypes that Coptic liturgy is out of date or worse, phony, (2) long-standing conflicts since the fifth century between Catholics and Copts, and (3) Coptic pride that hesitates to concede any measure of apostolic authorization to either Protestants or Catholics.

Despite these differences, all of them are in basic agreement that Mark was the first apostle to Africa. This is a fact that makes Mark:

- foundational for the Coptic patriarchal history
- honored and celebrated in explicit annual Catholic and ecumenical liturgical recollections of Mark as the first Christian martyr of Africa
- viewed by almost all varieties of African Protestants, despite their diversity, with great pride and joy as their earliest apostolic ancestor
- the delight of both African Pentecostals and Orthodox in celebrating the outpouring of the Spirit at the house of Mary the mother of Mark as the setting of the original Pentecost in Jerusalem

Those who are looking for an ecumenical beginning point for bringing together diverse Christian viewpoints of African Christianity will turn naturally to Mark. Mark's life and mission embodied the unity of the body of Christ. Mark remains a fixed point of reference for virtually all Christian believers in Africa today.

[3]For recent African discussions of African origins of religion, including Christianity, see works in the bibliography by Paul Bowers, María Elena González Galván and Filipe Miguel Oliveira Resende, Yosef Ben-Jochannan et al., John H. Johnson and Ogbu Kalu.

IS AFRICAN MEMORY DEFINABLE?

By *Africa* in its broader sense we refer to the whole of the great continent, not part of it. Those who arbitrarily reject as non-African the ancient Mauretanian culture or the great Nubian culture are missing a palpable and real historical expression of the African spirit. Those who treat them as if they were "not really quite African" are missing a magnificent part of Africa. When I speak here of Africa, I am not referring to one half or portion of the continent (such as sub-Saharan or Nilotic), but all of it. Nor am I referring only to contemporary African writers. I am talking about a shared African historic memory of John Mark. It focuses less on his ethnicity than his faith and witness. It has been a core aspect of the African mind for over two millennia.

Some who today live on the African continent are uncomfortable about being called African. Some would prefer to be identified as Ethiopians or Nigerians or Libyans. But the most fitting way of speaking circumspectly of the vast mass of cultures of the past two millennia dwelling on this continent is: Africa. This is so, whatever may be its etymology or developing history.

The majority of Africans and non-Africans call this continent Africa. All mapmakers agree: Geographically Africa is a continent. Culturally it is a vast medley of diverse cultures and languages, but all these are bound together in a single physical space, a continent, a unique land mass. I have seen this continent by sea, rail, air, automobile and bus from Mozambique to Senegal. I have flown over its vast spaces and walked its streets in many of its cities and villages. However varied in cultures, it is one continent. So I will use the term *Africa* unapologetically as a geographical description, a single continent, aware that there remain many tensions and incongruities within that single designation.

It is an odd but understandable question to ask: Just how African was Augustine, who grew up in Numidia? How African was Athanasius who was born and bred in Egypt? Were Tertullian and Cyprian truly Africans? However valuable their contribution to world history has been, their status as genuine Africans has for odd reasons remained under a cloud in some circles.

The argument for the recovery of early African Christianity cannot easily proceed unless it can be shown that these great intellects were truly Africans, not just in a geographical sense but in spirit and cultural temperament. They were not just temporary trekkers or occupiers, but centuries-rooted Africans born and bred on this great continent. They were nurtured in families living through untold generations of African life. There is nothing phony or lacking in their African Christian identity. Many were willing to die for that identity.

A debilitating prejudice has invaded the reputation of these great African leaders, as if they were not genuinely Africans, but foreigners in disguise. This is a fairly recent Western intellectual habit that would have seemed odd to worldwide believers of the early Christian centuries. It would be somewhat akin to saying that those of English, Irish, Polish or other heritage, whose families had lived in North America for over two centuries, aren't real Americans but are (even in the twenty-first century) merely transplanted Europeans. Such Americans would take understandable offense.

This bias suggests that the African intellectual tradition cannot even claim many of its own African-born sons and daughters. This prevents Africans from fully embracing even their own great heroes and minds and saints, such as Pachomius who contributed so much to the history of prayer and the life of holy living, and Perpetua, the mother with child who set the standard for Christian witness unto death not only in Africa but in the ecumenical community of faith. This bias has wrongly dishonored the Africanness of the Libyan-born Synesius and the Numidian-born Monica.[4]

FACING RESERVATIONS ABOUT MARK'S AFRICAN IDENTITY

Those who look at the world only through modern Euro-American eyeshades will easily bypass and miss Mark's African identity. They

[4]For recent African-based discussions of Africaneity/Africanness/Africanity/Négritude (Negretude)/Pan-Africanism, see works in the bibliography by Bénézet Bujo, V. Y. Mudimbe, Léopold Sédar Senghor, Nina Silvanus, Peter Thompson, David E. Wilhite and Josiah Ulysses Young.

may characteristically doubt that there is or ever was a coherent early African form of memory about Mark. The African view is thus peremptorily dismissed, often without being given a hearing, and without examining carefully its literary and historical sources. The bias of this view is easy to show by the absence of Western literature on the African memory of Mark. There is an abundance of secondary African literature on the African Mark, but little attention has been paid to it in the West.

Meanwhile modern Western historical skepticism appears as a recent arrival in the history of interpretation of sacred texts. It is not more than two centuries old at most. This Western skepticism is now being seriously challenged by competent historians.[5] Among the first tasks of the realistic studies of early Christianity in Africa is to explore anew the alleged African origin of Mark, attested steadily during the first nineteen centuries but rejected by the critical majority of academics in the last century. Regardless of how the questions of evidence might be eventually settled, Western readers ought to keep an open mind if they seek fairness. The prevailing Western picture of a Palestinian Mark would be enriched by taking more seriously the African view. My task is to review the facts that might serve this enrichment.

WESTERN HISTORICAL SKEPTICISM CONCERNING MARK IN AFRICA

Those who are irreversibly committed to modern Western critical historical assumptions may find huge stumbling blocks on the first steps right in the middle of this road. They will be called upon to exercise an openhanded empathy for ancient African cultural assumptions. If not, they may be so predisposed to doubt that they will be forever unable to hear. Western scholars who have not yet absorbed or even scanned any of the standard classic versions of *The Martyrdom of Mark* (*Martyrium*

[5]For recent African discussions of the difference between Euro-American (Western) and African historical viewpoints, see works in the bibliography by Kwame Bediako, Jean-Marc Ela, William Leo Hansberry and E. Harper Johnson, Obgu Kalu, John S. Pobee, Lamin Sanneh and Frans J. Verstraelen.

Marci, synaxaries, Shenouda III and Sawirus, *HP*) cannot be said to be already fully informed. Many have never yet heard the fuller version of the African story of Mark's birth, life and death. If this were a minority of scholars, it would be understandable. But sadly it is typical.

Those who have decided in advance that the narrative is "mere hagiography" have already in their own minds solved the question of this inquiry before they begin.[6] Listening to that ancient narrative is the essence of this study. How listeners make up their minds about it is up to them, but those who have already decided without examining the evidence have prejudged it.

African teachers and scholars, on the other hand, have hesitated to omit altogether the tradition of Mark in Africa, despite following Western historical cues in many other ways. They are constrained by the weight of time-honored ancient social memories that arise distinctly out of Africa concerning the martyrdom of Mark. This creates an unnecessary tension between a two-thousand-year-old memory and a two-hundred-year method of inquiry. This storm blows in constantly from north to south. It has created a prevailing wind that comes at a time when Africans themselves are looking for distinctly African motifs out of which to rethink their own history and current identity.[7]

Many significant voices in primitive ecumenical Christianity have attested Mark in Africa—"the ancient presbyters" recalled by Clement, as well as Eusebius, Jerome and John Chrysostom, and most other classic Christian writers. Now their voices are belatedly being reconfirmed by a spirited initiative within contemporary scholarship. There has emerged a small but growing number of scholars who are prepared to reexamine the evidence for Mark as founding father of the African church. It may be much more persuasive than it was once thought to be.[8]

---

[6]For serious discussions of hagiography, see works in the bibliography by J. K. Elliott, De Lacy O'Leary and Tito Orlandi.

[7]For recent Euro-American discussions of the Markan narrative, cultural location and theology, see works in the bibliography by Paul C. Boyd, Michael C. Kirwen, María Elena González Galván and Filipe Miguel Oliveira Resende, and Laurenti Magesa.

[8]Among African scholars who have prepared the way for this discussion among Euro-American

REEXAMINING THE SUCCESSION OF LEADERS FOLLOWING MARK

Properly setting forth the succession of leaders following Mark has been a central concern of African Christianity. Getting this succession right has been crucial to the establishment and transmission of apostolic truth in early African Christianity. This list was never treated casually. It was never secondary to other more important matters. It was never inconsequential. It was never until recently considered merely a matter of political manipulation but rather viewed as guided by the Holy Spirit. It had a firm biblical and theological base. To many modern writers these matters have been the opposite. Their starting point for understanding the importance of apostolic succession has been largely its political consequences, based on the need for the institution to acquire legitimacy. Core arguments for apostolic continuity have been steadily set forth from the earliest times, not only by Paul, Ignatius and Irenaeus, but also by Clement, Origen, Tertullian and Cyprian. All of these assumed continuous succession long before Eusebius (writing in the early fourth century), who is all too often cited as the primary source of the presence of Mark in Africa.

Where did the ancient ecumenical consensus obtain its strongly held views? Early African Christians answer with one voice: from the apostles themselves. Few writers before the eighteenth century would have suggested that the lists showing apostolic succession were mere matters of economics and power politics. Eusebius likely received his Alexandrian list from the primitive Church of Alexandria itself. But he could have easily confirmed it by consulting with Antiochene or Roman authorities. Least likely of all is that Eusebius guessed at it or invented it impromptu.

Eusebius was specific in holding that Mark's successor in Alexandria was Anianus by A.D. 62: "In the eighth year of the reign of Nero, Anianus was the first after Mark the Evangelist to receive the charge of the diocese of Alexandria" (Eusebius, *Church History* 2.24; hereafter *CH*). Atiya estimates the dates for Anianus as bishop of Alexandria at A.D. 68–82, assuming Anianus formally assumed the duties of bishop after Mark's

---

scholars are those who have long been working on the reassessment of African Christian identify, including Bénézet Bujo, Kwame Bediako and Lamin Sanneh (see bibliography).

martyrdom. Shenouda III sets the martyrdom of Mark as 30 Baramouda A.D. 68 (that is, the 26th of April by Western reckoning), consistent with the most common synaxaries. He, however, held that Mark ordained Anianus as bishop in A.D. 62, in agreement with Eusebius. Mark, then, according to African memory would have traveled and done missionary work outside of Africa, while Anianus served locally in Alexandria, until Mark's return to Alexandria where he was martyred in A.D. 68.

The influence of Walter Bauer has decisively affected the late-modern phase of historical studies of early Egyptian Christianity, calling into question this Coptic memory. Many of Bauer's assumptions and methods have been persuasively challenged, but his popular influence still remains. Bauer's view relies heavily on an argument from silence—that is, an argument that depends on what is *not* said, not what *is* said.

The decisive turning point in recent research came with the work of Colin H. Roberts in 1979 in his lectures published as *Manuscript, Society, and Belief in Early Christian Egypt*.[9] He showed how the earliest forms of paleo-Christianity in Egypt were developed out of the largest Jewish community in the Diaspora—in Alexandria, with a strongly Jewish vocabulary and outlook in their primitive phases. The scholars further developing this new perspective following Roberts are impressive: They are studies deftly set forth by Birger A. Pearson, Tito Orlandi, James Robinson, Roger Bagnall, Stephen J. Davis, James E. Goerhing, David Frankfurter and many others. From their studies have flowed a continuing stream of well-documented monographs on the history of Egyptian Christianity, Coptic liturgies, synaxaries and internal literary criticism. These have come from scholars in major universities from Oxford and Rome to Yale and Claremont. None of these has yet sought deliberately to argue the case for the historicity of Mark in Africa, but they have paved the way.

TOWARD A COMPOSITE CHRONOLOGY OF COMPETING MEMORIES OF MARK

What follows in table 1 is an attempt to provide a composite chronol-

[9]Colin H. Roberts, *Manuscript, Society, and Belief in Early Christian Egypt* (London: Oxford, 1979).

ogy that merges modern chronologies with traditional. No thoroughgoing attempt has yet been made to coordinate the texts of Mark, Luke-Acts, Peter, Paul, Eusebius and Jerome with the synaxaries and Sawirus, as we will in the ensuing discussion.

The African memory of Mark is an epic personal narrative. It begins with the birth and family of Mark, and their transit from Africa to Jerusalem. In traditional memory, Mark's family, fleeing civil disorder in Africa, moved to Palestine when Mark was young, sometime during the first three decades of the first century. He had joined Peter's mission by the early forties, and returned to Libya and Egypt in the forties or fifties to his death in the sixties.

The Coptic chronology places Mark back in Africa (either Libya or Alexandria) variously as early as A.D. 43 till his death about A.D. 68—earlier than most modern accounts. But assuming that Mark's appearance in Alexandria would have come after his likely service with Peter and Paul in Rome, and several years after the Council of Jerusalem in A.D. 49, his return to Africa would have occurred only after the martyrdom of both Peter and Paul. These dates are usually placed in the period of 64–68, which would have included the time of the burning of Rome under Nero and the martyrdom of Peter.

Significant indicators in early Christian traditions of Mark's very early presence in Alexandria are reportedly as early as the first years of Claudius (A.D. 41–44) or as late as the reign of Nero (A.D. 54–68, according to Eusebius, *CH* 2.24). Traditional Coptic sources hold that "the Coptic Church is based on the teachings of Saint Mark who brought Christianity to Egypt during the reign of the Roman emperor Nero in the first century, a dozen of years after the Lord's ascension. . . . Christianity spread throughout Egypt within half a century of Saint Mark's arrival in Alexandria as is clear from the New Testament writings found in Bahnasa [Oxyrhynchus], in Middle Egypt, which date around the year 200 A.D."[10]

---

[10]*Encyclopedia Coptica,* www.Coptic.net.

Table 1. Composite African chronology of Mark (*Italics* indicate disputed event or source; all dates conjectural)

Date (estimated)	**Event**	**Place** (established or traditional)	**Sources or Purported Evidence**	**Classic Consensual, Coptic and African Memory of Mark**
6 B.C.– A.D. 1	Jesus' birth	Bethlehem	Matthew 2:1 *Chrysostom* Dionysius Exiguus	consensus
A.D. 1–3	flight of Holy Family to Egypt	*Nile from Pelusium to Asuit*	Matthew 2:13-15	consensus
5–15	birth of Mark on the African continent as Diaspora Jew	*Cyrene, Pentapolis in Libya, Ebryatolis*	synaxaries, Sawirus	Martyrium Marci, Shenouda III, Girgis
5–20	civil unrest in Pentapolis, Libya, North Africa	Cyrene	Suetonius, Josephus	consensus
15–30	Diaspora Jewish Messianic movements in Africa	Freedmen's synagogue in Jerusalem, *including Jews from Cyprus, Cyrene and Alexandria*	Acts 6:9 and passim	consensus
20–30	*family of Mark immigrates from Cyrene to near Jerusalem*	Jerusalem *near Mt. Zion*	*Mark 14:12-26*, Acts 12:12	synaxary, Sawirus, Shenouda III, Girgis
33	disciples guided to Passover Supper crucifixion resurrection appearances ascension Pentecost	upper room (*Mary/Mark's home*) Golgotha tomb Mount of Olives upper room in Jerusalem—*Mary's safehouse = "where they had been staying"*	Mark 14:12-26 Mark 15:21-41 and parallel Gospel passages Mark 16:1-8 and parallel Gospel passages Luke 24:50-53; Acts 1:6-11 Acts 2:1-13; *cf. Acts 12:12; Mark 14:12-26*	consensus

Date (estimated)	**Event**	**Place** (established or traditional)	**Sources or Purported Evidence**	**Classic Consensual, Coptic and African Memory of Mark**
34–35	apostles arrested, warned, released Barnabas, Mark's cousin, lays proceeds of field sale at apostles' feet stoning of Stephen with Cyrenian and Alexandrian collusion	Jerusalem	Acts 4 and 5 Acts 4:36-37 Acts 6:8–8:1	consensus
41	gospel preached in Antioch first to Jews, then to Greeks by men from Cyrene and Cyprus	Antioch	Acts 11:19-21	consensus
43	Barnabas and Saul in Antioch *(with Mark)*	Antioch	Acts 11:22-30	consensus
43/44	persecution by Herod Agrippa martyrdom of James the Greater Peter's imprisonment Peter's flight from prison to Mary's home	Jerusalem the home of Mary, Mark's mother *(same upper room as Passover Supper and Pentecost)*	Acts 12:1-5 Acts 12:6-17	consensus
43/44	Peter departs to an "another place"	unknown	Acts 12:17	
43/44	Peter sends greetings from "my son Mark" to churches in Asia Minor	*pre-Roman refugee location—Babylon of Cairo*	1 Peter 5:13, Strabo's Geographica 17.1.30, Diodorus Siculus 1.56.3, Josephus's Antiquities 2.15.1	Girgis
44–48	famine in Jerusalem	Jerusalem	Acts 11:27-30	consensus

Date (estimated)	**Event**	**Place** (established or traditional)	**Sources or Purported Evidence**	**Classic Consensual, Coptic and African Memory of Mark**
47	famine visit of Barnabas and Paul from Antioch to Jerusalem *(with Mark)*	Jerusalem	Acts 11:30	consensus
	Herod's death	Caesarea	Acts 12:19-23	
	John Mark taken by Paul and Barnabas on first missionary trip	Jerusalem, Antioch, Seleucia, Cyprus, Salamis, Paphos, Perga	Acts 12:25–13:13	
47–48	Paul and Barnabas continue first missionary journey	Pisidian Antioch, Iconium, Lystra, Derbe, Attalia	Acts 13:14–14:25	
48	report to Antioch church	Antioch	Acts 14:26-28	consensus
49	conflict with Judaizing Christians prompts Council of Jerusalem	Antioch, Galatia and Jerusalem	Acts 15:1-21	consensus
	apostles' letter to Gentiles		Acts 15:22-29	
50–52	Paul writes Galatians	Galatia	letter to the Galatians	consensus
	Paul's second missionary journey with Silas and Timothy	Syria, Cilicia, Derbe, Lystra, Iconium, Pisidian Antioch, Troas, Philippi, Thessalonica, Berea, Athens, Corinth, Ephesus, Caesarea, Antioch	Acts 15:36–18:22 letters to the Thessalonians first letter to Corinthians	
	Paul refuses to take Mark	Antioch	Acts 15:36-38	
	Mark accompanies Barnabas to Cyprus	Cyprus	Acts 15:36-41	
53–57	Paul's third missionary journey	Galatia, Phrygia, Ephesus, Macedonia, Greece, Troas, Miletus, Patara, Tyre, Caesarea, Jerusalem	Acts 18:23–21:16	consensus

Date (estimated)	**Event**	**Place** (established or traditional)	**Sources or Purported Evidence**	**Classic Consensual, Coptic and African Memory of Mark**
56/57	Paul writes letter to Romans during three-month stay in Greece Paul greets Rufus *(of Cyrene, then in Rome, known to Mark)* and his mother (as a "mother to me")	Corinth	Acts 20:2-3 Romans 16:13	consensus
c. 57–59	Paul's arrest and trial Paul's trial before Felix Paul imprisoned Paul's trial before Festus and Agrippa	Jerusalem Caesarea Caesarea Caesarea	Acts 21:27–22:30 Acts 23:31–24:27 Acts 24:27 Acts 25:1–26:32	consensus
60–61	Paul imprisoned in Rome	Rome	Acts 28:11-31	consensus
61	*Mark in Rome during Paul's first imprisonment* Mark expected to visit Colossae	Rome Colossae	Philemon 24; Colossians 4:10 Colossians 4:10	consensus
61–62	*Mark preaches, heals and ordains future leadership for Libyan churches in the Pentapolis*	Cyrene and all of the Pentapolis	synaxary	synaxary, Sawirus, Girgis, Shenouda III
61–63	*Mark founds church in Alexandria*	*Alexandria*	synaxary	early synaxaries, Sawirus, Girgis, Shenouda III

Date (estimated)	**Event**	**Place** (established or traditional)	**Sources or Purported Evidence**	**Classic Consensual, Coptic and African Memory of Mark**
64	*Mark in Ephesus at beginning of Paul's second imprisonment* Mark requested by Paul to come to Rome with Timothy *Mark through Aquilea on his way from Ephesus to Rome*	*Ephesus* *Ephesus* *Aquilea*	2 Timothy 4:11; cf. 1 Timothy 1:3 2 Timothy 4:11 Sawirus	early synaxaries, Sawirus Girgis, Shenouda III *disputed*
64	*Mark in Rome* Nero burns Rome	Rome	Eusebius, Jerome	consensus
64–67	*Mark in Rome during Peter's second imprisonment*	Rome	*2 Timothy 4:11*	consensus
67	Paul arrested and imprisoned	Rome	2 Timothy 1:16-17; 2:9; 4:9-16	consensus
67–68	Peter and Paul martyred in Rome Mark writes Gospel *Mark evangelizes Aquilea*	Rome	Irenaeus John the Elder, Papias via Eusebius	consensus *disputed*
68	*Mark martyred April 26*	Alexandria	Eusebius, Jerome, Peter of Alexandria	synaxary, Sawirus, Girgis, Shenouda III
69	*successors of Mark in Alexandria beginning with Anianus*	Alexandria	*martyrdom sites*	synaxaries, Sawirus, Girgis, Shenouda III Martyrium Marci
70	fall of Jerusalem	Jerusalem	Josephus	consensus
71–78	Great Jewish Diaspora	ancient world	Josephus	consensus
70–120	further accounts of Mark writing the Gospel of Mark	Rome	John the Elder, Papias through Eusebius	Clement, Sawirus, Shenouda III

Date (estimated)	**Event**	**Place** (established or traditional)	**Sources or Purported Evidence**	**Classic Consensual, Coptic and African Memory of Mark**
100–120	accounts of Mark writing under Peter's direction	*Rome*	Eusebius on Papias Muratorian fragment anti-Montanist writings	consensus
130–150	Mark described as stump-fingered	Italy Rome	Muratorian fragment anti-Montanist writings Hippolytus's Philosophumena	consensus
180	vibrant presence of Christianity in Africa	Africa	Irenaeus's Against Heresies 1.10.2	consensus
c. 185–210	*references to Mark in Africa*	*Alexandria*	Clement of Alexandria's Outlines (Hypotyposeis), including Adumbrations and references to "earliest presbyters"	insufficiently examined
c. 200	*references to Mark in Africa*	*Alexandria*	Clement's presumed *Letter to Theodore* Mar Saba discovery by Morton Smith	*disputed*
190s–250s	*references to Mark in Africa*	Alexandria	Origen's homilies and commentaries	exegetical studies
c. 200s–300s	*account of Mark's martyrdom in Alexandria*	Alexandria	Martyrium Marci	liturgical hagiographic studies
320s	*account of Mark in Alexandria*	Alexandria	Eusebius's Church History	liturgical hagiographic studies
390s	*references to Mark in Alexandria*	Antioch, Bethlehem	Chrysostom's Homilies, Jerome's Lives of Illustrious Men	consensus

Date (estimated)	**Event**	**Place** (established or traditional)	**Sources or Purported Evidence**	**Classic Consensual, Coptic and African Memory of Mark**
2nd–10th centuries	transmission of proto-synaxaries in primitive forms	Egypt, Ethiopia, Rome, Antioch	calendars, synaxaries	liturgical consensus
9th century	synaxaries in Arabic	Egypt	Johannes den Heijer	Sawirus
960s–990s	History of the Patriarchs	al-Ashmunein	David W. Johnson, Johannes den Heijer, Stephen J. Davis	Sawirus

3

THE AFRICAN ROOTS

Although the evidences of Mark's birth are largely inferential and circumstantial, they are not easily dismissed. Four major ironies accompany the African traditions concerning Mark's birth, life and ministry:

- First, it is ironic that Mark's birth would take place in the most remote of the three known continents—Africa—and more so, that Mark's birth would occur in one of the most out of the way places in Africa—Libya.
- Second, it is ironic that Mark's family would be forced to flee from this most remote place to the vortex of Hebraic culture, the center of its history, its law, its social teachings and its religion.
- Third, it is ironic that this young man from nowhere would become known as the apostle to everywhere. It is from Libya that he became the universal evangelist. Geographically he covered more of the earth than Paul, witnessing on all three known continents.
- Fourth, after Mark had traveled all over the eastern Mediterranean world, it is ironic that he would then return to his own home on the African continent, and bring the embryonic form of early Christian catechesis to its greatest city, Alexandria, the intellectual and academic center of the Greek world.

The claims regarding an African Mark would be thought unimaginable if they had not been believed as true and transmitted from generation to generation by many millions of believers over such a long time.

The traditional birthplace of Mark on the African continent has always been of high importance to the long history of the churches of North Africa, and hence to subsequent Christians all over the African continent.

Here the traditional narrative is specific. The primordial narrative begins:

> There were two brothers living in a city of Pentapolis in the West, called Cyrene. The name of the elder of them was Aristopolus [elsewhere Aristopolis or Aristobulus], and the name of the other was Barnabas; and they were cultivators of the soil, and sowed and reaped; for they had great possessions. And they understood the Law of Moses excellently well, and knew by heart many of the books of the Old Testament. But great troubles came upon them from the two tribes of the Berbers and Ethiopians, when they were robbed of all their wealth in the time of Augustus Caesar, prince of the Romans. So on account of the loss of their property, and the trials which had befallen them, they fled from that province, in their anxiety to save their lives, and traveled to the land of the Jews. (Sawirus, *HP*, 135-36)[1]

Sawirus had found the core of this narrative repeatedly in earlier editions of the Orthodox synaxaries dating back to pre-Nicene times in the *Martyrium Marci*. Its primitive core has been repeated in subsequent synaxaries. "This Saint [Mark] was *born in Cyrene (One of the Five Western cities, Pentapolis—in North Africa)*."[2]

In this simple statement, the majority voice in traditional African memory points to Libya as the place of Mark's birth, likely in or near Cyrene, in the region of Cyrenaica (sometimes identified as Ptolemais

[1]Sawirus ibn al-Muqaffa, *History of the Patriarchs of the Coptic Church of Alexandria*, ed. and trans. B. Evetts, 3 vols., Patrologia Orientalis 1.2, 1.4, 5.1 (Paris, 1904–1910), 1.2:135-36. All the material on Mark is contained in PO 1.2, which will be cited from hereon as Sawirus, *HP*, with a page reference; available online at www.ccel.org/ccel/pearse/morefathers/files/severus_hermopolis_hist_alex_patr_01_part1.htm.

[2]Coptic Synaxarion for Baramouda [Ethiopic-Amharic Miyazia] 30, emphasis added. (Miyazia is one of the months in the Ethiopian Coptic year, similar to the Egyptian Coptic month of Baramouda; cf. Shenouda III.)

or Barka), in North Africa, shortly after the dawn of the first century.

From this tradition and its correlated inferences, we note that the members of the family of Mark were:

- Diaspora Jews
- wealthy cultivators and traders
- learned in Hebrew Scriptures
- living in Africa
- facing unwelcome social dislocation early in the first century
- refugees to Jerusalem, for Jews of that time a safer place than Cyrenaica

The likely inferences most congruent with the traditional narrative are based on corroborating evidence:

- the family belonged to a Diaspora economy that not only produced agricultural products but marketed them internationally
- they were pious Jews who memorized Scripture
- at the time we first explicitly meet the family of Mark in Jerusalem in Acts 12, they had already made the transition from their African homeland to "somewhere near Jerusalem"

The family of Mark mirrors the perennial vulnerability of Jews in history. It is best viewed in relation to the central deliverance narrative of Hebraic memory in Africa: the exodus. The promise of a land of milk and honey is then fulfilled in history following a long period of Israel's spiritual formation in the wilderness. Having fallen into bondage once again in the period of captivity, its recovery is promised and fulfilled in the incarnation. Africa again appears as a place of refuge in the flight of the family of Jesus to Egypt. Mark and possibly Peter flee to Africa in the Diaspora, and then return to the holy city whose center is the house of God.

In some accounts the specific location of Mark's birth is a site in Cyrenaica called Ebryatolis ("city of Jews"), but where is that? The place name may refer to the settlement where Hebrews lived in the outskirts of Cyrene, reflecting the etymology of the Hebrews as peoples descended from Shem, one of Noah's sons, through Eber ("Hebrew") and Abraham (Gen 10:21; 11:16-26), or to ivory workers, or those who lived near the waters, presumably of Cyrene, which had a celebrated flowing spring. The location of Mark's birth is reported by the African narrative most consistently, however, as the Pentapolis (the five cities of African Cyrenaica), and sometimes more specifically as Cyrene (a designation that could include the regions of the Pentapolis around Cyrene).[3]

Troubles had been brewing for decades for the Jews of Africa: wars, subjugation and rebellion. The family of Mark must have grieved in their goodbyes to African friends and neighbors. But they were going where Diaspora Jews all longed to be—the blessed temple to which faithful Jews constantly prayed to return. The holy city of Jerusalem had special meaning for the Diaspora Jews, a large number of whom had taken up permanent residence in Africa. However long their life as Jews had been rooted in the synagogue in Cyrene, they moved on to Jerusalem, with its great temple uniting Jews of all times and places. At that time the temple was the supreme architectural glory of the period of Herod the Great. Yet this very temple was soon to come to ruin, as prophesied. The Passover recorded in Mark 14 was only four decades before the temple's destruction by the Roman army of Titus.

Transit from the Libyan Pentapolis to either Alexandria or Jerusalem would have been well within their capabilities. It would be even simpler for a prosperous family proficient in sea commerce, connections and the pertinent international languages (Greek, Latin and Aramaic). These languages were necessary capabilities among the mercantile Jews of Cyrene. Small vessels could hug the seacoast of Africa, passing Gaza, continuing to Herod's spectacular port in Caesarea Palestina. From there they would travel overland the short distance to Jerusalem. If not by sea, the family in flight could have taken the well-traveled land route over established Roman roads whose milestones and settlements can still be identified between Pelusium and Gaza.

Mark is remembered as having been born to a well-traveled Diaspora

---

[3]Fr. Tadros Y. Malaty, *The Gospel According to St. Mark* (Alexandria: St. George's Church, 2003).

Jewish family of the tribe of Levi (Acts 4:36) who had sufficient trading skills, wealth and mobility to journey widely. It was an international family with crucial interests in Levitical Jewish piety and in the destiny of Jerusalem.[4]

THE AFRICAN MEMORY OF MARK'S FAMILY: FLIGHT FROM PENTAPOLIS TO PALESTINE

We are talking about a large extended family when we speak of the African narrative of Mark. What happens to John Mark as a child and youth? Though sketchy, this sequence of events is continued by Sawirus: "Now Aristobulus had a son named John [Mark]. And after they had taken up their abode in the province of Palestine, near the city of Jerusalem, the child John grew and increased in stature by the grace of the Holy Ghost." Where near Jerusalem did the young John Mark grow to maturity? No location is defined until we find his mother residing on Zion hill.

Sawirus continues: "And these two brothers had a cousin, the wife of Simon Peter, who became the chief of the disciples of the Lord Christ; and the said John whom they had surnamed Mark, used *to visit Peter, and learn the Christian doctrines from him* out of the holy Scriptures. . . . And Mary, the mother of Mark, was the sister of Barnabas, the disciple of the apostles" (Sawirus, *HP*, 136-37, emphasis added). Accordingly, Mark would be a relative of Simon Peter. The families of Mark and Peter appear to be close enough to visit and sustain an active relationship. Table 2 displays the family cast of characters as told by Sawirus and Shenouda III.

What might a reasonable observer make of the chart of family relationships in table 2? First, it is very long. It is interwoven. It is so detailed and interlaced that it appears to be a later legend with, at times, seeming contradictions, appended to a core of Gospel narratives. But what if only a small fraction of it is true? Suppose the families of Peter and Mark were in some way related, even marginally, which they would be if Peter's wife was a cousin of Mark's father and Uncle Barnabas.

[4]Samir Fawzy Girgis, *A Chronology of Saint Mark* (Cairo: St. John the Beloved Publishing, 2002), p. 27 (hereafter Girgis).

That would make it necessary to recast the Western version of the story of Mark's identity. That would be too important to ignore. But even if they were not related, the closeness of the two families is implicit in Mark's Gospel and in Luke's accounts in Acts concerning Peter, Paul, Mary and Barnabas.

We probably will never know. But some smart researcher might find a way to reassess this question by means of the frequency of family names, archaeological or epigraphic evidence, or some research technique not yet known.

The house of Mary, mother of Mark, in Jerusalem, was described in Acts as having a large room and gate and a servant, suggesting a family of wealth (Acts 1:13; 12:12-13). Jerusalem was a favored place of retirement for wealthy Diaspora Jews. Mark's relative Barnabas was also described as a person of means which he used in service to the church (Acts 4:36-37). Mark's family shows evidence of having strong religious commitments with means sufficient to motivate them to attend major Jewish liturgical festivals in Jerusalem. This was the time of the second temple before its destruction in A.D. 70. It was a time when the delight of returning to Jerusalem was dear to every pious Jew, including those in Cyrene. It was a solemn duty to make the joyful pilgrimage.

Mark was apparently handling multiple languages, according to Shenouda III.[5] His parents were able to provide him with a good education. He was able to explain Jewish customs and translate Semitic terms to a Greek or Latin audience. His mission and passion was for the Gentiles (Mk 7:3-4, 31).

The essential languages that Mark would have had or acquired must be at least Aramaic, Greek and Latin, in addition to his native Libyan tongue, and probably some Hebrew. That sounds formidable, but would not have been unusual to a well-traveled, relatively well-off Levitical Diaspora Jew.

---

[5]H. H. Pope Shenouda III, *Beholder of God: Mark the Evangelist: Saint and Martyr*, trans. Samir F. Mikhail and Maged S. Mikhail from the 4th ed. (Santa Monica, Calif.: St. Peter and St. Paul Coptic Orthodox Church, 1995), hereafter Shenouda III.

Table 2. Family relationships (*italics* indicate disputed information)

INDIVIDUALS	TEXTS	LOCATIONS
Aristopolus/Aristobulus of *Cyrene* and Rome, *father of Mark*	Romans 16:10	*Cyrene, Jordan Valley,* Rome
Mary, mother of Mark, of *Cyrene, wife of Aristopolus,* relative of Barnabas	*Mark 14:12-26;* Acts 12:12; Colossians 4:10	*Cyrene, Capernaum,* Jerusalem
Simon of Cyrene, father of Rufus and Alexander	Mark 15:21, *Romans 16:13*	Cyrene, Jerusalem, Rome
mother of Rufus *of Cyrene* living with Rufus in Rome	Romans 16:13	Rome
Paul of Tarsus who viewed the mother of Rufus as a mother to him	Romans 16:13	Rome
James and John, sons of Zebedee, fishing partners of Peter and Andrew, who were brothers mother of Zebedee's sons	Matthew 4:18; 10:2; 26:37; Mark 1:16, 19; Luke 5:10 Matthew 20:20	Capernaum Capernaum
Peter's close association with Mark, *son of his wife's cousin*, Mary of Cyrene	Matthew 8:14; Mark 1:30; Luke 4:38 as interpreted by later hagiographical literature (Sawirus), 1 Peter 5:13 hagiographic literature, Papias	Bethsaida, Capernaum
Peter's mother-in-law	Mark 1:29-31	Capernaum
Barnabas, Mark's cousin or uncle	Acts 4:36, 15:39; Colossians 4:10	Cyprus, Jerusalem, Antioch, accompanying Paul
Peter's wife (=*Strapola), cousin of Aristobolus, Mark's father*	Matthew 8:14; Mark 1:30; Luke 4:38 as interpreted by later hagiographical literature (Sawirus)	Capernaum

FROM MARK'S BIRTH IN AFRICA TO HIS RESIDENCE IN JERUSALEM

Though the references to Mark's mother are few, they come at crucial points with special consequences. The inferences surrounding these few references are staggering. Mary, the mother of Mark, is one of the most intriguing figures in the New Testament. Before the crucifixion or Pentecost or Antioch, Mark and his mother make an early appearance within the core circle of Jesus in Jerusalem. This inference hinges on the relation between the various passages that imply that Mary, the mother of John Mark, was identical with the owner of the house reported in Mark 14. If so, Mary the mother of Mark and probably her young son are reported by both Mark and Luke-Acts as residing in Jerusalem.[6] This residency appears to be established by the time when Jesus began to come forward in his active ministry, sometime around A.D. 30. Little is known of Mark's father, but the fact that only the mother and not the father of Mark is mentioned in Acts 12 may indicate that the father had died before the mother, or that the father for whatever reason was not present at the times reported in Mark 14 and Acts 12.

The constellation of New Testament texts suggest that Mark's mother Mary was devoting her energies to the observant Jewish life in the Levitical tradition. This life was almost certainly heightened by intense messianic expectations, apparently characteristic of some Cyrenaic Jews. The texts do not disclose how she became involved in the ministry of Jesus, but it is implied that she was a woman of a Levitical family with prominence among the Cyrenaic congregation, and lived in a house in Jerusalem. All these are significant limiting conditions. Pious and observant Jews would have wanted to be in Jerusalem in key times of seasonal celebrations such as Passover and Pentecost. It does not seem unusual that, given the importance of participation of pious Jews in the study and observance of Torah, they wanted to be in Jerusalem for the feasts.

[6]See Mk 14:14-15; Acts 1:13-14; 12:12. Cf. R. A. Guelich, "Mark, Gospel of," *DJG*, p. 514; A. Gelston, "Mark (John)," *NBD*^{3}, p. 731; J. R. W. Stott, *The Message of Acts* (Downers Grove, Ill.: InterVarsity Press, 1990), p. 210; R. A. Cole, *Mark*, TNTC, 2:296; I. H. Marshall, *Acts*, TNTC, 5:67; F. F. Bruce, *The Acts of the Apostles* (London: Tyndale, 1951), pp. 73, 246-47.

Messianic Jews from Cyrene would have had much in common with other known New Testament Jews from Cyrenaica, such as Simon of Cyrene, Lucius and likely Mark himself. The fact that Mark would specifically refer to Alexander and Rufus as sons of Simon of Cyrene (Mk 15:21) without further explanation makes it likely that they were well-known to his audience. Rufus and his mother may have been the ones referred to by Paul in Romans 16:13. These messianic Jews who came to Jerusalem from Cyrene were apparently ready to participate in the ongoing conversation surrounding the events of the Passover in Jerusalem at the time Jesus was crucified. They had lived through apocalyptic-like challenges in North Africa. They were motivated to draw near to the vortex of messianic activities.

THE DISPLACED FAMILY

The story of Mark is the story of a displaced family, fleeing first to the Diaspora from Palestine, and then amid troubles in Africa back to Palestine. The displaced family fleeing to Palestine became symbolic of the whole historic family of African Christians. The papa (father, abba, pope) of the family of churches of Africa was viewed, as were all ordained apostolic vessels of ministry, as a trustworthy father, thus called to be trustable to guide the family of God on this great continent.

Mark became the patriarch of the whole family of African Christianity. He was Africa's first evangelist, apostle and martyr. Here is the voice of the synaxarion: "He [Mark] was the first papa [pope] of Alexandria and one of the Seventy Apostles" (Synaxarion for Baramouda 30). The language of papa-of-the-family (pope) emerged in African Christianity during precisely the same period that it arose in Rome. *Papa* was not a term of defensive acquisition of power, but of caring love for each one in the extended family, and the right nurturing of the family toward the way, truth and life.

Imagine a map of Mark's travels as traditionally viewed (see chapter seven) compared to Paul's travels. It is apparent that Mark is more widely traveled than Paul, even if Paul's journey to Spain is included as an imagined dotted line on the map. Apart from Thomas, Mark is likely the most widely traveled of all the apostles. The ancient tradition called Mark the universal apostle because he appears in all three known continents: Asia, Europe and Africa. This differs from Thomas whose travels were focused traditionally upon a single continent, Asia, from the Near East to India. The traditional narrative assumes Mark's birth in Africa, ministries in Roman Asia and Europe, and his death in Africa. Viewed today in global perspective, this is a decisive point: Mark preached the same gospel in all three continents. He came from and returned to Africa. He was in Palestine at the crucial time of Jesus' death and resurrection. He then served in the early Christian mission that contributed to the primitive formation of the civilization of Europe. It is only when the implication of this is seen internationally that justifiable pride of African Christianity is instantly strengthened.

RECONSTRUCTING THE TRADITIONAL STORY

Why is this retelling of the events of the traditional African narrative of Mark necessary? Because it has not been told in the West. Few in the universities of the West have heard it in any detail. They do not recognize the names of Aristopolus and Lucius and Rufus of Cyrene. The texts for the story seldom appear in the syllabus of courses on Mark. The story has hardly been factored in, even modestly, in the current Euro-American literature concerning either Mark or Africa.

The historical critical questions surrounding Mark, even if urbane and fascinating, will not be complete if they do not grasp the primal story itself. It will be seen only from a Western evidentiary point of view, not from an African point of view as a story of a saint. I have told parts of this story many times on the continent of Africa, often to university students and faculties. I have seen in their eyes the moments of recognition and spiritual power. But when I tell it in North America the eyes tend to narrow toward suspicion.

The difficulty for Western Christians in listening to a non-Western account is evident, especially to those long-habituated to appeal first to historical-critical arguments. Even before listening to the story we are prone to dismiss it. This mindset prematurely rules out the traditional sources of early African Christianity before it has had a chance to be told. As a Western theologian born and bred on the assumptions of

Wilhelm Dilthey, Martin Dibelius and Rudolf Bultmann, I know how hard it was for me first to hear the African voice. As a result, it is almost impossible for us in the West even to *compare* the empirical view with the traditional view, if we have not first listened intently to the ancient story of the saint on its own merits.

By now it is easy to see that I am far more concerned about hearing the story in a way consistent with classic consensual Christianity than in trying to hammer out a shaky (and always disputable) consensus within modern scholarship. Westerners approach the ancient narrative with our own hardwired agendas.

Mark gives us an opportunity for a profound exercise in empathy. My intellectual conviction based on a lifetime of study of early sources is to trust the work of the Spirit in engendering the ancient ecumenical consensus of classic apostolic Christianity. Readers who have missed these classic arguments are able to examine them in *Classic Christianity*, where I offer an assessment of what is best and deficient about both modern and ancient methods.[7]

How much of this classic liturgical account can be confirmed or supported by other credible evidences? All the rest of these pages are devoted to an assessment of that question. In order to compare the modern evidences with the traditional narrative, it is first necessary to unpack and review the traditional narrative. This will be seen in relation to the independent evidence that can be supplied by literary, archaeological and epigraphic sources. I will be seeking simultaneously to trace these reasonable inferences as a pattern of circumstantial evidence. The quality of this evidence is comparable to most historical information consensually received on alleged ancient events.

No one can establish precisely when ancient documents passed from oral to written forms. It is our hubris that leads us to believe we can do so with high certainty. The transmission history of the synaxary narratives are clouded in the same way that the primitive oral transmission of New Testament narratives were clouded and remain forever disputable empirically. Nonetheless, the circumstantial evidence clearly indi-

---

[7]Thomas C. Oden, *Classic Christianity: A Systematic Theology* (San Francisco: HarperOne, 2009).

cates that the traditional narrative of Mark was passed along steadily, generation by generation, from the earliest decades of the Christian kerygma to the 200s A.D. when we begin to have some evidences of it in written form. With few exceptions, most of the earliest evidence, based on extant surviving documents, was diligently copied and archived from the fifth through the tenth centuries.

The Orthodox liturgy solemnly promises to tell the truth it has received. It seeks to report accurately and without addition or subtraction what it understood as having been known and remembered from the outset of ancient African Christianity. Orthodox teachers care about the apostolic ground of their truth claims. The fair and honest study of history is a necessary and useful exercise to guard those truth claims.

ANCIENT ECUMENICAL NORMS ON SCRIPTURAL AUTHORITY

The African remembrance of Mark, as seen in its liturgy and exegesis, stood strictly under the authority of Scripture (that is, texts of Paul and the Gospel writers that later became canonized as Scripture). From the outset this premise was operative. The most basic source of the information on Mark is the New Testament text itself—Mark's own Gospel and what other original apostles said about him. These occasional references are not numerous, but they are very telling. The earliest apostolic witnesses are considered normative in African Christianity. They outweigh all other forms of ecclesial memory. All subsequent traditionally remembered narratives are assumed to be accountable to and implicitly consistent with the texts of the Gospels, Acts and Paul's letters. Apostolic teaching is the judge and norm of subsequent forms of memory. The worshiping community trusts Scripture as the unique work of the Spirit in the communication of grace. The subsequent events in the African memory of its sacred tradition are also guided by the Spirit but never considered equal in authority to the four Gospels, Acts and Pauline Letters. These were early designated for reading in church, alongside the Septuagint version of Hebrew Scriptures. The same Spirit is at work in both the consensual exegesis of Scripture and its subsequent doctrinal expressions, as remembered ecumenically by the tradition of believers in Africa as well as in Europe and the Near East.

Any differences that may appear among apostolic witnesses are viewed as consistent with each other on the grounds that the apostolic testimony and its transmission was truly the work of the Holy Spirit. Articulating the internal cohesion of varied gospel texts is the task of the classic exegetes and homilists. Many of their patterns were primordially formed in Africa (especially by the Alexandrian Midrashic Jewish rabbinic and messianic traditions, and further developed by Clement, Origen, Tertullian, Augustine, Cyril the Great and their successors). The earliest postapostolic witnesses of the faith such as Ignatius and Polycarp have been remembered, recorded, guarded and transmitted with care. They became acknowledged first locally, then recognized universally in the measure of their faithfulness to the apostolic preaching. Recollections of saints and martyrs living after the time of the writing of the New Testament documents were valued as complementary to them, as seen through the prism of the African experience of martyrdom, catechesis and liturgy.

Though many alleged events that were woven into the African memory of Mark do not appear in the New Testament, they have their basis in the New Testament sacred texts as judge and arbiter of the boundaries of subsequent tradition. They have been respected for centuries as compelling recollections by the early Christians of Africa. Before formal canonization in the fourth century, all the documents that were ultimately judged as canonical were being read in church services and already received by ecumenical consent. In this way the canonical Scripture texts were echoed and reappropriated by the lives of the early Christian witnesses and writers. In Africa especially, these recollections have been preserved and carefully safeguarded through ancient liturgical rites and synaxaries. They are assumed to have reliably recorded the received tradition on Mark. In due time this narrative was received continentwide in Africa and virtually worldwide until modern times.

The most direct way to test the evidence of Mark's identity is to ask whether his good news was consistent with the earliest apostolic testimony. This pattern of appeal is seen as early as Paul's letter to the Galatians in 1:8-9. Obviously Mark's Gospel is apostolic, since it was the first to be received as such, and that with the special blessing of Peter, as well as Luke and Matthew who likely followed Mark's pattern, as is held by the majority of today's New Testament scholars. Mark comes with impeccable credentials as an apostolic witness.

Those who were chosen in the first generation of eyewitness believers had accompanied Jesus personally during his earthly journey (Acts 1:21-22), had met the risen Lord and had shown their readiness to testify to him to the ends of the earth (Lk 24:48; Acts 2:32; 3:15; 10:39-43; 13:31). These elements were considered constitutive of the first generation of witnesses, whose recollection subsequent generations would scrupulously transmit. Accurate recollection of apostolic testimony was understood to be ensured by the guidance of the Holy Spirit. Subsequent generations of witnesses are perennially pledged and bound to recall accurately the salvation event as received (Gal 1:19-20; 1 Thess 2:3-8). A direct eyewitness to an unrepeatable event depends upon the Spirit to conserve and sustain the integrity and truthfulness of the previous eyewitnesses.

All Christian testimony and experience stands in this Spirit-led succession (Origen, *First Principles* preface). The disciples at second hand (noneyewitnesses) do not receive a new, separable, improved or different revelation but attest to the original revelation centered on the events of cross and resurrection, and upon personal meeting with the unique person—Son of Man and Son of God. The task of the apostolic successor is not to improve upon the message or embellish it or add to it one's own spin, but rather simply to remember and attest it accurately, credibly and intelligibly.

To assist in correct remembering, the Holy Spirit has enabled the apostolic testimony to be written down in due time in a canonically received body of writings ecumenically received by lay consent in all locations of the church as normative apostolic teaching. Amid each cultural variation, subsequent apostolic witnesses are solemnly pledged and bound to the apostolic canon as norm of Christian teaching. By the end of the first century, that norm included at least the four Gospels and the Pauline letters. Thus Mark and Luke-Acts, which are most crucial for the African memory of the identity of Mark, were likely written and received consensually as inspired Word by the time of the earliest apologists (Ignatius, Justin and Irenaeus). Paul made a strict distinction between his own opinions, which were to be duly considered, and those received from the apostles, which were to be obeyed (1 Cor 1:1; 4:1-7; 7:12, 40).

The authenticity of this testimony is preserved by the Spirit. The appeal to novelty is forever tempted to heresy (from *hairesis*, which meant an alternative choice different from the received apostolic tradition—Tertullian, *Praescr.* 4–6). Contrary to modern assumptions about progress, that which is closest to apostolic testimony is truest, since the good news is about events of history and hence grounded in eyewitness testimony (Tertullian, *Marc.* 4.5).

Paul viewed his own witness as inseparable from the consensual pre-Pauline apostolic tradition, as is evident from his own admonition: "But even if we, or an angel from heaven, should preach to you a gospel contrary to that which we preached to you, let him be accursed" (Gal 1:8 RSV). Paul did not invent a new gospel. His gospel was a clarification of pre-Pauline teaching of the Jerusalem church, which he viewed as the binding norm for his own mission and proclamation (Gal 1:13-20; 2:2; 1 Cor 11:23-29; 15:5-8). He delivered to the Corinthians the tradition he had received from the pre-Pauline apostolate: that Christ died for our sin, was buried, was raised and appeared "to all the apostles."

This point on the priority of Scripture to tradition is especially important for Protestant evangelicals. The most obvious critique the Copts get from evangelicals is that they seem to expand the weight of tradition at the expense of Scripture. My perspecitve is both Orthodox and evangelical. The Gospel of Mark has been regarded as apostolic since the time of its writing. Protestant analyses such as this one are scrupulous in requiring that the Scripture text trumps subsequent recollections. Careful reading of the Alexandrian exegetes on the plain or historical sense of the Scripture makes it clear that they too formally approve of the priority of sacred text to later tradition or oral interpretation of it. Origen sought out the spiritual sense of every text of the Word of God, but that spiritual sense depended upon a proper understanding of its literal or plain sense. In doing so, he was utilizing an earlier Jewish tradition of midrashim, investigating the meaning of the sacred text on what is left unsaid by the text or is felt to be missing or not made explicit in the text.

Two dissimilar ways of approaching the narratives of saints are hard to reconcile.

1. Approached as a liturgical document, these narratives have been revered and trusted and passed to ensuing generations. Many of these copies were destroyed over centuries. Efforts at preservation were continuous, especially under conditions of persecution.
2. Approached with modern eyes as an empirical task of verification, these same documents require an attitude of caution. Hence it is not surprising to see modern scholars handle these narratives in an entirely different way than the tradition itself has valued them. Scholars trained in the methods of modern historical scholarship often feel mandated by their own methods to approach the documents with suspicion, doubt and disbelief until proven wrong, willing to listen only to corroboratory facts based on external documentary evidence.

The only way to get inside the African memory of Mark is to allow it to tell the story of a saint. Otherwise the reader might mistake the saintly narrative intended for liturgical use as if it were a modern empirical historical description. If we limit our knowledge of the earliest decades of Christianity only to such empirical descriptions, we are apt to conclude that we can know virtually nothing except what is by speculation conceived to be the probable situation existing among the probable rememberers. But the liturgical-catechetical purpose of the stories of saints was not simply to report history or validate data, but rather to engage in a much more consequential action: to worship God as made reliably known in the life and death of his Son Jesus.[8]

[8]For recent discussions of issues relating to biblical history in relation to African history and consciousness, see the works in the bibliography by Paul Bowers, Paul C. Boyd, and María Elena González Galván and Filipe Miguel Oliveira Resende.

4

THE LITERARY SOURCES OF THE AFRICAN MEMORY OF MARK

The African narrative of Mark fills in many blanks that have remained perplexing when we limit ourselves only to hearing the modern Western narrative. Today young Africans are discovering their own African roots. They are actively retrieving this epic story. To aid them, it is useful to clarify where readers can find this story in its primitive forms, and in its developing stages.

Chief among the sources of this story are the liturgical synaxaries of early African Christianity. Here is the crucial summary of the synaxary that deals with Mark's life:

> After the ascension . . . [Mark] accompanied Paul and Barnabas to preach the Gospel in Antioch, Seleucia, Cyprus, Salamis, and Perga Pamphylia where he left them and returned to Jerusalem. After the Apostolic Council in Jerusalem, he went with Barnabas to Cyprus. After the departure of Barnabas, with the order of the Lord Christ, St. Mark went to Afrikia, Berka [Barca], and the Five Western cities. He preached the Gospel in these parts, and they believed. He laid his hands on most of its people. From there, he went to Alexandria in the first of Bashans 61 A.D. (Coptic Synaxarion for Baramouda [Ethiopic-Amharic Miyazia] 30)

The synaxary versions of Mark's life became common all over Africa in antiquity and remain so today. Hence this is properly designated as the primary African memory of Mark, as distinguished from the Western historical memory. The textual base of the "African memory" of Mark is extensive but not always critically edited. The most frequently referenced classic texts that attest the narrative of Mark are four accounts that largely confirm each other. I will discuss these sources specifically in this order:

- Coptic liturgy, especially in its synaxaries
- *Martyrium Marci*
- Sawirus ibn al-Muqaffa of al-Ashmunein
- Anba Shenouda III, current patriarch of Alexandria

SYNAXARIES

A *synaxary* (Lat. *synaxarium*, Gk. *synaxarion*) is an account of a martyr or saint—to be read at an early morning service—or a compilation of such accounts organized according to days of recollection of the Christian year in the ancient African church tradition. These accounts are brief recollections of the lives of saints for liturgical use in celebrations of saints in an annual cycle of memorials. They give official form to the received version of the traditional lives of the saints. They reveal commonly remembered events of the saints' lives. Of these Mark holds the distinction of always being the first in Africa. As with Peter in Rome, it gives Mark the foremost place among apostolic figures for Africa. This ratification is not an historical judgment but a liturgical confirmation of received tradition.

The standard African memory of Mark is clearly and concisely set forth in these ancient official accounts meant for public reading in church services. They were also used for private devotions. Only those most generally and consensually received in the larger worshiping community were collected and liturgically summarized for reading at annual feast days of the saints and martyrs. Since these brief accounts are liturgical summaries, they do not pretend to be full-length biographies, as we have for many of the later African saints.

Synaxary editions have appeared in the languages of both lower Egypt and upper Egypt at various times, to accommodate cultural variations, in Coptic, Ge'ez, Amharic, and later in Arabic and other languages.[1] Virtually identical narratives are found in Ethiopian and Armenian versions. This confirms that they were ecumenically received. They are similar to the *Acta apostolorum apocrypha* in the Western Latin traditions and to the narratives of the saints in the Eastern Orthodox traditions. The African chronicle of Mark's life and death is among the most important founding documents in African Christian history. It is fundamental and constitutive for Egyptian, Libyan, Ethiopian and Nubian Christian history.

Mark is remembered annually with high esteem in the ancient Christian calendar. The Coptic Synaxarion was being circulated in sustained editions over many centuries before the extant reproductions of it were preserved. Despite the obstacles of war, plunder and fire, its core narrative has been conserved. The nucleus of the synaxary narrative was later woven into the longer version found in the tenth-century narrative of Sawirus. All editions appearing in different languages and in different periods report in much the same way the pivotal events of the life of the saint: his birth, holy life, mission to Africa and his death.

Several editions and translations of the Synaxarion have been published. Among the earliest was that by the Arabist H. F. Wüstenfeld, an edition with a German translation of part of al-Maqrizi's Khitat under the title *Macrizi's Geschichte der Copten* (Göttingen, 1845). He followed that with a German translation of al-Sinaksari, published as *Synaxarium das ist Heiligen-Kalender der Coptischen Christen aus dem Arabischen Übersetzung,* 2 vols. (Gotha, Germany, 1879), relying upon an Arabic manuscript of a Lower Egypt recension. For those who are seeking out translations of the original texts, an English translation of early Coptic original documents was published in six volumes in the 1870s by Salomon C. Malan, under the series title *Original Documents of the Coptic Church.*[2]

---

[1]For discussion on the history and development of synaxaries, see the entries in the bibliography by René M. J. Basset, O. H. E. (Khs-)Burmester, Jacobus Forget, Youssef Habashi and H. F. Wüstenfeld.

[2]Salomon C. Malan, *Original Documents of the Coptic Church,* vol. 1, *The Divine Liturgy of St. Mark the Evangelist* (London: D. Nutt, 1872); vol. 2, *The Calendar of the Coptic Church* (London: D. Nutt, 1873); vol. 3, *A Short History of the Copts and of Their Church* (London: D. Nutt,

The standard modern critical editing of the Arabic text of the synaxarion of the Coptic Orthodox Church was initiated by Jacobus Forget in the Corpus Scriptorum Christianorum Orientalium, Beirut, 1904–1912, and continued by René Basset in Patrologia Orientalis in French translation as *Le Synaxaire arabe jacobite* (rédaction copte/text Arabe), begun in 1904, completed in 1929.[3] Corpus Scriptorum Christianorum Orientalium produced a Latin translation, *Synaxarium alexandrinum,* in 1905, amalgamating two different recensions. The Coptic-Arabic Synaxarion follows the patterns found elsewhere in the martyr records of Antioch, Rome and Constantinople.

The earliest Greek and Coptic compilers and subsequent editors of the ancient Coptic Synaxarion have left few traces of their identities, but it is reasonable to assume that they had the approval of the highest officials of the See of St. Mark. In 1935–1937 a widely used, two-volume edition of the synaxarion was published in Cairo taken from manuscripts not yet known in Europe. Titled al-Sinaksar, it was based on several Egyptian manuscripts and the Paris edition, and the Ethiopic Synaxarion. In 1994, a German translation appeared (*Das Synaxarium: das koptische Heiligenbuch mit den Heiligen zu jedem Tag des Jahres,* trans. by Robert and Lilly Suter [Waldsoms-Kröffelbach: St. Antonius-Kloster, 1994]).

The critical study of the Ethiopian Synaxarion was begun by Ignazio Guidi (1844–1935), an Italian professor who learned Ge'ez and wrote *Storia della letteratura etiopica* in 1931. The French critical edition begun by Guidi was continued by Sylvain Grébaut, Geneviève Nollet and, most recently, Gérard Colin, culminating in a general index published in 1999 in Patrologia Orientalis (48.3). The full set of synaxaries may be found in the Patrologia Orientalis.[4] The Ethiopian edition followed the Egyptian pattern of synaxaries, adding Ethiopian saints of regional interest.

E. A. Wallis Budge published a translation of the Ethiopic Synax-

---

1873); vol. 4, *The Holy Gospel and Versicles* (London: D. Nutt, 1874); vol. 5, *The Divine Euchologion* (London: D. Nutt, 1875); vol. 6, *The Divine Liturgy of S. Gregory the Theologian* (London: D. Nutt, 1875).

[3]These works can be found in PO 1.3, 3.3, 10.5, 16.2, 17.3, 20.5.

[4]PO 1.5, 7.3, 9.4, 15.5, 26.1, 43.3, 43.4, 44.1, 44.3, 45.1, 45.3, 46.3, 46.4, 47.3, 48.3.

arion entitled *The Book of the Saints of the Ethiopian Church* based on manuscripts preserved in London.[5] The oldest surviving manuscript of previous editions is dated A.D. 1581.

The Armenian Synaxarion of Ter Israel was published at Constantinople in 1834. It similarly recalled the martyrdom of Mark in Alexandria.

PRIMITIVE TEXT OF *MARTYRIUM MARCI*

The Martyrdom of Mark (sometimes called the Acts of Mark or History of Mark, *Martyrium Marci* or *Passio Marci—Acta Sanctorum* 12:352; PG 115:163-170) awaits fuller inquiry. It is of Egyptian provenance, likely a very early writing, thought to be second to fourth century, recalling earlier written forms of documentation, carefully guarded and passed on through sacred tradition. Its account corresponds with the other known ancient editions of synaxaries. We are not here comparing vastly different accounts of Mark, but a sustained tradition that appears to hark back to the events it reports.

The Acts of Mark (including *Martyrium Marci*) may be found in R. A. Lipsius and M. Bonnet, *Acta Apostolorum Apocrypha* 2:431-53; *BHG* 2:1035-6; Sawirus, *HP*, 141-48; and *Acta Sanctorum* 9:344-49; cf. Alla I. Elanskaya, ed., *The Literary Coptic Manuscripts in the A. S. Pushkin State Fine Arts Museum in Moscow* (Leiden: Brill, 1994); P. Hubai, "The Legend of St. Mark: Some Coptic Fragments," in *Studia in honorem L. Fóti*, Studia Aegyptiaca 12 (Budapest: Chaire d'Égyptologie, l'Université Eötvös Loránd de Budapest, 1989), pp. 165-234; and E. A. Wallis Budge, ed., "The Martyrdom of St Mark the Evangelist" in *The Contendings of the Apostles*, vol. 1, *The Ethiopic Text* (Oxford: Oxford University Press, 1899), pp. 257-64, and vol. 2, *The English Translation* (Oxford: Oxford University Press, 1901), pp. 309-18. For another English translation, consult R. McL. Wilson, *New Testament Apocrypha*= ET of 6th ed. of Wilhelm Schneemelcher, *Neutestamentliche Apokryphen*, 2 vols. (Louisville: Westminster/John Knox Press, 1991–1992).

The Martyrdom of Mark (Martyrium Marci) was repeatedly received

[5]E. A. Wallis Budge, trans., *The Book of the Saints of the Ethiopian Church*, 4 vols. (Cambridge: Cambridge University Press, 1928).

for the next six centuries following Eusebius and confirmed in the history of Sawirus. We deal with it here because it summarizes the core of the earlier streams of African tradition concerning Mark (cf. T. Baarda, "Het martyrium van Marcus," *Benedictijns Tijdschrift* 52 [1991]: 168-77). The still disputed account has likely survived in various forms from the period between Clement and Athanasius. It is a conflation of previous traditions relating to the martyrdom of Mark in the first century. Its antecedents were the now-lost documents on which the earlier synaxary summary relied.

Martyrium Marci became one among many sources for Sawirus, who wrote the definitive history of the Coptic Patriarchs near the end of the first millennium (Birger A. Pearson and James E. Goehring, eds., *Roots of Egyptian Christianity*, hereafter *REC*, 142). Only a few recensions of the original text of *Martyrium Marci* survived the hazards of transmission from the versions of the fourth century (The Acts of Mark, *Martyrium Marci, Acta Sanctorum* 12:352, PG 115:164-69). This narrative also was found in Coptic, Ethiopic and Arabic (*REC*, 140). However widely it was once circulated in the East, it has been given minimal attention in the West. Since Sawirus incorporates the core of the *Martyrium Marci* into the early parts of his history, I will frequently reference them together.

The Roman martyrology similarly summarizes the martyrdom of Mark as a disciple and interpreter of Peter. It reports that Mark was born in Africa, wrote the Gospel of Mark in Rome, preached in Egypt, established the church in Alexandria, where he was imprisoned and suffered, and was comforted by an angel. In prison the Lord himself appeared to Mark to call him to his celestial home. This happened in the eighth year of Nero (*Vetus martyrologium romanum*, April 25).

The pre-Arabic (before 636) documentation of the African memory of Mark was transmitted from sources dating back to Eusebius and to his pre-Eusebian sources. It took a consistent and stable written form, and was transmitted uniformly by the fourth century and in a definitive form by the end of the first millennium.

SAWIRUS IBN AL-MUQAFFA

The most ancient and authoritative accounts were gathered together from previous liturgical texts and historical accounts, and edited under the direction of Sawirus ibn al-Muqaffa (hereafter Sawirus; variously spelled Sawirus ibn al-Mukaffa', Sawirus ibn al-Muqaffa', Sévère d'Aschmounaïn, Sévère ibn al-Moqaffa). I prefer the transliterated Arabic name Sawirus, since its spelling as *Severus* leads toward confusions with either the Roman Severian regime or Severus of Antioch. Many modern readers will know Severus of Antioch, but few have ever heard of Sawirus of al-Ashmunein, one of our most important sources for the Coptic memory of Mark.

Sawirus was the scholar-bishop of al-Ashmunein (variously El Ashmunein, Al-Ushmunain, Ashmunayn, Nastora, the ancient Hermopolis Magna in the district of Antinopolis, near modern Asyut). Sawirus was writing from about A.D. 955 to about 987. Traditionally he is celebrated as the author of the classic *History of the Patriarchs of the Coptic Church of Alexandria.*[6]

The Greek codex of Sawrius was found in the Vatican library (gr. 866) and was published in Acta Sanctorum in Antwerp in 1675 (vols. 46-47). The Greek codex of Sawirus in Paris (gr. 881) was published in PG 115. Major translations and critical editions of Sawirus ibn al-Muqaffa include, in English, *History of the Patriarchs of the Coptic Church of Alexandria,*[7] or in French, *Histoire des patriarches de l'Église d'Alexandrie* continued as *History of the Patriarchs of the Egyptian Church,*[8] as well as in other languages *Alexandrinische Patriarchengeschichte von S. Marcus bis Michael I (61–767),*[9] *Historia patriarcharum Alexandrinorum,*[10] *Réfutation de Sa'id ibn Batriq (Eutychius)* and *L'histoire des conciles de Sévère ibn al Moqaffa.*[11]

[6]For discussion of Sawirus (Severus) and the *History of the Patriarchs of the Coptic Church of Alexandria,* see the bibliographic entries by Farag R. Farag, Johannes den Heijer and David W. Johnson.

[7]See chap. 3n1.

[8]Sawirus ibn al-Muqaffa, *History of the Patriarchs of the Egyptian Church,* ed. Yasa 'Abd al-Masih, O. H. E. Burmester, A. S. Atiya and Antoine Khater, 4 vols. (various publishers, 1943–1974).

[9]Sawirus ibn al-Muqaffa', *Alexandrinische Patriarchengeschichte von S. Marcus bis Michael I (61–767), nach der ältesten 1266 geschriebenen Hamburger Handschrift im arabischen Urtext herausgegeben,* ed. Christian F. Seybold (Hamburg: Lucas Gräfe, 1912).

[10]Severus ben el-Moqaffa', *Historia patriarcharum Alexandrinorum,* ed. Christian F. Seybold, 2 vols., CSCO 52, 59 (Louvain, 1904–1910).

[11]Sévère ibn-al-Moqaffa', *Réfutation de Sa'id ibn Batriq (Eutychius),* ed. P. Chébli, PO 3.2 (Paris, 1909); *L'histoire des conciles de Sévère ibn al Moqaffa',* ed L. Leroy and S. Grébaut, PO 6.4 (Paris, 1911).

Sawirus (d. between 987 and 1003) was the leading editor of a series of documents that had many prior and subsequent editors. Despite contested viewpoints regarding the edited document attributed to Sawirus, I will only focus on compelling reasons why the history ascribed to him has remained the definitive late version of the African memory of Mark. The subject matter of the account of Mark by Sawirus is concisely described in the title of the first section of his lengthy chronicle on the history of the patriarchs: "The history of Saint Mark, the Disciple and Evangelist, Archbishop of the great city of Alexandria, and first of its Bishops" (Sawirus, *HP*, 135). In the extensive research project organized by Sawirus, he and his associates avidly collected documentation from ancient oral and written traditions. Upon these Sawirus based his history. His account is based on documents and recollections that in his time had text-supported reasons for his narratives being given official sanction in Coptic liturgical and patriarchal history. I say "in his time," since many of these anteceding documents were available to Sawirus but have been subsequently destroyed. This means we have very limited evidence of their earlier transmission history. What is clear is that after Sawirus, virtually all Egyptian Christian authorities agreed on the authenticity of his information, and assumed that their oral traditions extended back to the very beginning of the church in Alexandria.

Some modern critics prematurely suppose that since Sawirus was writing centuries after Mark, this suggests that his sources must have also been centuries after Mark. But that assumption misunderstands the stated purpose of Sawirus in his historical writings, namely, to gather together the earliest extant sources from all ancient accounts existing in the tenth century, including pre-Eusebian, and to bring them into a cohesive, official record for the formation of worshiping believers and the fitting liturgical recollection of the saints and church leaders of Egypt.

Why do I quote Sawirus, who lived much later, who was quoting documents that have been subsequently destroyed? The weight of evidence indicates that Bishop Sawirus himself and his main editorial assistants and successors had documents extant then that we do not have now. Some of these documents were destroyed over the early centuries of the Arab conquest, but many survived to the tenth century. It is unwarranted speculation to make the assumption that Sawirus was simply inventing stories, rather than holding himself accountable to documentation that had been long guarded through the years leading up to and beyond the Arab conquest, but after which they could no longer be safeguarded.

There are many examples in historiography of well-attested events whose primary documentation is irreparably lost, yet they are taken for granted by the consensus of secular historians—events such as Homeric authorship and the battle of Masada, to mention only two, yet few historians would question that there was a battle at Masada or that there was a book of epic poetry attributed to Homer.

The Sawirus narrative of Mark had to withstand internal criticism in its own time from all quarters in order to secure its extraordinary repute as official Coptic history. If Sawirus had been inventing the narrative of Mark in the tenth century, his account could not have been regarded as acceptable or received by his contemporary authorities and scholars who were well informed about this documentary history. The purpose of his historical labor is specifically stated in the prefaces to the *History* and in the early chapters that openly set forth the method of its research. The author acknowledges that he had reluctantly taken on a task that was far beyond him, but did so because of an urgent need for textual recovery amid an unfavorable political order.

Sawirus was called to this special vocation: to organize all available documents of Coptic patriarchal history into a single cohesive narrative. To do this he determined to assemble the most worthy scholarly associates who could help him gather the documents and texts that he would draw together in an integral account. This appears to be the first time that the history of all the patriarchs had been written down in concert as an integral project of historical narrative. That was his task—not to make up these stories or to artificially bridge gaps in the data, but rather to utilize the normative and consensually received texts that had been passed down throughout the entire history of Coptic leadership. By the time he went to work, there likely was a huge collection of almost a thousand years of documentation.

SAWIRUS AS TRANSLATOR, EDITOR AND RESEARCH DIRECTOR

Sawirus was among the greatest of Coptic writers who was completely at home with the Arabic language. He provided a literary pattern that would be followed over the last thousand years of Egyptian Christianity under Islam. His life spanned most of the tenth century. His father was called al-Muqaffa (the Bent-Backed). He was educated at a time when the Copts were beginning to write in Arabic, the language of their rulers. He had served as a scribe in civil administration until he decided to retire to monastic life. It is likely that he at one time resided at Dayr Anba Maqar, the monastery of Macarius in the Nitrian Valley, where there was even then an unexcelled library in Christian history and Coptic hagiography. With vast knowledge of the classic Coptic tradition, history, Scripture and moral philosophy, the fame of his scholarship spread. The leaders of the city of al-Ashmunein selected him as their bishop. There he made extensive contributions to historical studies and scriptural exegesis.

His most lasting contribution has been his definitive account of the history of the patriarchs of Alexandria. It sometimes bears the title "Biographies of the Holy Church." This text, which can rightly be viewed as the official history of the Coptic Orthodox Church, "should be defined," according to J. den Heijer, "not as one book representing a structural unity, but rather as a tradition of historical writing" extending through many epochs.[12]

The early historians anteceding the work of Sawirus wrote primarily in Coptic. Their successors wrote chiefly in Arabic. The text as we know it today consists partly of Arabic translations of Coptic originals and partly of original Arabic works that cover subjects from the first to the eleventh centuries. Sawirus's *History of the Patriarchs* constitutes our main literary source for much Coptic history, and for much Egyptian history, especially that after the Arab sweep across North Africa.

With few exceptions modern scholars regard Sawirus as the redactor of these earlier sources written in Coptic, which he collected in order to

[12]Johannes den Heijer, *Mawhub ibn Mansur ibn Mufarrig et l'historiographie copto-arabe: Étude sur la composition de "l'Histoire des Patriarches d'Alexandrie"* (Louvain: Peeters, 1989).

supervise their translation into Arabic. However, some think his role was largely honorific. In particular, recent attention has been paid to the redactional activity of the Alexandrian deacon Mawhub ibn Mansur ibn Mufarrig.[13] As early as 1890 Alfred von Gutschmid had already examined many of the Coptic sources for the *History of the Patriarchs*.[14]

The portions of the Sawirus history in which this study has special interest are those on the life and martyrdom of St. Mark.[15] Mark appears first in all lists of all known editions of the saints of the Nile.

The dependence of the Sawirus history on Eusebius of Caesarea, among other sources, was recognized early by Oskar Eduardovich Lemm and W. E. Crum.[16] Cyril the Great (412–444) was also prominent among the contributors to the documents assembled by Sawirus. Others included Jirja (George) the Archdeacon, spiritual son of the patriarch John III (677–686) and scribe of the patriarch Simon I (689–701), and another editor, John, the spiritual son of Bishop Moses of Aswan. Johannes den Heijer, in particular, has argued that early sources were composed in Coptic and subsequently translated into Arabic by Mawhub ibn Mansur ibn Mufarrig.

Many of the cohorts of Sawirus scanned monastic libraries for manuscripts that they translated under his direction into Arabic, including the deacon Mikha'il ibn Bidayr al-Damanhuri (later bishop of Tanis) and the presbyter Yu'annis ibn Zakir, abbot of the Nahya monastery. Sawirus did not compile his work by accepting a single manuscript for each of his subjects, but by comparing various manu-

---

[13]Heijer suggests ascribing all redactional work to Mawhub; see Johannes den Heijer, *Mawhub ibn Mansur;* idem, "Sawirus ibn al-Muqaffa', Mawhub ibn Mansur ibn Mufarrig et la genèse de *l'Histoire des Patriarches d'Alexandrie*" *Bibliotheca Orientalis* 41 (1984): 336-47; cf. Tito Orlandi, *Storia della Chiesa di Alessandria, Testo copto, traduzione e commento, I. Da Pietro ad Atanasio, II. Da Teofilo a Timoteo II,* Testi e documenti per lo Studio dell'Antichità 17 and 31 (Milan and Varese, 1968–1970); David W. Johnson, *Coptic Sources of the History of the Patriarchs of Alexandria* (Ph.D. diss., Catholic University of America, Washington, D.C., 1973).

[14]Alfred von Gutschmid, "Verzeichnis der Patriarchen von Alexandrien," in *Kleine Schriften von Alfred von Gutschmid,* ed. Fritz Rühl, 5 vols. (Leipzig: B. G. Teubner, 1889–94), 2:401-3.

[15]Hugh G. Evelyn-White, *The Monasteries of the Wadi 'n Natrûn,* 3 vols. (New York, 1926–1933).

[16]Oskar Eduardovich Lemm, *Koptische Fragmente zur Patriarchengeschichte Alexandriens.* Mémoires de l'Académie impériale des sciences de St. Pétersbourg, 7th series, 36.11 (St. Petersburg: M. Eggers, 1888); W. E. Crum, "Eusebius and Coptic Church Histories," *Proceedings of the Society of Biblical Archaeology* 24 (1902): 68-84.

scripts in search of the most reliable historical facts.

The monastery libraries and patriarchal records came from Scetis and the Fayyum and the Eastern Desert, and then south all the way to Meroe. The central location of the research was al-Ashmunein. There the al-Ashmunein monastery had been founded near the ancient site previously known as Hermopolis Magna. Hermopolis is in the middle Nile region of al-Minya. In that central location it is was close enough to relevant documents and monastic archives along the entire stretch of the Nile Valley. These sources came from libraries and monasteries from Alexandria south to Asyut, Sohag, Akhmim, the Thebaid and beyond.

An official request had been made to the most highly qualified scholars to seek to produce a unified history of the whole patriarchate of the See of St. Mark. To do that, they had to go back into the earliest known documents that describe that history. That meant beginning with Mark. So what we have in Sawirus is a summary of what he regarded as the most reliable aspects of the narrative of the Egyptian church based on its earliest documents from its very beginnings. He was dealing with a huge number of documents and narratives, and many people were likely assisting him. His aides were bringing him documentation, gathering and ordering it and assessing its reliability.

THE METHOD ASCRIBED TO SAWIRUS AS SET FORTH IN ITS PREFACES

Before plunging further into the actual content of the Markan narrative presented by Sawirus, we take note of the methodological information embedded in the prefaces. In the first preface it is clear that *the whole history hinges on the successors of St. Mark.* That is the subject matter of the detailed history that follows. The larger work is all about the trials and challenges of the See of St. Mark over its first thousand years. This shows the affinity of the whole work with the ground laid in its early sections on Mark.

This first preface ascribed to Sawirus reports that Mark preached the gospel in Alexandria first and then in the various regions of Egypt but also in Ethiopia, Nubia and the Pentapolis. During much of late antiquity the Libyan Pentapolis was viewed as a satellite of Egyptian influence. Mark was, according to Sawirus, also specifically responsible for the pastoral care of what we now call Tunisia, which in Roman nomenclature would be Proconsular Africa. This apparently was not the limit of the diocese of Mark, however, since after listing these regions he then evocatively adds to these "the neighboring territories" which hypothetically would have included whatever he knew of sub-Saharan Africa (Sawirus, *HP*, 105).

Since the beginning point of this vast history was the biography of Mark, it was the key to all that followed. Sawirus recorded what Mark did, what he preached, what happened to him as a result of it, his successors, and what this means for believers not only of the Nile region but for believers everywhere. Sawirus did not write all of these accounts. Rather, he collected and unified them. The first preface says, "These histories here given were collected from various places by the care of . . ." Sawirus, the bishop of Ashmunein. From which archives did he obtain them? Many came from the monastery of St. Marcarius. Happily, Sawirus was given a long life. He did not complete this remarkable effort until the end of his eightieth year. It appears he spent most of his later life on this project.

The second of four prefaces is a fervent invocation for the arduous labor to be done and a confession of its limitations. It acknowledges God as the origin and source of learning, who calls and guides his servants who are shepherds of the worshiping community to tell the truth. The history of the See of St. Mark is filled with tragedy and glory and blood and the overcoming of adversity. So it is fitting in this invocation for the liturgist to pray fervently to the one "who lifts up the poor from the ground, who delivers the weak from the mighty, who rules with justice and truth," that the truth might be told accurately.

The whole story of the ten centuries from the original Mark to Sawirus himself is a story of ordinary people who risked their lives for the truth. Many died. Many were imprisoned. Many were tortured. Many were sent to work in the mines. From its first chapter to its last, Mark's people tell a narrative of struggle. The believers who followed the apostolate of Mark in Africa have learned faith through his history.

In the second part of the second preface the writer makes it clear that Mark was the first one "who fed the flock of Christ" and it was Mark's pattern that was followed "generation after generation" (Sawirus, *HP*, 109). All who have been known to be called into the leadership of the See of St. Mark were tried with adversity. They were called to resist the enemies of the truth. Their acts show that they followed the narrow way of Christ.

To demonstrate the continuity between Mark and the whole history of the See of St. Mark, the second preface surveys the kinds of adversity the church has had to undergo in order to manifest the Christian life. They were scourged and stoned and crucified. They were shipwrecked. They were burned by fire. They had to suffer wounds. They were thrown off high places down to the ground. They were killed by the sword. "All kinds of torment [came], which if we were to relate in detail, our narrative would be too long . . . and volumes would not contain even a small part" (Sawirus, *HP*, 110). These are the successors of Mark in Africa. Those who took up this succession of Mark's apostolate were not theorists or church bureaucrats. They put their lives on the line generation after generation.

In the third preface Sawirus refers to himself as the complier of these primary sources (Sawirus, *HP*, 114). He claims no worthiness to take on this task but rather sees himself as a penitent who grieves over his negligence. Meanwhile he remains in the office of a bishop of the church in Egypt where he stands in a tradition of accountability to the One who chose the twelve and the seventy and all who came after them.

How did Sawirus reason that the See of St. Mark embraced the whole of the continent? Sawirus knew that he was addressing not just the Egyptian church but all the churches of the region. He specifically noted the Libyan church, mentioning in particular the regions from Barka in the Pentapolis to Kairouan. This is a telling reference. It speaks of the great early medieval center of learning in Tunisia in Kairouan where the Great Mosque, built on the site of a Byzantine Church, became an embryonic university and a world pattern for Islamic higher education. Then he also mentions Tripoli, between Tunisia and Cyrenaica, as belonging to the See of St. Mark. He specifically includes

Ethiopia and Nubia. Sawirus says all of these lands were drawn by the power of the Holy Spirit into the orbit of Mark's preaching. Finally, he refers also to "Africa" as within the See of St. Mark, probably a reference to Roman Proconsular Africa, yet symbolically suggests the entire African continental mass as far as it was known in the tenth century.

SAWIRUS'S ASSESSMENT OF THE OUTCOMES OF THIS METHOD

Sawirus had assessed the fitness of scholars all over the region to assist him. He thought he and they had located the most ancient and reliable sources and translated them into the contemporary language of the realm: Arabic. Most of these sources were earlier written in Greek or Coptic but he is trying to get them into the current vernacular of the people of his day who did not any longer (by law) read Coptic.

Apparently a large part of his research project was simply copying documents, for he says, "I copied that which I knew not from the men of old, in agreement with the canons of the church" (Sawirus, *HP*, 116). He is retaining the memory of the ancient documents as they had been approved not just by Sawirus personally, but by those who had given ecumenical consent to saint's stories that had been repeatedly approved to be publicly read in churches. These were regarded as valuable year after year and rehearsed annually in the African church. Sawirus humbly asks God to pardon him for anything that is his own personal bent or distortion, namely any contribution from myself "relating the accounts of those whose meanest disciple I am unworthy to be." He asks God's forgiveness for his own originality and disclaims that if it is something innovated by him, he pleads for divine mercy.

Sawirus came late in late antiquity, but his sources were early. He was an editor, a reporter and a translator of writers and transcribers from the second, third, fourth, fifth and sixth centuries. As a medieval writer he cannot be expected to provide modern-style documentation for his reader, as we would today. That would misunderstand the nature of the documents that he was dealing with, which were primary documents. He was attempting to see the whole history of the See of St. Mark in relation to its first exemplar and prototype. He was putting in order a vast outlay of ancient sources in order to do this. Many of these sources were available only in one or perhaps a few editions or extant manuscript copies.

SHENOUDA III

Shenouda III is the present patriarch of the See of St. Mark, and a leading interpreter of the Coptic narrative of Mark.[17] He has drawn together all the traditions relating to Mark that are taken into account in the received Coptic sources. This is the most complete statement of the traditional narrative, combining into a synoptic view all the ancient and modern sources on Mark that correspond with Coptic Orthodoxy. No one has articulated the Coptic consensus on the memory of Mark better than Shenouda III. Few in the current New Testament guild regard Mark as an eyewitness. Yet virtually all in classic African memory have remembered Mark as the "beholder of God"—that is, of God incarnate in the flesh.

Since today the Gospel of Mark is widely regarded as the first Gospel written, it must have been circulating while some other original eyewitnesses were still living. Thus Mark's Gospel would not have been taken seriously by contemporary eyewitnesses if it had differed widely from other contemporary recollections of Jesus.

Mark's martyrdom did indeed take place in a great city, Alexandria, but his range of responsibility extended to a vast territory—the continent of Africa. His successors were following his authority to shepherd the flock over the whole unknown continental region, in so far as possible. Sawirus was thinking almost a thousand years after Mark and a thousand years before Shenouda III. They were telling the story of how the people of God have continued to be led by the apostle "who had seen Christ's face." This is why Mark is uniquely remembered in Coptic tradition as "the beholder of God," the title of Shenouda III's book. This means that of all those who attested God in the flesh in Africa, Mark holds a unique place of having beheld the Son of God face to face. This perennial African title for Mark assumes that Mark himself

---

[17]See chap. 3n5.

was an eyewitness. While many modern scholars have reservations about this, I think it is worth taking into consideration. It is an ancient premise in Africa that the one from whom all of Africa has received this apostolic ministry is one who had, as an eyewitness, beheld the face of Christ (Sawirus, *HP*, 115).[18]

[18]For discussion of Coptic history and other early African literary sources, see the bibliographic entries by Frank E. Brightman, O. H. E. (Khs-)Burmester, Stephen J. Davis, David Frankfurter, James E. Goehring, C. Wilfred Griggs, Peter Grossmann, Jill Kamil, Otto F. Meinardus, Birger A. Pearson and James M. Robinson.

PART TWO

The Identity of the Biblical Mark Viewed from African Tradition

5

A PORTRAIT OF MARK

It is time to paint a more complete African portrait of Mark as we know him from many sources. We know already from traditional sources that he was from Cyrene and that his family moved to Jerusalem, driven there by turmoil in their homeland. What else can we learn of Mark as he grew to be the patriarch of the church?

THE YOUNG MARK—FROM CAPERNAUM TO JERUSALEM

If Mark spent most of his youth in Cyrenaic Africa, he would have known the local Punic-Berber dialect as well as Greek. If he spent some of his youth in Jerusalem as the son of a displaced Jew of the tribe of Levi, as the traditional story goes, he would surely have learned common Aramaic, and if well-educated, perhaps some Latin. In either case he would likely have been dutifully introduced to the Torah in Hebrew.

According to the traditional narrative, Mark came under the tutelage of Peter of Capernaum who was a son of Jonah (Mt 16:17). The relation of the Cyrenaic family of Mark with the Galilean family of Simon Peter is strongly affirmed in the traditional African narrative. This is odd to Western eyes: "They [the family of Mark] were Jewish in faith, rich and of great honor. They educated him [Mark] with the Greek and Hebrew cultures. He was called Mark after they emigrated to Jerusalem, where St. Peter had become a disciple to the Lord Christ." The relation was close, with alleged visits of Mark to Peter in his youth: "St. Peter was married to the cousin of Aristopolus. *Mark visited St. Peter's house often*, and from him he learned the Christian teachings" (Synaxarion: Baramouda [Ethiopic-Amharic Miyazia] 30, emphasis added). Since Peter did not have a house in Jerusalem, where was "St. Peter's house" where these visits took place? In the African narrative, Mark appears to be visiting Peter at Capernaum.

It was then that Mark played a part in enabling the conversion of his own father: As father Aristopolus (Aristobolus) and son John Mark were walking near the Jordan River in a wilderness area, they were attacked by two lions. The father cried out to the son to "escape to save himself." All we know of the character of Mark's father according to tradition is condensed in this selfless cry of a father to protect the life of his son. But what ensues following this legend is all about a relationship: one between a father and son, and between the heavenly Father and the incarnate Son. To his father's cry, Mark answered, "Christ, in whose hands our lives are committed, will not let them prey on us." Mark then prayed to "Christ, Son of God" for preservation. The lions were rendered harmless. This prompted his father to ask Mark to explain to him more "about the Lord Christ." He then "believed in the Lord Christ at the hands of his son, who baptized him" (Synaxarion, Baramouda [Ethiopic-Amharic Miyazia] 30).

Mark apparently had learned this teaching from Peter. In the African narrative the father "believed in the Lord Christ *at the hands of his son*." This is viewed typologically by way of recollection in relation to the crucifixion/resurrection, where the Father accepted the sacrifice of the Son on behalf of the sins of the world. The encounter with the lions is often discounted by Westerners, but not necessarily by the African mind. Though post-Enlightenment observers tend to easily dismiss this sort of story, it is the pivotal first step in the African narrative. It is the only glimpse we have into Mark's youth. But already by means of it, from the outset we learn of Mark's burgeoning faith, and of his emerging vocation, and of his special relation with Peter, who first led him to Christian teaching and discipleship.

Figure 1. Statue of the apostle Mark on Saint Isaac's Cathedral, St. Petersburg, Russia

From this episode a major symbol emerges that will pervade the iconic memory of Mark for all subsequent centuries: the lion as the symbol of Mark's youthful faith in the fulfillment of God's promises to Israel through Jesus of Nazareth. Mark's memory is associated with the lion due to:

- Mark's courage in mission and witness
- his father's conversion

This symbol is seen today all over Africa, and especially in Ethiopia where the entire history of its governance has been legitimated on the basis of this visual metaphor. Similarly, the lion is found all over Venice because of the ninth-century stealing of the remains of Mark from Alexandria and his central place as the patron saint of the city and republic since that time. Of course, as one of the four Gospel writers, Mark is remembered throughout the Christian world (see fig. 1 for a magnificent statue of Mark in St. Petersburg, Russia).

Consider this curious detail, which though conjectural, shows how the New Testament references to Mark were interwoven inferentially with the African traditions of Mark. In Coptic tradition, Mark's father Aristopolus was related by marriage to Simon Peter. Quoting from the Coptic scholar Samir Fawzy Girgis: "Peter was married to Strapola, a relative of Mark's father," and the family lived "together with Mark's mother and her brother Barnabas," which "might explain the close intimacy between Mark and Barnabas on the one hand, as well as between Mark and Peter, who called him 'son,' on the other" (Girgis, 27; cf. 1 Pet 5:13). That sentence alone, if true, would require a thousand shifts in our Western picture of Mark.

HINTS OF MARK'S IDENTITY WITHIN THE GOSPEL

In Mark's Gospel we find suggestions or indicators of the possible identity of the author and further information about him. According to Coptic hagiography, the author of the Gospel was present among the eyewitness disciples. Hints of Mark's mandate to report these events, or Peter's testimony to these events, are dropped at crucial moments of the story. Jesus is already in Jerusalem on the way to the cross when some of the main hints appear. Notably, at the very beginning of Mark's Gospel (Mk 1:1, 11) and at the end (Mk 14:61-62), Mark reveals the secret that has been intriguing the hearer throughout the narrative: Jesus is Son of God, walking freely as fully human in accord with the divine plan. He is baptized with us and risen for us. He is offering to his family of believers remission of sin and union with him by faith.

Jesus' divine Sonship is anticipated at the beginning and demonstrated at the end of Mark. Only with his resurrection is it clear without doubt who this one is. He has been proclaiming the coming kingdom of God but withholding, for good reason, full disclosure of his identity. The resurrection lifts the veil. It is this divine Sonship in human form that is being received and joyfully celebrated in the new family of God, according to African liturgy: the body and blood of Christ himself who is crucified for us, who arises from the dead on the third day to confirm his Sonship. Through the Son the Father's forgiveness is being offered.

The new family participates in his body and blood by faith through the institution of a meal of bread and wine, interpreted messianically. The kingdom of God is revealed in the ensuing cross and resurrection. This recognition unfolds dramatically in a particular room, the upper room. The African memory holds that this was Mark's house.

In some forms of Alexandrian spiritual exegesis, Mark is thought to be the "young man" referred to in Mark 14:51 in a strange episode between Gethsemane and the Sanhedrin.[1] After Jesus' arrest: "A young man, wearing nothing but a linen garment, was following Jesus. When they seized him, he fled naked, leaving his garment behind."

One of Jesus' disciples, unnamed in the text, but named Mark in the exegetical imagination, was there with his normal outer garment on. During the seizing of Jesus a scuffle occurred and the young man fled leaving the outer garment behind. Matthew reports that *all* the disciples fled (Mt 26:56). Mark alone, however, with anonymity and modesty, reports *about himself*, a young man who fled without his clothes, with a feeling of total vulnerability and exposure. This is a characteristic of Mark's style: self-effacing and penitent. His nakedness symbolized his loss of defenses, his shame at fleeing. Had he better known the prophets, he would not have fled. Based on Coptic hagiography Anba Shenouda sets out the definitive Coptic view: "All the references pointed that St. Mark was the young man who followed Lord Christ the night He was arrested" (Mk 14:51-52, Shenouda III).

On the third day after the death and burial of Jesus, an anonymous "young man" once again appears in Mark 16:5-7, after Jesus' resurrection, when the women at the tomb find the stone rolled away: "As they entered the tomb, they saw a young man dressed in a white robe sitting on the right side. They were alarmed. 'Don't be alarmed,' he said. 'You are looking for Jesus the Nazarene, who was crucified. He has risen!'" Though nothing in the text identifies this young man, African memory has sometimes posited that it could have been Mark, who was reporting the event, although others have held it was an angel, taking their cue from the parallel in Matthew 28:5-7.

---

[1]This possibility is entertained by modern exegetes as well; see Donald English, *The Message of Mark*, BST (Downers Grove, Ill.: InterVarsity Press, 1992), pp. 222-23; R. A. Cole, *Mark*, TNTC (Downers Grove, Ill.: InterVarsity Press, 1989), pp. 307-8.

Might the young man of Mark 14:51-52 be Mark himself? Might this curious episode contain some kind of parable or hidden instruction? The Carpocratians, in a view later declared as heresy, may have taken this strange story as an opportunity to speculate on the salacious aspect of Mark's narrative, the nudity of the young man in flight after the arrest and his transformation after the resurrection, now clothed in white. This was questioned in the Letter to Theodore attributed to Clement. This speculation is discussed in chapter nine, where it fits more clearly, along with Clement, into the chronological sequence we are following. In Clement's view there is no consensually received allusion to initiation into a sexually perfect way of life.

Why is the young man clothed in white? He is clothed because, upon beholding the empty tomb of the risen Lord, he is a new man, bathed in Christ's mercy, clothed in Christ's righteousness. He is clothed in white to point toward the redeemed celestial community of praise. Why is he sitting on the right hand side? "What does the left hand side mean but this present life; and the right hand side, if not life eternal." Why? "Our redeemer has now passed over beyond the mortality of this present life," hence the one who came to "announce his entry into eternal life, sit[s] on the right side."[2]

This young man is again unnamed, but within the African exegetical imagination there were some who assumed that there were indicators pointing toward Mark himself, the same one who fled naked at the arrest, who is now clothed at the resurrection. Again Mark in humility and self-effacement does not identify himself, but remains anonymous.

THE EXTENDED FAMILIES OF MARK, BARNABAS AND PETER

The interfacing of extended families among the earliest disciples is intriguing. This interface, as elaborated by the African memory of Mark, has vast implications for Markan studies, even if only a fraction of it is historically verifiable. Among the known facts of the text of Acts are the following details:

[2]Gregory the Great, *Homilies 21,* as quoted in ACCS NT 2:231.

- Mark was the cousin or nephew of Barnabas, and accompanied him on his missionary journeys.
- Mark's mother was closely related to Barnabas.
- Barnabas brought both Paul and Mark into the mission to the Gentiles in Antioch.
- Barnabas and the mother of Mark were generous to the earliest disciples, offering hospitality and resources to them.
- Barnabas apparently regarded the younger man, John Mark, as a helper or assistant.

Thus it is not mere fantasy to claim that Mark was exceptionally well-positioned to know what was happening in the earliest days of Christianity.

Consider the international implications of this group of associates: One was from Cyprus (a Greek island), one from Tarsus (in Roman Asia) and one from Cyrene (in Africa). Already all continents of the known world are involved. The key salvation event occurred in Jerusalem. The proclamation of this event to the rest of humankind was taken up by a representative group of international broadcasters: Barnabas, Paul and Mark. None were born in Jerusalem.

Cyprus was associated by language and political affiliation with Europe; Tarsus was in Cilicia of present day Turkey in the orbit of Syria in the East. Cyrene brought into the world mission the gifts and languages of the great southern continent—Africa. The Orthodox imagination reasoned: Only the One omniscient God could have brought together such a intermingling of gifts flowing from the multilanguage outpouring of Pentecost.

There is little record of dispute over the report that Mark was a relative (Gk. *ho anepsios*) of Barnabas. In Colossians 4:10, Paul writes: "My fellow prisoner Aristarchus sends you his greetings, as does Mark, the cousin of Barnabas. (You have received instructions about him; if he comes to you, welcome him.)" In various versions the Greek is rendered differently—in the KJV, "Marcus, sister's son to Barnabas"; or in Young's Literal Translation, "Marcus, the nephew of Barnabas"; or in the Revised English Version, "cousin of Barnabas." Barnabas, like John Mark, had two names: *Joseph* (or Joses), but the name by which he was called by the disciples was *Barnabas*, or son of encouragement or consolation or comfort.

Thus Mark and Barnabas were bound together by:

- sharing deep bonds of kinship
- sharing their family resources together with the disciples
- sharing in their faith that Jesus Christ is Lord
- sharing a special calling from God as called and empowered by the Spirit: taking the good news of Jesus to the Gentiles (Acts 15:37-39)

Mary the mother of Mark was known to be a close relative of Barnabas—depending upon the translation either his sister or cousin or sister-in-law. Peter sought refuge from Herod's persecutors in this same house of Mary the mother of Mark. When Peter was rescued from prison by an angel, he immediately "went to the house of Mary, the mother of John whose other name was Mark, where many were gathered together and were praying" (Acts 12:12).

Even as a young man, John Mark would have been positioned close to the leading disciples of Jesus Christ. When was Mark converted? The text does not say. It was surely by the time he appears with Paul and Barnabas. But it could just as plausibly have been, as the African memory holds, as early as Peter's calling in Capernaum or the disciples' gathering in Mary's house for the Last Supper, or for Pentecost and the birth of the church. Whether earlier or later, we do not know, but we do learn from African tradition that his father was converted in the Jordan Valley not far from Capernaum after Mark's conversion. Certainly by the time of the first missionary journey from Antioch to Cyprus, Mark was known and trusted by the apostles.

Barnabas and Mark went to Cyprus with Paul. Barnabas and Mark would later go back to preaching ministries in Cyprus. It should not be overlooked that Diaspora Jews of Cyprus had many affinities with those of Cyrenaica. Barnabas ("the son of consolation/encouragement") was so surnamed "not only on account of his so largely assisting the poor with his fortune; but also of those peculiar gifts of the Spirit, whereby he was so well qualified both to comfort and to exhort."[3] And with this assessment, many African exegetes concurred. While Barnabas gave the proceeds of the sale of a field belonging to him (Acts 4:36-37), his relative Mary the mother of Mark apparently offered the use of her home as a meeting place for the disciples in Jerusalem (Acts 12:12). According to the leading African exegetes, these events were taking place on another level of understanding. They were nurturing a new family being raised up to a new inheritance. They have no continuing city. They are looking for a city which is to come (Heb 13:14). Their citizenship is in heaven (Phil 3:20). They are ready to face death with the messianic Lord, trusting in his grace, carrying his cross.

For three discrete reasons, even if of unequal weight, the ancient tradition has led us to think that Mark was a member of a priestly family, that is, in Jewish terms, a Levite.

- Barnabas was known to be a Levite, as the book of Acts clearly reports: "Joseph, *a Levite from Cyprus, whom the apostles called Barnabas* (which means Son of Encouragement), sold a field he owned and brought the money and put it at the apostles' feet" (Acts 4:36-37, emphasis added).
- If Barnabas and Mark are cousins (or possibly uncle and nephew), then it is highly likely that the family of Mark would also be from the family of Levi. This would identify them with the priestly class, including its learned traditions, zeal and influential prestige in the first century A.D. From an early tradition, the Vulgate preface to Mark's Gospel assumed that Mark himself was a Jewish priest: "Mark the Evangelist, who exercised the priestly office in Israel, a Levite by race."
- If so, it is likely that both Mark and Barnabas might well have had priestly relatives in Jerusalem. This priestly identity may correlate

[3]John Wesley, *Explanatory Notes Upon the New Testament,* s.v. Acts 4:36. These notes have been published in many editions over the years.

with the apparent location of the house of Mary the mother of Mark on Zion hill where many Levitical priests apparently lived.

Add to these another intriguing speculation: Early in the third century Hippolytus of Rome referred to Mark as stump-fingered or mutilated in the finger or toe (*ho kolobodaktylos*).[4] If Mark did have a shortened finger, it could have been caused by many forms of disease or accident. The "Anti-Marcionite Prologue" (A.D. 160–180, Rome) notes that Mark was "called 'stump-fingered,' because he had rather small fingers in comparison with the stature of the rest of his body." This has elicited a speculation in the tradition of exegesis that this epithet was applied to Mark because he may have damaged one of his fingers to make him unsuitable for the Jewish priesthood, which required bodily integrity. The premise of this argument is that if Mark was a young Jewish son of a priestly tradition who was studying for the priesthood, who later met Jesus' disciples and was converted, he might look for some way to make himself ineligible for the priesthood. This is based on a strict interpretation of the Torah that no priest who is blemished—blind or mutilated, possessing an injured hand or foot and so forth—was permitted to perform the duties of a priest (Lev 21:16-23).

From one perspective, we might expect an account of Mark's life to tell of miracles through healing or extraordinary events beyond natural explanation. Yet the composite narrative of Mark portrays him as an ordinary individual whose life and death and heavenly rebirth so fully refracted the life of Christ that he was remembered as a "saint," as were many in the New Testament. More so it is the story of the first saint of Africa, who was born, abided, returned and died in Africa. Mark is the first and most important conveyor of the earliest apostolic tradition to Africa. His Gospel narrative was assumed to be inspired by the Holy Spirit in all classic Christian traditions. Mark was then far more decisive for the history of Jesus and for doctrinal teaching than later Christian writers who depended on Mark. Mark's history became a crucial pattern for African Christian history.

[4]Hippolytus, *Philosophumena* 7.30 (PG 16.3:3334, where the work is attributed to Origen as *Contra Haereses*).

In his "good news" he was first to reveal the human appearance of the Son of Man of apocalyptic expectation, the fleshly coming of the divine Word. Mark was the one who first directly conveyed the divine Word from eyewitnesses not only to Africa but to all subsequent readers of the New Testament.[5]

[5]For recent discussions of the crucial role of African Christology in African theology, see Tokunboh Adeyemo, Ukachukwu Chris Manus, Takatso Alfred Mofokeng and Tito Orlandi.

6

THE AFRICAN MOSAIC OF THE LORD'S SUPPER AND PENTECOST ACCORDING TO MARK

A crucial test case for the African memory is the exercise of connecting the major events that occurred in the upper room:

- how the disciples came to this location
- whose place it was
- where it was
- what happened there (the supper and the washing of feet)
- whether the birth of the church at Pentecost occurred in the same place
- and whether the disciples returned to this room—most dramatically in the case of Peter's escape from prison

The African narrative links these events and treats them as intrinsically connected. The prevailing Western narrative tends to treat them as discrete and separable.

In this chapter we review the Markan report of the events leading up to the Eucharistic institution and Pentecost. It is two days before the Passover in Jerusalem on the Feast of the Unleavened Bread (Mk 14:12). The chief priests and scribes were trying to arrest Jesus and kill him (Mk 14:10-11), but were afraid of the tumult of the people (Mk 14:1-2).

In Bethany Jesus was anointed with an ointment of pure nard, very costly, by a woman. She broke the alabaster jar and poured it over his head, as if announcing his messianic office anticipatively (Mk 14:3-9). Jesus said she had "done a beautiful thing" (Mk 14:6). When questioned why the perfume was wasted, he replied: "She poured perfume on my body beforehand to prepare for my burial" (Mk 14:8). Jesus is revealing his identity as Messiah. Mark had announced from the beginning of his Gospel that this would be the subject matter of his good news (Mk 1:1). But trouble is ahead: Judas goes to the chief priests immediately after this anointing to tell the chief priests, betraying Jesus and receiving a promise of money (Mk 14:10-11).

The disciples ask: Where do we go to eat the Passover (Mk 14:12)? Where do we go to celebrate God's grace toward our new family, the believing community that follows the Messianic Lord? Jesus gives the gathering family of God a specific instruction: Go into the city. You will see "a man carrying a jar of water" who will meet you. Follow him. Where he takes you, enter. Say to the householder: "The teacher asks, *Where is my guest room*?" (Mk 14:14, emphasis added).

For what providential purpose could this hospitality be provided? What becomes clear later, according to African memory (rooted in Acts 12:12, as understood by Sawirus and Shenouda) is that the house is the residence of Mary the mother of Mark. The room is to become remembered as the "upper room." It has been prepared in advance. According to African interpreters, the room was symbolically offered up as a gift of community and expectation from a distant place, from a continent away in Africa, for the use of the Lord and his disciples.

"He will show you a *large upper room*," Jesus says, "furnished and ready. Make preparations for us there" (Mk 14:15, emphasis added). There is reason to conjecture that Jesus had been to this house before and knew of its upper room. If so, does this imply that Jesus had some previous relationship with the householder? If so, might that reinforce the premise that he may have had some family connection with the owners, or some reason to know they would be hospitable? Even if he did not know them previously, he was certain that they had a room ready. The African imagination ponders: Could Jesus have known the family of Mark previously, or Mark himself, who would be guided by the Spirit to write the first account of the gospel?

The African narrative grasped an obvious confluence of texts (Mk 14:14-15; Acts 1:13; 12:12) that Mark's mother lived there in that very house. The disciples then go into the city, find the man carrying the jar of water, follow him to the house where they find that the Passover location is already prepared for them. As prophesied, the messianic Servant Lord would not have a place to lay his head. No place to call his home. And yet, he is gathering together a new family. Everything is being supplied.

Is it a symbolic or typological hint that a Diaspora Levitical family from the African continent supplied the place? Something special is happening. Does it pertain to Africa's gifts? The answer is given by this inference so crucial to the African memory of the flight of the Holy Family to Egypt: *Just as Africa had given the family of Jesus a home in his childhood in flight from Herod, so now a family in flight from Africa is giving Jesus a home in the last hours before his death.* In both the Old and New Covenants, Africa is serving as host. An astounding African irony is thus woven into the Jerusalem story. Jesus is fed and sheltered by a family from Africa. Everything is prepared.

In African memory, the man carrying the jar was Mark himself, who was writing the narrative. The rabbinic tradition of exegesis, especially in Alexandria, paid special attention to the spiritual meaning of each phrase of each sacred text. Accordingly, in every sentence of the sacred text, indeed every word, everything said and unsaid, God is seeking to convey the mystery of his providential purpose for humanity. This is a mystery more profound than we are able to grasp. It is always deeper than the surface indicators. The water metaphor suggests that "Wherever waters enter, the waters of holy baptism, Christ stays there." They "wash us from all the stains of sin . . . that we might become a holy temple of God and participants in his divine nature."[1]

In order to get the impact of this sort of prefigurative or typological mode of reasoning, we can compare this episode with another analo-

[1]Cyril the Great, *Commentary on Luke,* Hom. 141, quoted in ACCS NT 3:329.

gous "water jar" scene, as remembered by the African exegetes. According to African memory, Mark was thought to be present at the wedding in Cana (Jn 2:1-11), appearing as "the servant who poured out the water which Our Lord turned into wine." The typological imagination quickly got the point. The water of baptism and the bread and wine of the Eucharist are being conveyed first by Mark, before any of the other eyewitnesses. Thus this same unnamed figure (who some African exegetes thought might be Mark himself) appears in connection with the pouring out of water and wine, anticipatively summarizing the elements of the two sacramental acts, as the man "carrying a pitcher of water" into the house of Mary the Cyrenian, at the time of the sacramental Supper, in preparation for the Passover (Mk 14:13).

Thus in the early African tradition, the pitcher of water anticipates the coming baptism of the faithful into the Son's yet to be revealed crucifixion and resurrection. According to Euro-Amerian historicist criteria, of course, these nuances should be ignored for lack of hard evidence. But from an African perspective they are viewed as providential and confirming. The interwoven connection between the displaced family and baptism and water and wine would all burst through to the African imagination. The most telling fact: the sheltering family was from Africa. Whatever the connections, it appears that as a young man, Mark became deeply and permanently drawn into the teaching and ministry of Jesus. His linguistic aptitude in particular may have made him extremely valuable to the community led by Simon Peter of Capernaum and to the mission of St. Paul.

Earlier Mark had made it clear that this varied international family of believers, including African Jews who expected the Messiah, was Jesus' true family. "Whoever does God's will is my brother and sister and mother" (Mk 3:35). Whether it was Jesus' blood family or a symbolic family is less important than that this was the new family of those who believe that God has come personally in human history in Jesus. This eschatological kinship is far deeper than any blood bond. It is the new emerging family of the people of God, following the command of the messianic Lord. They have no design except to do his will. His will is to gather his family for Passover in Jerusalem. This is just as the Teacher had taught—this new family is coming into being through a new relation with the heavenly Father through his Son. Each believer is being born into a new life, a new creation. They are now coming to the table of the Father. He invites them as the eternal Son. They are bound in unity of love based on their relation to the Son through the Spirit.

THE HOUSE OF THE MOTHER OF MARK

Though details are disputed, at least four major events are understood to have occurred in this particular house in Jerusalem: the Lord's Supper, the Lord washing the feet of his disciples, the outpouring of the Holy Spirit at Pentecost, and the flight of Peter to this house after his imprisonment.

Here is the narrative in the language of the Coptic Synaxarion: "His [Mark's] house was

- the first Christian church,
- where they ate the Passover,
- where they hid after the death of the Lord Christ, and
- where in its upper room the Holy Spirit came upon them" (Synaxarion: Month of Baramouda [=Ethiopic-Amharic Miyazia] 30).

The African narrative offers plausible reasons to infer that these pivotal events occurred in Mark's house where the mother of Mark was a presiding figure. If all of these foremost events of early Christianity may be shown to have a direct connection with a family from Africa, that would have stunning implications for believers in Africa today. But is there a case for all these events to be reasonably connected? Their correlation is dependent upon the exegesis of Mark 14 in conjunction with Acts 1–2 and especially Acts 12, which we will look at in detail in the next chapter. I will show how they are interrelated.

The African narrative recalled the names of both of Mark's parents. This is unusual for ancient sources: His father's name was Aristopolus (Aristobulus) and his mother's name was Mary (Sawirus, *HP*, 135-37). The synaxarion gleaned the name of Mark's mother from the narratives of Luke-Acts (Acts 12:12). As important as she is, she is identified to the hearers in relation to her son, who would become known to all the disciples, all the Antiochene missionaries, as well as the churches of Rome and Alexandria.

The first written reference to Aristopolus is found in Paul's letter to the Romans: "Greet those who belong to the household of Aristobulus" (Rom 16:10). In traditional recollection, the household of Aristobulus included Mark, his son. Was Mark in Rome in about A.D. 56—the time of the writing of Paul's letter to Rome? Were some of Mark's relatives living in Rome at the time Paul wrote his letter? Or was this a different Aristobulus than the one from Cyrene? Might it be that Aristobulus (father of Mark) was living in Rome, and Mary (the mother of Mark) was living in Jerusalem? When or whether the mother of Mark was with Aristobulus remains unclear and disputed. All these questions are speculative and unresolved.

One indicator that it was the same family as that of Mark is Paul's mention in the same letter of two others who are traditionally presumed to be from Cyrene, namely, "Rufus, chosen in the Lord, and his mother, who has been a mother to me, too" (Rom 16:13). Does this suggest that there was an enclave of several Cyrenaic families in Rome by the time Paul wrote his letter? Were Rufus and his brother Alexander and his father Simon of Cyrene and his mother in any way related to Aristopolus and Mary? The text is silent, but regardless of the answer, Paul says he has benefited from a very warm and perhaps even familial relation with the mother of Rufus of Cyrene. She treated Paul as a son.

Moreover, Mary the mother of Mark appears in Jerusalem in the New Testament texts as a generous woman who offered hospitality to the disciples after the resurrection, and (if the African narratives are correct) prior to the crucifixion as well, and then during the early years of mission, first to the Jews, then to the Gentiles. She shared with most Cyrenaic Jews high messianic expectations. She is perceived as a hostess to the earliest Christian believers of Jerusalem.

She is thought by traditional sources to be among the women who ministered to Jesus with their possessions and resources (Lk 8:2-3). If Mary the mother of Mark was welcoming to the disciples as early as the time of the Lord's Supper, she could have been one of these women in the earliest circle of Jesus. She was remembered in Africa as among the women who had kindred or friendship relations with Mary the mother of Jesus. These supportive women may have included Mary the mother of James and Joses, Salome, Joanna, Susanna, or Mary Magdalene (Mt 27:56; Mk 15:40-41).

Mary the mother of Mark displays all the marks of belonging to the women that ministered to Jesus with resources and support. In Acts she is portrayed as ready to open her residence to the core of his faithful followers who would subsequently congregate there regularly for prayer (Acts 12:12). If so, Mark's mother Mary was among the earliest of Jesus' disciples, even if Mark himself was not overtly specified as such in the text. Mary the mother of Mark is clearly distinguished in the text from all the other Marys of the New Testament as the one who freely made her Jerusalem house available to the apostles. None of the other Marys were known to have guest space in Jerusalem. Mark's mother may or may not have been known to Jesus before the Last Supper but surely she was after it. There is no reason to rule out the premise that Jesus knew in advance to whom he was sending his disciples for the Passover Supper.

From the account in Acts 12 we draw the further reasonable inference that Mary was an influential woman who possessed a large house with servants, spacious enough care for more than a dozen guests. This was happening at a time when the persecutions of Christians had already broken out, as we see with James and Peter. But already by this time the church had grown to include thousands, according to Acts 2:41. Mary's house, presumably also Mark's house, was the place where its key leadership was safe to gather. There they prayed for the release of Peter from prison (see map 2 for the traditional location of Mary's House on Zion Hill).

Even the specific location of Mary's house in Jerusalem is known today with some reasonable probability. After dozens of destructions of Jerusalem we do not have her actual standing house, but we do know its probable location, because it was identified very early (by the third or fourth century, with epigraphic evidence from the sixth century) as the

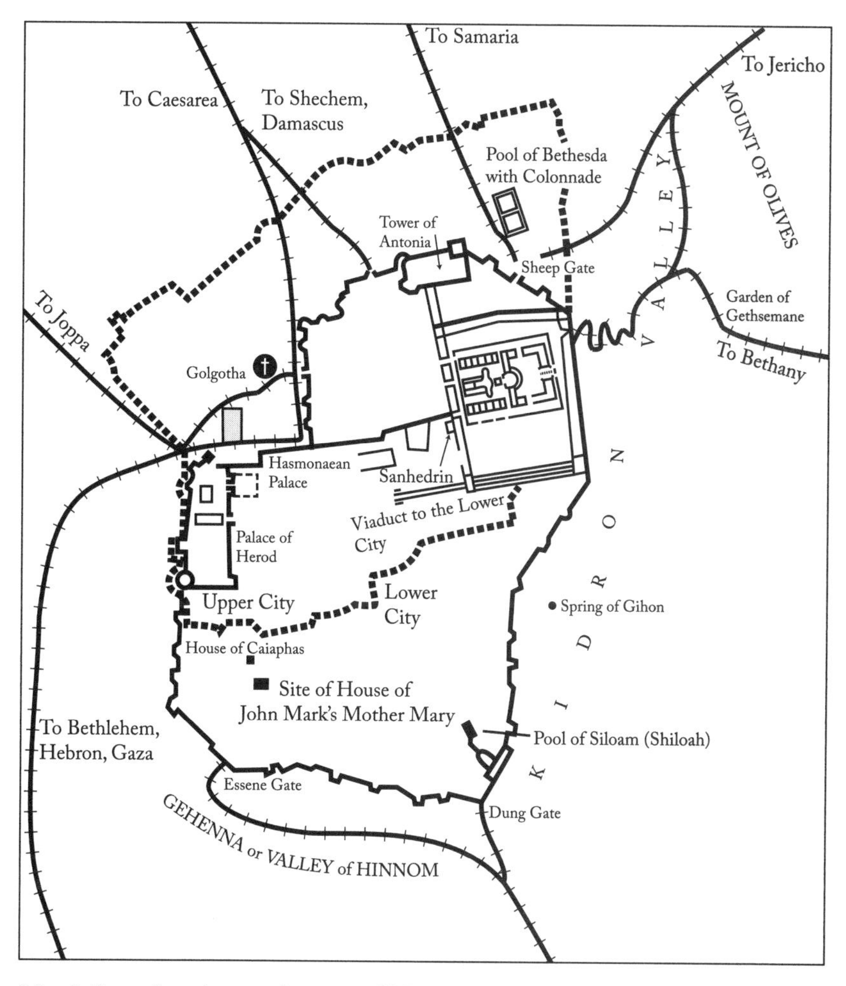

Map 2. Jerusalem showing location of Mark's mother's house

house of Mary, the mother of John Mark, on or near Zion Hill, Jerusalem, the place where the disciples gathered and where a very early pilgrimage site was located. Since the family had Levitical connections, it would make sense that their home was located in the city near Zion where many priests lived.

This house evidently was approached by a porch and had an outer door or property gate. The house was large enough to require the servant girl Rhoda (we know her name from Luke's narrative) to go to the gate, a distance far enough away that those inside did not hear the conversation in the outer area (Acts 12:13). The remnants of a first-century house partly hidden, partly exposed, lies in the upper city on the southwestern heights of Zion Hill. There St. Mark Monastery now stands on the ancient site of the house of St. Mark the Evangelist according to a sixth-century inscription which was discovered in 1940.

WHETHER REMNANTS OF THE HOUSE REMAIN

This is not exclusively an African memory, but has also been held by many other tradition bearers and empirical archaeologists to be the location of the Last Supper. Syrian Orthodox Patriarch Mar Aghnatius Yacoub wrote:

> His [Mark's] mother had a house in Jerusalem, through tradition and documented history it is confirmed that in it God gathered His apostles, celebrated the Passover, washed the feet of His disciples and gave them the mystery of His Body and Blood. There He talked to them. The apostles waited in it till the Lord came back to them after His Resurrection, while its doors were closed. There He gave them the ecclesiastics [sacrament], and the priesthood authority, and filled them by His Holy Spirit. Later the house was consecrated to be a church with the name of Mother of God. . . . It became the seat of Jerusalem. St. James, became the first Bishop of Jerusalem, and stayed there.[2]

Thus the house of Mary and her son Mark became the first church in the world. This was celebrated very early by both the Jerusalem community of faith and the African tradition. It was consecrated by the presence of the Lord himself in his first and prototypical sacramental action of gathering together the new people of God. This was the first great gift of Africa to Jesus' ministry: the providing of a house and a space of hospitality in which to gather and pray. There they partook of the Passover Meal. The dwelling toward which Jesus pointed the disciples for their last supper with him would provide hospitality for many more events to come. There Jesus washed their feet and offered them

[2]Mar Aghnatius Yacoub, "Beth John Mark, The First Christian Church," quoted in Shenouda III, p. 119.

the bread and wine that would become the model for all subsequent celebrations of the Eucharist.

The place is today often called the Monastery of St. Mark, or the house of Mary, mother of Mark. Within the monastery are a Byzantine church and the offices of the patriarch. The church was largely, but not completely, wrecked during the rule of the sixth Fatimid Caliph Abu 'Ali Mansur Tāriqu a-Hākim, also called bi Amr al-Lāh, in A.D. 1009. The monastery was abandoned during the Turkish rule, but the Syrians renovated it in 1855, and extended it in A.D. 1880. The house is still regarded as the first baptismal place, and the Seat of St. James the apostle, the first bishop of Jerusalem (*History of Jerusalem*, 4).[3]

I have twice visited this location. There I conferred with Coptic, Ethiopic, Armenian and Syrian Orthodox bishops. There I learned of the history of the house. As a young scholar, I scoffed at this evidence, but when physically there I found it compelling. Apparently the church of the first four centuries (between A.D. 30 and 333) had remembered this hallowed location explicitly, due to its liturgical significance, its relation to the Eucharist and Pentecost, and to Mark's Gospel.

This specific site was identified as a long-known site of pilgrimage as early as the time of Cyril of Jerusalem in A.D. 348, and before that by the Bordeaux Pilgrim (*Itinerarium Burdigalense)* in A.D. 333, and by the Spanish nun Egeria in 385, and by others. The Bordeaux Pilgrim described the area as it looked in A.D. 333: "Within, however, inside the wall of Sion, is seen the place where was David's palace. Of seven synagogues which once were there, one alone remains; the rest are ploughed over and sown upon, as said Isaiah the prophet."[4]

Did the Jerusalem faithful at the time of Cyril fabricate this location? In my view it is implausible to make the assumption that the Christian believers of Jerusalem would have forgotten the location of the place where the first Lord's Supper was instituted. Of all specific locations in Jerusalem, this would be among those least likely to be forgotten. If so, the Jerusalem Christians sustained a continuous his-

[3]*The History of Jerusalem* is a booklet published by the See of Jerusalem.
[4]*Itinerarium Burdigalense,* in reference to Is 1:8 and Mic 3:12; English trans. by Aubrey Stewart, *Itinerary from Bordeaux to Jerusalem,* annotated by Charles William Wilson (London, 1887).

tory from the first to the fourth century. What the pilgrims saw is what the church of Jerusalem consensually remembered.

At the site of this sacred place, "the house of Mary, mother of John Mark," a church was built in the sixth century, a very ancient basilica, of which a portion of one wall still remains, which has this inscription: "This is the house of Mary, mother of John, called Mark; Proclaimed a church by the holy apostles under the name of the Virgin Mary, mother of God, after the ascension of our Lord Jesus Christ into heaven; Renewed after the destruction of Jerusalem by Titus in the year A.D. 73."

Among all the disputed sites of early Christian Jerusalem, this is one of the most reliably authenticated by epigraphic and literary and archaeological sources in combination. There is far greater reason to doubt the precise location of the empty tomb than of this specific site, whose subsequent buildings have been destroyed and rebuilt on the same location without destroying the foundational wall. After the Syriac Orthodox Church lost its other churches and properties in the Holy City, St. Mark's became the seat of the Archbishop of Jerusalem. It is indeed true that one can still write a letter to the ancient house of Mark and Mary, to that address—P.O. Box 14069, IL-91140, Jerusalem, Old City, Israel—and have it delivered to that location.

To summarize: Mary of the upper room was the mother of John Mark, whose Levitical family had quarters in Jerusalem where Jesus came to meet with disciples the last time before his crucifixion, the same room where the first sacrament of the Lord's Supper was instituted, the same room where the Holy Spirit was poured out upon the disciples on the day of Pentecost.

HOW THE LORD'S SUPPER IS REENACTED IN EARLY AFRICAN LITURGY

Early African exegetes were keenly attentive to the details of Lord's Supper. Origen was first to observe that Jesus waited patiently until all the disciples were at the table until he said: "One of you will betray me—one who is eating with me" (Mk 14:18). Why wait, asked Origen? Because the Eucharist is itself a testing. This was asked in order that "the character of each might be tested by the witness of his astonished heart" (*Comm. Matt.* 50). The moral implication, according to the African memory, is that all who come to the Lord's Table are tested in conscience as to their faith. Eleven of the Twelve were disturbed by this confrontation. One lied. Cyprian of Carthage commented on the patience of Jesus: "He could eat calmly with his betrayer" (*The Good of Patience* 6).

Jesus then made an allusion to Psalm 41:9 "Even my bosom friend in whom I trusted, who ate of my bread, has lifted his heel against me" (RSV). Mark echoes this psalm in reporting Jesus' comment: "It is one of the twelve, one who is dipping bread into the dish with me" (Mk 14:20 RSV). "The very one who was being generously received to a common table betrayed Jesus who had embraced him with such great affection" (Origen, *Comm. Matt.* 50).

The food and drink which is being prepared presumably in the upper room by the mother of Mark is viewed in African liturgy as well as exegesis as "the blood of the grape" and "the bread of the word" (Origen, *Comm. Matt.* 85). They anticipate his ensuing death and rising again. The bread is "the word of Christ made from that corn which, falling onto the good ground, brought forth much fruit," in reference to Mark 14:22: "As they were eating, he took bread, and blessed, and broke it, and gave it to them, and said, 'Take; this is my body' " (RSV). Mark is either remembering or reporting words that Jesus himself said on that occasion, words that would be recalled in all subsequent celebrations of the Eucharist. These are words that Peter himself surely must have heard, and that Mark, as the son of the household, could have heard.

Body and blood refer to the word spoken through Christ's death and resurrection. Jesus is prefiguring an event yet to come: His body is going down like grain into the earth and will be raised again as living Bread for all time to come. "He was not speaking of the visible bread alone which he was holding in his hands as he called it his body. It is the Word in the mystery [in relation to] which that bread was to be broken" (Origen, *Comm. Matt.* 85). In this upper room what he held in his hand was bread. He "blessed it, broke it, and gave thanks, saying, 'Take it. This is my body.' " His whole body is soon to be offered up in his crucifixion and death. His whole body suffered. He died on the cross.

What he is offering to his true family, children of the Father, is "the blood of the grape cast in the wine press" (Origen, *Comm. Matt.* 85). Remember that the root word for Gethsemane on the Mount of Olives is to "press" for the extraction of fluids, such as oil or more frequently wine. His life is being squeezed out of him. His seed is being buried and brought back to life. The grape gives its blood in the winepress of the Passion. "For to what else could the body and blood of the Lord refer other than the atoning Word that nourishes and gladdens the heart" (Origen, *Comm. Matt.* 85).

Bread nourishes and wine makes the heart glad. Our souls are nourished by the coming, preaching and wonderful deeds of Jesus. By the mystery of his birth and death and resurrection, this new covenant family is filled with the new wine of the Spirit. Our hearts are made joyful with "a stream of gladness" (Clement of Alexandria, *Christ the Educator* 2.32). To this place Jesus came with the Twelve who represent this new family, this new Israel, these new twelve tribes.

Tertullian of Carthage comments on Marcion's docetic temptation to turn the bread into a symbolic figure only: "Having taken the bread and given it to his disciples, he made it his own body by saying, 'This is my body.' . . . A figure, however, there could not have been, unless there had first been a palpable body. A phantom or a mere void is not capable of embodying a figure" (Tertullian, *Marc.* 4.40).

Now we have a clear window to see the connection between the African hospitality tradition and the Jerusalem community of hospitality: at the very location of the institution of the Eucharist. It happens in a large room provided by an African family for the Lord who has no place to lay his head. Jesus is offering his body to be broken, yet soon to be resurrected, offering it to the new family to participate in his life. So take the bread, eat it, this is my body. Take the cup. Give thanks. Drink it. This is my blood of the new covenant shed for many (Mk 14:22-24). "As they were eating" the Passover, he was offering the new family an entirely new form of the divine-human covenant, an enriched food for the soul, and in doing so transforming the Passover. He is offering his own body and blood, a once for all true sacrifice, ready to be given to the whole world on the cross.

In Mark 14, Jesus made it entirely clear what is meant by this blood: "This is the blood of the covenant, which is poured out for many. Truly, I say to you, I shall not drink again of the fruit of the vine until that day when I drink it new in the kingdom of God" (Mk 14:24-25 RSV). This is the last time Jesus will eat and drink before the kingdom comes in his death and resurrection. That coming kingdom would be revealed the next day on the cross and then its truth vindicated in his resurrection. He is the lamb to be taken out of the herd to be slain and buried by night.

The reign of God was coming, announced by Jesus' preaching and inaugurated by his death and resurrection. Of the millions of sacrificial meals in salvation history, this was the most definitive. It fulfilled the covenant promise that had been embedded in what up to that time was the most significant meal in Hebraic history—the Passover. The bread and the wine in that upper room provided the central core of the sacramental life for all the subsequent centuries of Christian worship. It was the first house church. Thus it is pertinent to listen carefully to how Mark himself first reported this event. Mark's next scene provides details on the location and preparation for the Passover.

THE WAY TO GETHSEMANE

It is useful to rehearse the sequence of locations of Mark 14, and then the events reported in Acts 12.

First, recall the sequence of events in Mark 14:

- the anointing in Bethany
- the betrayal by Judas
- the institution of the supper
- Gethsemane arrest
- the young man following Jesus fled
- the trial

Following the resurrection, the disciples are found in what appears to be the same upper room (Acts 1:13), where they continued to meet for Pentecost (Acts 2:1), and afterward for continuing prayer, according to the early chapters of Acts. It is crucial to the African narrative that it was from this same house of the supper, that Jesus and the disciples went directly to the Mount of Olives. They sang together. He prayed. He was betrayed. The next day he offered up his body for the sins of the world. His blood was shed for all humanity.

African exegetes did not miss any tiny aspect of the narrative. For example, the singing. The deep symbolism hidden in the event is revealed: When you receive this word in faith, this bread, this wine into the depths of your soul, your whole life turns into a flute, a lyre, an instrument of music played by the Holy Spirit. The faithful join with the singing of the disciples on the way to the Mount of Olives, in anticipation of songs they will sing in the heavenly gathering (Gen 31:27; 1 Chron 15:29; 16:5; Mk 14:26).

Were Mark and his mother among the disciples who continued from her home toward Gethsemane? The African exegetical imagination thought so. They were going directly from Mark's house. As the people of God were called and enabled to sing amid adversity in Isaiah (Is 44:23; 49:13; 51:11), so the disciples sang on the way to the cross. "Break forth, O mountains, into singing" (Is 49:13). After they received "food to profit their souls," they sang. As Cyril of Alexandria wrote: "After God took mercy on them, however, a feast has been prepared for them in the choir school of spiritual good things" (Cyril, *Commentary on Isaiah* 4.4.49.8-12).

By our eating of his body and drinking of his life-blood, we are participating in him, walking with him through his death and resurrection, walking with him to the cross, descending to burial and ascending in resurrection, by faith through grace. So they walked and sang to Gethsemane, where the Lord sweated and prayed he would be enabled to receive this cup, even with all its bitterness.

The African imagination savored the sacred text, each word of it. The company of the disciples could see from the Mount of Olives the great buildings of the temple. Those enormous stones. The Lord is teaching them: "Not one stone here will be left upon another" (Mk 13:2). The old era will be replaced by a new era. This will all be thrown down. That would occur in fact in A.D. 70, as a confirming sign of the end of the old age and the coming of the new (Eusebius, *CH* 3.5-7). From that same Mount of Olives he would ascend to heaven. When we participate in his body and blood, taking his bread and wine into our bodies, eating and drinking gladly, we show our willingness to share with him in his love and mercy. In this way our bodies become a new temple of the Spirit. We see the temple in a new way—from the viewpoint of its end, its being transcended. We participate in the death of the old man and resurrection of the new. We embody the new temple, and live thereafter with the Lord who will come again.

THE GATHERING PLACE OF THE CHURCH IN MISSION

When the apostles returned to Jerusalem from the Mount of Olives, where did they go? They immediately "went to the upstairs room of the house *where they were staying*" (Acts 1:13 NLT, emphasis added). Where were they staying? The last place we have heard about is "a large upper room, all furnished" (Lk 22:12)—indicating a large house not unlike the house of Mary the mother of Mark (Acts 12:12-13). Luke 22:7-13 echoes the description of Mark 14:12-16. The gathering place of the apostles before and after the resurrection was Mark's house. So the text was understood in Africa. Why else would Luke have added the phrase "where they were staying"?

The central postresurrection activities of the disciples most likely occurred in the same place, the same upper room where the Cyrenaic disciples would later gather after the ascension of Jesus with the other believers. There they awaited, as instructed by the Lord, for the outpouring of the Spirit at Pentecost.

Note the significance of this: If the African memory is received, the disciples were meeting in the home, somewhat surprisingly, of a displaced Jewish family of the priestly order whose previous residence was in Libya. After the Last Supper, we begin to see the footprints of Jews of the African Diaspora all over the New Testament. By common African memory the ensuing events happened in the upper room of the house of Mary the mother of Mark. What hints of this common memory can we find in the canonical text? We begin with the upper room language that appears in Mark 14:15, Luke 22:12 and Acts 1:13.

Weymouth renders Acts 1:12-13: "Then they returned to Jerusalem from the mountain called the Oliveyard, which is near Jerusalem, about a mile off. They entered the city, and then went *to the upper room*, which was *now their fixed place for meeting*" (emphasis added). Notice the repeated language regarding the upstairs room: The disciples were returning from the Mount of Olives (Acts 1:12). To where? "When they arrived, they went *upstairs to the room [hyperōon] where they were staying*" (Acts 1:13).

Luke in his Gospel follows Mark's lead in speaking specifically of "a large room upstairs, all furnished" (*anagaion mega estrōmenon*—Mk 14:15; Lk 22:12) as the location of the Last Supper. Is this location in Acts 1 then the same as that in Mark 14 and Luke 22? It seems unlikely that there was more than one upper room where the earliest disciples repeatedly gathered. Thus all references to "the upstairs room" or "large room upstairs" likely point to a single location. Later in Acts we hear the name of the one to whom that house likely belongs: "Mary, the mother of John Mark" (Acts 12:12). She was the hostess obedient to the command of the Lord. She was a mother whose son would soon be deeply involved in a mission that would change his life and send him all around the Mediterranean to all known continents.

The identification of the upper room (*anagaion*) in Mark 14:15 and Luke 22:12 with the upper room (*hyperōon*) in Acts 1:13, of course, would be stronger if they were linguistically the same. Furthermore, it must be acknowledged that there is no specific mention of an upper room at the home of Mary the mother of John Mark (Acts 12:12). Nevertheless, the two terms for an "upper room" are clearly synonymous, and the tradition remains strong that they were one and the same place and properly identified with the house of Mary. While detractors suggest we have no positive evidence to conclude they were one and the same, it can equally be said there is even less positive evidence to suggest they were different.

All the standard forms of the African narrative (from synaxaries to Sawirus to Shenouda III) make the inference that "where they were staying" (RSV; or "the upper room they had been using as a meeting place," *The Message*) was the same house where the Lord's Supper was instituted. There they returned to await the coming of the Holy Spirit, as Jesus had directed them.

The disciples did not meet just in any nondescript room. They "went up to *the upper room where they were lodging*" (*eis to hyperōon anebēsan hou ēsan katamenontes*, Acts 1:13, emphasis added). There is no hint in any episode of the narrative between Acts 1:13 and 2:1 that they had changed their location. Thus if this room is properly identified as the upper level of the house of Mark's mother, it is indeed in Mark's house that the Holy Spirit descended on the disciples after the crucifixion, resurrection and ascension of Jesus. And if this is so, then the African component of the earliest layers of Christian memory of the gifts of Pentecost cannot be dismissed. Since Independent Pentecostal Christianity is Africa's fastest growing form of worship, this connection has immense implications. Though the Mark text is not sufficiently explicit to make this an absolute and unqualified assertion, the reasonable correlation of the texts of Luke 22:12, Acts 1:12-13 and Acts 12:12 make it a compelling argument, far more plausible than the alternatives.

If these correlations lead to a proper conclusion, then the upper room remained the center of mission and apostolic activity from Pentecost to Peter's flight from prison. Who was there? The Twelve (less Judas) along with the family of Jesus, his mother and the women who had been accompanying Jesus (Acts 1:14). Mary the mother of Mark could well have been among "the women who had been accompanying Jesus." Thus it seems reasonable to accept or at least reevaluate the ancient tradition that the upper room was the upstairs part of the house of Mary the mother of Mark and that it provided the place where a host of major events took place: the Last Supper and footwashing, the gathering place for prayer, and as we will see, much more.

THE UPPER ROOM AS THE LOCATION OF PENTECOST

The next reported event states: "When the day of Pentecost came, they were all together in one place. Suddenly a sound like the blowing of a violent wind came from heaven and filled the whole house *[holon ton oikon]* where they were sitting" (Acts 2:1-2). Which "one place"? It appears to be the same place "where they were staying" (Goodspeed), "their fixed place of meeting" (Acts 1:13 Weymouth), the upper room in which they had gathered for the Last Supper.

African memory took this as a clear signal that African voices were among those at Pentecost. They were clearly cited (Acts 2:10). The hostess was a woman named Mary, living in Jerusalem who had come from Libyan Cyrene. The location for all these events was previously identified and described as the house of Mary the mother of Mark. There the Spirit filled the whole house. They spoke "as the Spirit enabled them."

It is explicit that believers from Libya were present at Pentecost: "These cities [the five cities of the Pentapolis of Libya] were represented at the time the disciples received the Holy Spirit on the Pentecost, 'And the parts of Libya about Cyrene.'" (Acts 2:10; Shenouda III, chap. 5n4). What were the Pentecost participants saying in their different languages—including Libyo-Punic or Berber? People were "telling in our own tongues the mighty works of God" (Acts 2:11 RSV).

People of many different language groups were present. They were coming from all over the remote places of the Jewish Diaspora to the house of a Diaspora Libyan woman. But despite the wide differences in their languages, they could understand each other. The Acts narrative names some of those languages known to be present at Pentecost. Among them were those "from Libya in the area of Cyrene" and from Egypt.

What was occurring at Pentecost was the opposite of Babel, where the power of language, which due to human arrogance had become idolatrously reinforced, was broken up, collapsed, dysfunctional and grossly impaired. Amid all the failures of human language, all the misunderstandings that come from human miscommunication are being overcome by the power of the Spirit (cf. comments from Origen, Cyril, Augustine, ACCS NT 5, s.v. Acts 2:4).

It is folly to explain miracles, but the historic fact is that something miraculous was happening at Pentecost. Was it a miracle of human hearing, or was it a miracle of human speaking? Or was it a miracle preternaturally enabled by the Spirit? Whatever, it was beyond our understanding, immersed in mystery. This premise makes more sense than that of unknown word sounds or senseless phonemes being blurted. It was an event of hearing and speaking and accord clearly among people who could not speak these different languages but could understand. Even today, the vast African body of believers is still marveling at the Pentecostal event, hosted by an African woman.

7

MARK WITH PETER AND PAUL

Taking the premise that Mark was likely living, at least intermittently, at his mother's house at Pentecost, the sequence of events invites the question: *Where was Mark* during the events reported in the first twelve chapters of the Acts? Recall that at Pentecost there were people speaking the languages of "the parts of Libya near Cyrene" (Acts 2:10). When the church was born at Pentecost, Africans were there. If this event occurred in Mark's house, as African memory holds, Mark was likely with them.

No one can say with certainty whether Mark was at this time already implicated in the apostolic ministry, but there is no reason to rule it out. It is more likely than not. African memory, however, clearly places him among the disciples gathered at Pentecost at his mother's house. From their perspective, Mark was an apostle and eyewitness who had beheld the Lord face to face. If so, he would have had to be among the disciples from before the ascension and through Pentecost to the events that occurred in his family home.

And if Mark was in Jerusalem, then, he would have heard Peter proclaim his Pentecost message to the multitude: "God has raised this Jesus to life, and we are all witnesses of the fact" (Acts 2:32). If Mark had a close, perhaps familial, relation with Peter, Peter's call to "repent and be baptized" could have prompted Mark himself to be baptized at

Peter's hand, as the African narrative suggests. If Peter's reference to "my son Mark" (1 Pet 5:13) implies "my son in the faith whom I baptized," Mark may have learned apostolic teaching from Peter himself.

THE AFRICAN MEMORY OF MARK'S JOURNEYS WITH PAUL AND PETER

Where was Mark from Acts 5 to 12? We can only proceed by reasonable inference. Between Pentecost and Antioch come the crucial narratives (see table 1 for a likely chronology):

- the persecution of the apostles in Jerusalem (Acts 5)
- the stoning of Stephen (Acts 7) with Saul consenting
- the outbreak of persecution against the Jerusalem church (Acts 8)
- the scattering abroad of believers, "except the apostles"
- the rapid spread of the gospel in Samaria through Philip's preaching
- Simon the Magician rebuked by Peter
- Peter and John's mission to Samaria to pray for the Holy Spirit to come upon the new believers
- the mission of Peter and John in the area of Jerusalem (Acts 8:25), in which Mark might have been a participant, as the African memory holds
- Philip converting the Ethiopian who was returning to Africa on the road to Gaza
- the conversion of Saul on the road to Damascus (Acts 9:1-9) and his mixed reception when he returned to Jerusalem
- Barnabas, Mark's relative, defending Saul before the apostles
- Peter's vision in Joppa and the conversion of Cornelius (Acts 10:1-48)
- Peter's explanation of his actions to the apostles and brothers "throughout Judea" (Acts 11)
- Barnabas and Saul's year-long preaching and teaching in Antioch (note the precedence of Barnabas to Saul)
- Barnabas and Saul's carrying of a gift to Judean Christians

- Peter's arrest and imprisonment (Acts 12)
- Peter's miraculous escape and flight to the house of Mary the mother of John Mark
- Peter's flight to "another place" (Acts 12:17)

These narratives from Acts 5–12 set the scene for a key detail that again connects Mark with Africa: the flight of Peter from Herod Agrippa II's imprisonment and his dazed return (Acts 12:12-17) to the house of the family of Mark. We have already made note of how revealing this episode is, especially regarding the possible identity and relationship between Peter, Mark, and Mary the mother of Mark. The African memory places Mark side by side with Peter, Paul and Barnabas during this period. According to the official Coptic narrative of Anba Shenouda: "St. Mark preached in Judea, Lebanon, Syria, Antioch and in Cyprus. He reached Paphos, Pamphylia, Rome, Colossi, Venice and Aquila" (Shenouda III, 20).

Shenouda III, in accord with Luke's account in Acts, places Mark in the middle of all this missionary activity, saying that Mark

> accompanied St. Paul and St. Barnabas on their first trip. They went to Syria, and particularly to Antioch. [Acts 11:27-30]; "And took with them John, whose surname was Mark." Thus he handled with them the Word of the Savior to Antioch about 45 A.D. . . . He went with them to Seleucia, [Acts 13:4] which was the port of Antioch. St. Mark came again to Antioch with Barnabas the apostle, [Acts 15:37] after the council of Jerusalem. (Shenouda III, 21)

PETER'S LEADING ROLE AMONG APOSTLES

Peter's leadership position among the disciples is evident:

- He is the leading figure among those called by Jesus to discipleship (Mk 1:16-20).
- He is the rock of the eyewitness testimony upon which Jesus promised to build his church (Mt 16:13-18).
- He delivers the first public sermon proclaiming the resurrection, winning a large number of converts (Acts 2:14-41).

- After Saul's conversion Saul came to Jerusalem "to see Peter" (Gal 1:18-20).
- After James's martyrdom, Peter was the first to be imprisoned.

Peter's mission among the Christians of Antioch is revealed in an episode concerning the observance of the Jewish ceremonial law by Christians reported by Paul in Galatians (Gal 2:11-21). The "pillars" of the apostolic church—Peter, James and John—had confirmed Paul's mission to the Gentiles, while they themselves focused largely on teaching among the Jews. Peter came to Antioch to see what was happening there, sharing their meals and looking for discernment. This raised questions about food laws. These may have been a part of Mark's tension with Saul of Tarsus.

When the Christianized Jews from Antioch came to Jerusalem, Peter was sensitive that the Jewish ceremonial law might be offended. Peter's standing among Judaizing Christians may have appeared vulnerable. Peter avoided eating with the uncircumcised, as did Barnabas (and if Barnabas, likely Mark). Paul opposed them, defending converted pagans from being compelled to become circumcised. Nevertheless, when divergent opinions were expressed in the Council of Jerusalem, it was Peter who spoke the deciding word. Though at first aloof to Gentile converts out of concern for the Jewish Christians from Jerusalem, Peter did not give his approval to the extreme Judaizers, who opposed Paul. No enduring doctrinal differences can be supposed between Peter and Paul in their understanding of salvation for both Jews and Gentiles.

Recall that Peter was one of the first to be directly called by Jesus into discipleship at Capernaum (Mk 1:16-17; cf. Jn 1:40-41). After Jesus' Jerusalem ministry, Peter's time in Jerusalem came to an end with Herod's persecution. After the martyrdom of James, Peter was thrown in prison, miraculously freed, and in a confused condition immediately found his way. Where? Precisely to the house of the mother of Mark, the same house where the faithful were gathered for prayer. Afterward, Peter departed to "another place" (Acts 12:1-19).

We come back to our question: Where was Mark throughout these events? The deeper we go, we sense the paradox of the ubiquity and anonymity of Mark, to be further discussed in chapter eleven. The text is largely silent, except for incidental allusions and inferences. But we have good reason to guess that Mark was a confidant of Peter and a participant of some consequence in these mighty events stretching from Jerusalem to Antioch to "another place," to be discussed next.

John Mark was not named among the Twelve, and not chosen among the seven deacons, but this could be because of his younger age and perhaps his more recent entry into discipleship. Looking at the names of the seven, it appears that it includes Jews who come from the international Diaspora—the Hellenists. There is not sufficient reason to rule out the view that Mark could have been among the pool of Diaspora Jews from which the seven were chosen to serve tables in order to free the Twelve to preach the good news.

It seems almost an afterthought when Luke, having described the gruesome death of Herod Agippa I, notes: "When Barnabas and Saul had finished their mission, they returned from Jerusalem, taking with them John, also called Mark" (Acts 12:25). Note again the implied priority: Barnabas, Saul, Mark. This was at a time when the word of God was continuing to "increase and spread." Then followed the first missionary journey with Mark joining Barnabas and Paul. Why did they take Mark? The next episode, found in Acts 12:1-17, will bring us closer to solving the puzzle.

BABYLON OF EGYPT AS THE PLACE TO WHICH PETER MAY HAVE FLED

The location of Peter's flight to "another place" is the subject of our investigation now. In particular, we explore the possibility that Mark may have accompanied Peter on his flight and what implications that might have for its location. The most logical location for that other place, according to Egyptian reasoning, would have been Babylon of Egypt (later "Old Cairo"), which for many years before the Roman occupation had been a place for receiving refugees (see table 1 for a chronology of the events).

The hypothesis that Peter fled to Babylon in Egypt has for the most part been ignored or discounted by Western scholars, but there are good reasons to reexamine it. Three reasons in particular must be considered:

- If Mark was indeed accompanying Peter directly from his own mother's house to another place, another safe house, and probably one far away—out of Herod's reach—and if Mark knew the lay of the land in Africa, his presumed place of birth, he could have guided Peter safely to Old Cairo.
- If Mark was a close relative of Peter, as traditional African memory holds, then he might well have been given responsibility for Peter's safety.
- If Mark was from a well-traveled and wealthy Diaspora family, as traditional African memory holds, he would have the means and know-how to get Peter safely away from Jerusalem and into a safe house, perhaps at Babylon of Egypt.

What do we now know about Old Cairo as a refugee center before Roman times based on current research? What sources are available now that were not previously in circulation? What new hypotheses seem plausible?

- We now have the Genizah Papers.
- The metaphor of "Babylon" had been a symbol of flight and persecution and refugee safety prior to Roman occupation.
- After the building of the Roman fort under Trajan, the ancient pre-Roman location retained the name of Babylon and had typological meaning, as perceived by Christians under persecution in Palestine.

Babylon of Egypt had been an essential military site and a port for economic transit for centuries long before Roman occupation—indeed since Egypt's Old Kingdom. Many battles were fought over this crucial location, now called Old Cairo (Kheraha). Though few residents of Cairo know its Christian history, it is well known to Coptic Christians whose Coptic Museum is located there. It was its strategic location, due to its access to the Nile and the Persian-built canal that linked Old Cairo and Heliopolis, that made it so important over the centuries before the Romans ruled. Human settlements near the southern apex of the delta go back to the sixth millennium B.C. First-century Jews in flight from Roman authorities had over a long period of time streamed into the Nile region south of the Delta. Old Cairo was one of their first stops. It was an entryway to all points south, where safe houses for refugees were hidden away.

Kheraha was the root word for Cairo. The word itself refers to a "battleground." The fort was first built by the Persians in the sixth century B.C. on the heights near the river. When the Romans came, they first used the remnants of the old Persian fort, until in Trajan's time they relocated it to a nearby spot closer to the Nile. The Romans built on this site a bastion that had long been referred to as "Babylon" in pre-Roman and pre-Christian times.

Diodorus of Sicily in his *Bibliotheca historica* (1.56, 49 B.C.) writes that this settlement was populated by prisoners from the Mesopotamian city of Babylon. When Strabo later visited Heliopolis, he noted, "Going higher upriver, you come to Babylon, a stronghold where a number of Babylonians rebelled and, after negotiations, obtained the kings' permission to settle. Today however it is the garrison town of one of the three legions stationed in Egypt" (*Geographica* 17.1.30). Today the old fort is the entrance to the Coptic Museum. Contiguous with the fort is one of Egypt's oldest and most famous Coptic churches dedicated to the Virgin Mary and known as Mu'allaqa (the Hanging Church). After being a refugee location in pre-Christian times, Babylon in due time became a Christian stronghold, the sacred location of Cairo's earliest Christian churches, and for a time the center of the patriarchate, the See of St. Mark. It continued to serve as a refuge for Coptic Christians persecuted by Roman and Byzantine authorities.

The Synagogue of Ben Ezra is Egypt's oldest surviving synagogue. It is only a few steps away from where the former Roman fort, commonly called Babylon of Egypt, was built. Its antecedents may have preceded the building of the fort. Today, the only visible trace of Roman occupation is the Fortress of Babylon of Egypt, known as Misr al-Qadima in Old Cairo. At the south gate excavations have revealed a quay, indicating that commercial and military activities were going on around the harbor in Roman times. Much remains in doubt, but what has been confirmed is that a Jewish community had existed in this same area long before the ninth century when the synagogue acquired a Coptic church property. This church had been dedicated to St. Michael until the conquest of Egypt by Chosroes in A.D. 616.

What were Diaspora Jews doing in Babylon of Egypt before this time? They were building up a significant library. A collection of almost 280,000 manuscripts dating from A.D. 870 onwards was discovered there. They were found in a hidden store room of the Ben Ezra Synagogue in Fustat, in Old Cairo, and from the Basatin cemetery east of Old Cairo. When the synagogue was repaired by the Cairo Jewish community, during the renovation an old depository was rediscovered. It was in a secret chamber at the back of the east end of the synagogue and was approached from the farthest extremity of the gallery by climbing a ladder and entering through a hole in the wall.

A genizah is a storeroom in a synagogue, often hidden. The purpose of a genizah, or synagogue depository, is to preserve good things from harm and bad things from harming. It protected worn-out copies of sacred Jewish writings and set aside heretical writings. The normal practice for preserving antique sacred texts was to bury them in a cemetery. Since the Hebrew sacred script was considered to be the literal writing of God, the texts could not be destroyed even long after they had served their purpose in worship. The area surrounding the Fort of Babylon contained numerous extensive cemeteries—Jewish, Christian and Muslim.

The Genizah of the Ben Ezra Synagogue, often simply called the Cairo Genizah, contained a thousand-year accumulation of Jewish manuscript fragments that constitute one of the most important sources for understanding the daily life of Jews in the region surrounding Babylon of Cairo. The documents that survived, many of which are now in London, Oxford, Cambridge and other libraries, included copies of texts and manuscripts that had been written much earlier. The Jews who wrote the materials stored or buried in the genizah were familiar with the culture and language of their contemporary society and to some extent of former times for Jews in Egypt. These documents deal with not only Hebrew and Jewish literature but virtually every aspect of life in the Mediterranean. They show that the Jewish community was a part of the general society, which, by the time of the storage of these texts, included Christians and Muslims. They were engaged in the same trades as their neighbors: farming, trading, renting, selling goods and services. Some of these documents came from Palestine, Syria and Italy, and as far away as India, Morocco and Samarkand. Records relating to Marseilles, Genoa, Venice and Kiev were referenced.

What might this collection have to do with Peter and Mark? To explain, we must have a look at the earliest known Christian quarter in the same area.

THE EARLY CHRISTIAN QUARTER OLD CAIRO

Old Cairo is the ancient Christian center of the city. The oldest churches in Cairo are there. The pre-Islamic church dates back to a Christian community existing at least in the fourth century and probably much earlier. Here we can see remnants of the beginning of Christian architecture in Egypt. Before the churches were built, the displaced Jewish and Christian congregations met in houses. Many churches of great antiquity still stand there, including the Hanging Church (al-Mu'allaqa), suspended over the south gate of the fort.

The Coptic patriarchate was centered there during early times. The Church of St. Barbara, originally dedicated to Sts. Cyril and John, was built in the fourth or fifth century. The Monastery of St. George (Maris Girgis) was integrated into the northern of the twin western towers of the Roman fort. Inside the fortified area were the Churches of St. Sergius/St. Bacchus and St. Barbara, and the Synagogue of Ben Ezra. Nearby is the Coptic Museum, where many early Christian artifacts are displayed.

The site of Old Cairo was apparently a refugee haven long before the fort was renovated by the Romans under Diocletian in A.D. 300. There were pre-Roman settlements along that part of the riverbank as early as the Persian occupation. Later, the Romans built a fortress here, which we know today as "Babylon," the walls of which are still visible today (see fig. 2). As the Jewish Diaspora to Egypt intermittently increased during the first century, this central port location, connecting the upper and lower Nile, once again became a refugee center. Similarly with the spread of Christianity, and perhaps as early as Peter and Mark themselves, the region around Babylon of Egypt served as a welcoming center for pilgrims of many nations. By the third-century persecutions it was likely a predominantly Christian refugee center. By the fourth century the patriarchate itself, the See of St. Mark, was located there. Why would the See of St. Mark be moved to Babylon of Egypt unless there were recollections of the earlier importance of the site?

Figure 2. Roman fort at Babylon of Egypt, Old Cairo

Over time as many as twenty churches would be built within a compacted area of just one square mile. Why so many churches? It was a place to receive foreign visitors. Of these many churches only five remain, along with the earliest mosque ever built in Egypt. After the fall of Jerusalem in around A.D. 70, the area saw an influx of Jews. It is there in Babylon, where Egypt's oldest synagogue, Ben Ezra, is located, that the Genizah papers were found.

A refugee from Palestine seeking safety in Egypt in the first century would ordinarily come by land or sea to the Egyptian coastal city of Pelusium in the northeasternmost part of the rich Nile delta. They would go down the Pelousiakos River through Boubastites (Bubastis) south toward Heliopolis and Memphis where the river from the south divided into the delta. One of the first places on that trajectory where the refugee would likely find Jewish enclaves would be the area around Heliopolis to the east and Letopolis to the west of the Nile, with Kerkasoros and Babylon as protected cities directly on the river. This is likely the way Peter and Mark would have come if they were fleeing Herod Agrippa II for Egypt. The river valley between Babylon and Pelusium was in the Bible called Goshen.

Turning back to 1 Peter 5:13, we read: "The church that is in Babylon, elected together with you, salutes you, and so does *Marcus my son*" (KJV, emphasis added, Gk. *Markos, ho huios mou*). Where is this church that is in Babylon? Only two options are plausible: Rome or Babylon of Egypt. Rome has been overwhelmingly assumed by the West. Babylon of Egypt has been mentioned in African tradition as the place of Peter's writing.

Recall that Peter was an escaped prisoner under pain of death when he sought out the family of Mark. *Might he have left from Mark's home and perhaps with Mark himself as his companion and helper?* So speculates one strain of the Coptic memory. Since this would have been intrinsically a covert operation, we have no record of it either in Scripture or historical chronicles.

Let us *suppose that Peter's motive in coming to the house of Mary was not only to reestablish contact with the disciples but also to pick up her son Mark to accompany him and assist him to another safer place.* If this were the case, the likelihood that Babylon of Egypt is where they fled is not surprising. Among the reasons we might suspect this to be true are the following:

- Mark could assist Peter in whatever he needed: logistics, travel, food and lodging, etc., as well as being a spiritual companion grounded in the gospel.
- If Mark was a young man helping out an older man, he could make

the way easier for Peter wherever he wished to go.

- If Mark happened to have been a family member, even distant, of Peter in Capernaum, Peter would already have knowledge of Mark's temperament and competencies.
- If Mark himself had come from African Cyrenaica, as the African memory of Mark proposes, he would be well-prepared to accompany Peter to safety in Africa.
- If Mark was courageous, as we learn from the legend of the lion and lioness and from the willingness of Mark later to take on the mission to Libya and Egypt, he may have been viewed as a sort of "special operations" person capable of ensuring Peter's safety.
- If Mark had come from a well-traveled Levitical family, he would be well-positioned to make contacts with Diaspora Jews, many of whom were in Egypt.
- If several items or all of the above were true, it might have been Mark himself who suggested the location of Babylon of Egypt and found an emergency way to get Peter there in safe hands.

Admittedly with all these "ifs," we move toward speculation and cannot claim historical certainty. But it is this kind of imagination that African Christianity offers to world Christianity.

Between his imprisonment and death, Peter appears to be very active in widely distant locations building up the churches. That one of them could have been Babylon of Egypt should not be ruled out. The apostles' calling, after all, was "to the ends of the earth." During this same time, Mark appears to be very active in widely distant locations building up the churches.

Peter's possible presence in Babylon of Egypt cannot be said to be a standard aspect of the African memory of Mark. But it remains in the hypothetical background. Samir Fawzi Girgis comments on the location of Babylon of Old Cairo in connection with 1 Peter 5:13 in this way:

> This very spot [Babylon of Egypt] had been one of the main centers of Jewish communities in Egypt for ages. It was just the spot to which the Holy Family had taken refuge a couple of decades earlier. . . . Following

> the example and footsteps of the Holy Family, they [Peter and Mark] might have taken refuge in the Egyptian Babylon. This might explain the existence of some Christians at that place during the later visit of St. Peter and St. Mark, where the former wrote his first epistle. (Girgis, 69)

Concerning Peter's immediate subsequent activity, we have minimal further connected information from the extant sources, although we possess short glimpses of individual episodes of his later life.

MARK'S JOURNEYS

How do these observations impinge upon the African memory of Mark? In order to answer, it would be useful if we could confidently correlate the above sequence with the missionary journeys of Peter (and possibly Mark) away from Jerusalem and Antioch prior to the Apostolic Council of Jerusalem of A.D. 49, and then following the Council. Many attempts have been made, but few with the hypothesis of Babylon of Egypt as a potential component.

As noted earlier, the record of Luke-Acts does not report precisely where Peter went when he went to "another place" after his imprisonment. The chronology is unclear, but it is clear that Peter remained for a time at Antioch and may have gone in and out of Antioch several times. From episodic references, it appears that Peter made various widespread missionary journeys which may have extended within the very broad range of Pontus, Antioch, Caesarea, Jerusalem and Rome. Peter appears to have been very mobile between longer residences in Jerusalem, Antioch and Rome. Since the First Epistle of Peter was addressed to believers in central and northern Anatolia (from Pontus and Galatia to Cappadocia and Asia), it is reasonable to suppose that Peter had engaged in ministries in at least some of these provinces, as well as Jerusalem and Antioch.

Much testimony from sources of the first, second and third centuries suggests that Peter himself came to Rome, but there is little speculation that Peter was ever in Alexandria. These were the two leading cities of the empire. While most scholars think that Luke's "another place" refers to Rome and some speculate that Peter may have come to Rome around A.D. 42, the African story prefers to hold it possible that Egypt could have been Peter's destination of refuge. In this he would be following the biblical types of Abraham, Joseph and the Holy Family.

After Barnabas and Paul left Jerusalem, they proceeded "*with* John Mark" to Antioch (Acts 12:25, emphasis added). Mark was apparently viewed by both Barnabas and Saul as a younger, trustable coworker who could serve as a general helper (*hypēretēs*) or attendant or hazzan in the synagogue. It is likely that Mark in due time came to assist them in the teaching of new converts and perhaps even in the preaching of the Word (Acts 13:5).

The text does not explicitly say that Mark was selected by the Holy Spirit or sent by the church of Antioch, as were Barnabas and Saul (Acts 13:2-4). But he was by this time an active participant in the believing community of Antioch, and was commissioned and sent along with Barnabas and Paul on their first missionary journey. The African memory has not hesitated to speculate that Mark was deeply involved, along with Peter, at some undefined points in this immense transition of paleo-Christianity from Jerusalem to Antioch and beyond.

The African narrative of Mark begins with Mark's birth in Africa and his family relationships. The sequence of Mark's Gospel begins with Isaiah, the beginning of the public ministry of Jesus, the call of the disciples, and the miracles of the Galilean phase of his ministry. The Western sequence begins with the historical evidences for date and authorship and stylistic characteristics, and moves through the historical and socio-political evidences for the communities of faith that Mark presumably was speaking to. I am attempting to take a combination of these approaches, seeking for plausibility that would not neglect any of these approaches.

CYRENAIC LEADERSHIP IN THE FIRST MISSION TO ANTIOCH

The Cyrenaic Jews of Jerusalem were argumentative and divided. Some were furious at Stephen. They were outraged at something Stephen must have said about the temple being destroyed (Acts 6:8-15). They were even more incensed when he had a vision of "the Son of Man standing on the right hand of God" (Acts 7:56). Others regarded Stephen as "full of the Holy Spirit" (Acts 7:65). The fanatics shouted louder. Stephen was dragged away and stoned to death, Saul of Tarsus watching and consenting. (Again see table 1 for a possible chronology of events.)

We cannot help wondering where Mark might have been within this conflict situation. If Mark was a Cyrenaic Diaspora Jew in Jerusalem during the time of the martyrdom of Stephen, he likely would have known the principal voices in the argument. It is plausible that Mark would have felt the huge and tragic consequences of Stephen's speech and his martyrdom as did Paul later. Some of these Cyrenaic Jews in Jerusalem were destined to play a major role in the transition of the gospel mission from Jerusalem to Antioch.

The next scene of Acts that could have involved Mark occurred immediately after Cornelius's and Peter's visions of the inclusion of the Gentiles in the messianic mission, when Peter said of the Gentiles in Joppa who believed in the Lord: "So if God gave them the same gift as he gave us who believed in the Lord Jesus Christ, who was I to think that I could oppose God? . . . So then, God has granted even the Gentiles repentance unto life" (Acts 11:17-18). Peter saw in his vision "three men who had been sent to me from Caesarea" (Acts 11:11). Who were these three, and might they have included Cyrenians, as in Antioch?

The next clue is in Acts 11:19. Apparently many in the Cyrenaic congregation fled from Jerusalem, but did not at first proclaim the gospel to the Gentiles, only to the Jews: "Now those who had been scattered by the persecution in connection with Stephen traveled as far as Phoenicia, Cyprus and Antioch, telling the message *only to Jews*" (Acts 11:19, emphasis added). Mark could easily have become caught up in this maelstrom of conflict. He was likely prepared linguistically and spiritually to help the mission. He would sooner or later make a choice: preach the good news to the Gentiles.

Then came the decisive turning point: "Some of them, however, *men from Cyprus and Cyrene*"—likely believers much like Barnabas and Mark—"went to Antioch" (Acts 11:20, emphasis added). These were the first Christians to be reported as going to Antioch. The African exegetes did not fail to note this intriguing detail. Is it likely that Mark was among them? It seems plausible, if not probable. Or if not, it would be preached by others with whom Mark had a close relationship—those from Cyprus, such as Barnabas, and those from Cyrene such as Lucius, or perhaps Rufus or Alexander who were known to Mark's audience.

What did they do that was so ground-breaking for Christian mission? They "began to *speak to the Greeks also*, telling them the good news about the Lord Jesus" (Acts 11:20, emphasis added). Those from Cyprus and Cyrene had long experience with both Diaspora Jews and their Greek neighbors. They were linguistically and emotively prepared to make this decisive transition, far more than the Palestinian-born apostles. The implication for African Christianity: Cyrenians from Libya were among those who first took the Christian message to Antioch. Their efforts were profoundly blessed: "The Lord's hand was with them, and a great number of people believed and turned to the Lord" (Acts 11:21).

The next crucial scene concerning Cyrenians: The news "reached the ears of the church at Jerusalem, and they sent Barnabas to Antioch" who confirmed that the grace of God was converting hearts of "a great number of people" (Acts 11:22). It is possible that Mark of Cyrene and perhaps Lucius of Cyrene arrived exceptionally early in Antioch. If so, they would have been among the very first Antioch Christians. Barnabas then fetched Saul from Tarsus and brought him back to Antioch. "So for a whole year Barnabas and Saul met with the church and taught great numbers of people" (Acts 11:26). Was Mark with his uncle/cousin during that year? The text is silent. But it would be unreasonable to rule this out. Learning of the famine in Judea, the disciples in Antioch sent their gift to the elders of Jerusalem with Barnabas and Saul (Acts 11:29-30). Mark may have accompanied them, according to African memory.

MARK'S PIVOTAL ROLE IN PREACHING TO THE GENTILES

Whether Mark was present in Antioch during Barnabas and Saul's year-long ministry there is not specified in Scripture, but the following indicators make this likely. These were especially noted in the traditional African memory (see table 1 for a possible chronology of the events):

- Mark's close relative, Barnabas, was in Antioch with Saul (Acts 11:25-26).
- Mark may have accompanied Barnabas to Jerusalem to offer relief during famine.
- "When Barnabas and Saul had finished their mission, they returned from Jerusalem [to Antioch] taking with them John, also called Mark" (Acts 12:25).
- Mark then accompanied Barnabas to Cyprus and Perga (Acts 13:4-13).
- Mark left Barnabas and Saul in Perga and returned to Jerusalem (Acts 13:13).

It is hard not to conclude that Mark's itinerary had been from Jerusalem to the regions around Jerusalem, then to Antioch, then to Cyprus and Perga, then back to Jerusalem. He had come all the way from his mother's house in Jerusalem—the central place of meeting in Jerusalem for the disciples since the Last Supper and Pentecost—to join actively with the nascent mission in Antioch. There he would have been among the first believers to take the good news to a distant Gentile audience to whom the Law was unfamiliar. If so, this is an extraordinary moment of Christian history in which Mark may have been a participant.

Prior to this Mark may have been with Peter as his assistant in Samaria, or perhaps in Syria among Hellenizing Diaspora Jews, proclaiming the good news. Either before or after these times in Antioch, Mark could have been accompanying Peter as a refugee to Babylon of Egypt. The puzzle of Mark takes on greater clarity when his pivotal role in Christian mission is grasped. A momentous event had just occurred. The gospel was being taken by some African Christian believers for the first time to Gentiles in far away countries. The world mission had begun. Mark appears to be already at the center of it.

We might ask whether Mark's joining Barnabas and Saul on their way to Cyprus occurred before or after Mark had begun his ministry in Libya? The early tradition as reported by Sawirus indicates that it was after; that is, Mark's return to Libya and leadership took place even earlier than is usually thought. We have little indication of precisely what Mark had been doing between his work in Jerusalem and his work with the Gentiles in Antioch and to the north. I have offered reasons why he may have already been in Egypt with Peter. He may have been in Syria among the Hellenizing Diaspora Jews proclaiming the good news. After Paul's harassment of the church, Mark may have accompanied "those who had been scattered [who] preached the word wherever they went. Philip went down to a city in Samaria and proclaimed the Christ there" (Acts 8:4-5). Here Philip is not the only preacher active, but an instance of many. There was a period of peace reported in Acts 9:31, where "the church throughout Judea, Galilee and Samaria" became established and grew in numbers. Peter "traveled about the country [and] went to visit the saints" (Act 9:32). Shenouda III suggests that Mark may have accompanied Peter in his early mission in the region surrounding Jerusalem. In any event, for the first time the good news was being proclaimed to a distant Jewish and Gentile audience. There are no compelling reasons to imagine that Mark was inactive during this period.

Barnabas and Saul returned to Jerusalem to bring relief to those who suffered in the famine of A.D. 45–46. Mark could have been with them, since he was clearly with them on their return.

MARK'S MISSIONARY TRAVEL

When Paul and Barnabas landed with Mark at Perga (now Turkey) on the first missionary journey and began to push inland, Mark departed from them alone and returned to Jerusalem (Acts 13:13). We do not know the reasons why—possibly because he was ill or had an emergency. Perhaps he had to take care of his mother or thought it necessary to consult with Peter about proclaiming salvation to the Gentiles. Or, maybe he had some of his own ideas about the direction of the mission. But for whatever reason, Paul did not forget his action and later declined to take Mark along on his second journey. Barnabas and Mark then sailed to Cyprus (Acts 15:37-40). (Consult table 1 for a possible chronology of events.)

Was Mark in attendance at the Council of Jerusalem? Though not specified in the text, it seems likely, due to the known itineraries of Paul, Barnabas and Mark before and after the Council. Before the Council, Mark had returned to Jerusalem (Acts 13:13). We hear nothing further of the presence of Mark until he appears likely in Rome with Peter, or possibly in Colossae around the time when Paul wrote the Colossians alerting them to welcome Mark if he comes (Col 4:10). Samir Girgis reflects the African memory that Mark did in fact go to Colossae (Girgis, 89).

Mark's journeys took place between about A.D. 33 and 68, over about thirty-five years. The journey commonly called his "first missionary journey" with Paul and Barnabas was about A.D. 45, but it likely was not Mark's "first." Before Cyprus there were the likely missionary journeys to Judea, Antioch and other locations. (See map 3, page 135, for a synopsis of Mark's travels as viewed within African tradition.)

At the time Mark was traveling, the Mediterranean regions were protected by the peace of Rome. If he was from a well-traveled family, Mark would have had little difficulty in using seaways and well-preserved roads guarded by Roman garrisons. Koine Greek was spoken as a common language throughout the eastern Mediterranean. Correspondence by mail was a regular and ordinary method of communication in the empire. Many North African ports were on open sea lanes connecting with Rome, Antioch and Caesarea Palestina. Scattered but well-organized communities of Jews were found throughout the eastern Mediterranean. Regular communication was maintained between the leadership in Jerusalem and these Jewish communities. In their early ministries, Mark and Barnabas would have been free to move among these communities. Only later would they be unwelcome in the synagogues.

WAS MARK IN ROME WITH PETER AND PAUL?

The historical foundation of the claim of the bishops of Rome to primacy is the martyrdom of Peter in Rome. Similarly, the historical premise of the claim of the bishops of Alexandria to equal apostolic status with those in Rome is based on the martyrdom of Mark in Alexandria. In both cases the chronology and the facts are disputed. Their resolution lies in hypotheses more or less plausible. While the case of Peter in Rome has been fully explored in the West, the case of Mark in Africa has not been.

That Peter suffered martyrdom is widely confirmed on the basis of a series of distinct testimonies extending from the end of the first to the end of the second centuries, and issuing from several lands. Among the chief sources are those from Africa—Tertullian and Clement. The key evidences are these:

- It appears that the manner and place of Peter's death was known in widely extended circles of believers by the end of the first century.
- The earliest confirmation in writing is that of Clement of Rome (*To the Corinthians* 5, written ca. 96) who says: "Let us place before our eyes the good Apostles—St. Peter, who in consequence of unjust zeal, suffered not one or two, but numerous miseries, and, having thus given testimony has entered the merited place of glory," a martyrdom which he suffered "among us" (i.e., among the Romans).
- The testimony of Papias and Clement of Alexandria prior to Eusebius confirming this wide recollection.
- Bishop Dionysius of Corinth, writing in the time of Roman Bishop Soter (165–174), says: "You have therefore by your urgent exhortation bound close together the sowing of Peter and Paul at Rome and Corinth. For both planted the seed of the Gospel also in Corinth, and together instructed us, just as they likewise taught in the same place in Italy and at the same time suffered martyrdom" (Eusebius, *CH* 2.25).
- Tertullian appeals, in his arguments against heretics, to the proof that is confirmed by the martyrdom of Peter and Paul in Rome: "If you are in Italy, you have Rome, where authority is ever within reach." There "the Apostles have poured out their whole teaching with their blood, where Peter has emulated the Passion of the Lord, where Paul was crowned with the death of John [the Baptist]" (*Praescr.* 36). He also states that there is "no difference between that with which John baptized in the Jordan and that with which Peter bap-

tized in the Tiber" (*Bapt.* 5), both by water and by death.

- Caius, who lived in Rome under Zephyrinus (198–217) wrote in his "Dialogue with Proclus" (Eusebius, *CH* 2.25): "I can show the trophies of the Apostles. If you care to go to the Vatican or to the road to Ostia, you will find the trophies [*tropaia*, graves of the apostles] of those who have founded this church."

Though the time of Peter's death remains disputed, it was likely between July A.D. 64 (when the persecution arose under Nero) and the beginning of 68 (when Nero took his own life). In the "Chronicle" of Eusebius the thirteenth or fourteenth year of Nero is given as that of the death of Peter and Paul (67–68). This date, accepted by Jerome, is still widely held. The year 67 is also supported by the statement, also accepted by Eusebius and Jerome, that Peter came to Rome under the Emperor Claudius (according to Jerome). If Peter's death in Rome is taken as historic fact, and if Mark received his commission from Peter to write Peter's Gospel for the benefit of the whole faithful, then Mark was likely in Rome with Peter at that time.

PART THREE

Mark in Africa

8

THE CALL OF MARK TO CARRY THE GOOD NEWS TO AFRICA

If we permit ourselves to take seriously the African narrative, here is what has been repeated over many hundreds of years:

> After his [Jesus'] Ascension into heaven, Mark went with Peter to Jerusalem, and they preached the word of God to the multitudes. And the Holy Ghost appeared to Peter, and commanded him to go to the cities and the villages which were in that country. So Peter, and Mark with him, went to the district of Bethany, and preached the word of God; and Peter remained there some days. And he saw in a dream the angel of God, who said to him: "In two places there is great dearth." So Peter said to the angel: "Which places do you mean?" He said to him: "The city of *Alexandria* with the land of Egypt, and the land of *Rome*." (Sawirus, *HP*, 140, emphasis added)

Accordingly the trajectory of Mark with Peter was from Jerusalem to nearby villages to Bethany. Then they split to the two great analogous destinations: Alexandria and Rome. The writer of the earliest Gospel was sent to the world's oldest civilization. What Mark found in his relation with Jesus under Peter's guidance, he shared with Africa. The significance of this in global perspective: Both continents (Europe and Africa—centered in Rome and Alexandria) were destined to hear the good news coming out of the vortex of the Near East (Asia—Jerusalem). The preached word was conveyed by two of the apostles' ablest voices: Peter and Mark. (See map 3 for a synopsis of Mark's travels as viewed within African tradition.)

LAUNCHING THE PREACHING MISSION WEST AND SOUTH OF ANTIOCH

The most fundamental insight we derive from the earliest sources regarding Mark (Papias, Irenaeus, Clement and Eusebius) is the presumed strong connection between the founding of the church of Rome and the church of Alexandria. Mark at some point reconnects with Peter in Rome.

Peter preached; Mark wrote down Peter's preaching and Mark then went to Africa under the guidance of the Spirit. In this account the enduring apostolic connection between Roman Christianity and African Christianity hinges specifically on a personal link—that between Peter and Mark. The churches of Rome and Alexandria were apparently founded at about the same time, at least within a half decade, according to this narrative. This assumption gained general consensual approval in early Christianity. It signaled to all new believers that the church's core message is the same the world over. The same good news was proclaimed in Africa on the premise that it was not "another gospel" but the identical gospel that had been preached by the apostles in Roman Asia and Europe. These ministries were synchronous from their origin and coordinated founding. The unity of European and African Christianity is embodied in the close relation of Peter (Rome) and Mark (Alexandria).

Note the wide scope of Mark's ministry. It took him through the major power centers of the Mediterranean world: Jerusalem to Antioch to Rome to Cyrene to Alexandria and back to Cyrene. All of these were vital centers of culture, learning, piety and political authority. All were urban focal points that had to be addressed in the founding of the worldwide faith. As Rome was the fitting setting for final witness of Peter and Paul, so was Alexandria to become the uniquely proper arena for the final witness of Mark.

Where was the most obvious place for the Christian mission to go immediately after having been proclaimed in Antioch, Ephesus, Athens and

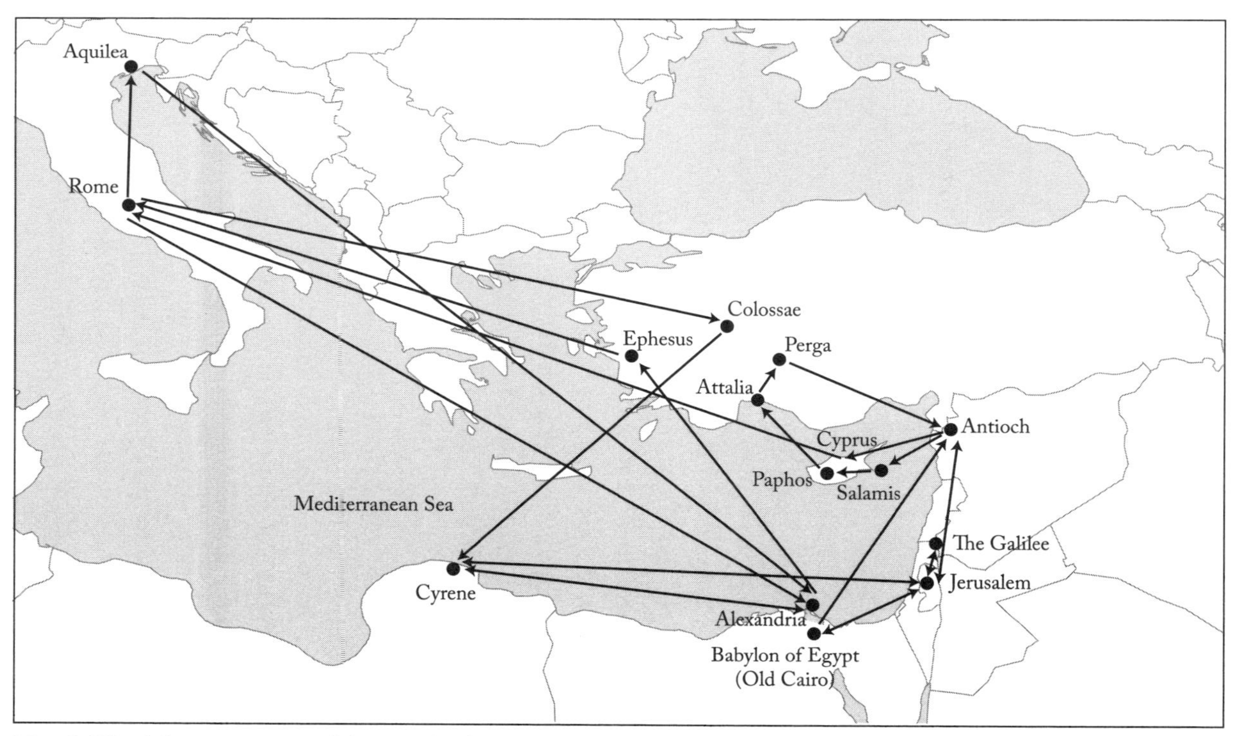

Map 3. The African memory of the travels of Mark
Birth in Pentapolis near Cyrene of Libya, to Jerusalem, to Capernaum in the Galilee, to Jerusalem, to Babylon of Egypt, to Jerusalem, to Antioch, to Salamis on Cyprus, to Paphos on Cyprus, to Attalia, to Perga, to Antioch, to Jerusalem, to Antioch, to Cyprus, to Rome, to Colossae, to Libya, to Alexandria, to Libya, to Alexandria, to Ephesus, to Rome, to Aquilea, to martyr's death in Alexandria. *Consult the composite African chronology of Mark in table 1 for conjectured times of phases of the sequence.*

Rome? No one could ignore the known world's second largest city: Alexandria. It was among the most cosmopolitan and learned, and had many Jews with messianic hopes. It must have been felt consensually as a matter of major urgency for gospel seeds to be planted in Africa. But who was prepared to lead such a challenging effort? The Spirit was guiding. Peter was led by an angelic visitor to see Africa as the most urgent mission.

The question can be put pragmatically: Who would reasonably be the obvious person to undertake this difficult and arduous mission? Who had the linguistic skills? It could not be someone who knew nothing about the vast African continent. It would have to be a tested leader who had served through a long learning process with the most respected of the apostles. Perhaps . . . Mark?

Who would have been sufficiently prepared by international experience, language competencies, indigenous credentials and cultural awareness of conditions in Africa? Maybe someone born there. Maybe someone who had been closely woven within the fabric of the early disciples. Maybe someone who had beheld the Lord face to face, who had been eyewitness to the earliest layers of Christian mission. Maybe someone who was among the first to preach to the Gentiles in Antioch, then with Barnabas and Paul in Asia Minor, and very close to Peter. Most likely it was Mark. It does not require vivid imagination to see Mark as the obvious answer. The Lord's command came through an angelic visitor, prompting Peter to send Mark from Rome, according to the remembered ecumenical consensus.

Mark appears to have been the right choice. He was a Cyrenian Christian teacher, evangelist and prophet already tested in Antioch. He was well prepared spiritually to undertake a dangerous and demanding task. He possessed crosscultural understanding and communication skills. He had deep connections with the distinctive African ways of looking at reality. He may well have been born on the African continent. Any or all of the above would have suited him to the task.

Why did such an obvious recognition take so long for Western scholarship to examine? Is it due to xenophobia, cultural myopia or racism?

These are not assertions I am alleging. The charge of racism is a volatile simplification. It tends to be inflammatory in a way that we least need at this hazardous moment of history. Though some may boil it down to a single cause, I see many. These causes have to do with silent cultural conceits and prejudicial assumptions in which racial prejudice may play a part but hardly the whole. They arise out of cultural egocentrism and nativism that are so common as to be almost endemic to the human condition of every race and latitude. These tendencies may mutate into the hidden demons of the "knowledge class" (Peter Berger, Erasmus Lecture, 1990) that are hard to detect and harder to extract. Why was it neglected so long? Here I can only hope that future investigators who understand social analysis and class dynamics and psychological habituations will seek clearer answers.[1]

The African memory is clear: Mark, after traveling extensively *northward* as a cherished assistant to both Peter and Paul, was directed by the Spirit to go *southward* to Africa, likely on Peter's commendation. The Spirit would provide a way. Before going back to Africa, however, Mark may have accompanied Peter first to Rome: "Peter and Mark went to the region of Rome, and preached there the word of God. And in the fifteenth year after the Ascension of Christ, the holy Peter *sent* Saint Mark, the father and evangelist, to the city of Alexandria, to announce the good tidings there" (Sawirus, *HP*, 140, emphasis added). If Peter could go as far as Rome and Paul could have the intent to go as far as Spain, why couldn't Mark go as far as Africa?

An apostle is, by definition, one who is *sent*. No one chooses on his own to be sent. He must be sent by a Sender—in this case the Lord of glory who died on a cross. The apostolic mission sought to bring the good news to *all* the world. *All* the world could never have excluded the great continent of Africa. Too much was known about North Africa in the first century to ignore it. Africa was too big to overlook, even in the earliest decades of Christian mission, even before the New Testament was written. Whoever was first sent to bring the good news to Africa and lead the church in Alexandria would have been given a crucial task.

---

[1]See David Wilhite, *Tertullian the African* (Berlin: De Gruyter, 2007).

It would require a well-trained, energetic young man already tested in character, apostolic preaching, ministry and courage.

MARK'S CALLING TO THE AFRICAN CONTINENT

Now back to the core of the African narrative of Mark. He returned after his missionary journeys to the north and west with Paul and Peter at a date not known precisely. He proceeded under Peter's guidance toward the most southerly reach of the known world: Africa. Mark was returning to the Pentapolis. He knew it well. Africa was not a foreign country to him. Through this more familiar experience he would be better prepared to take on the real challenge: one of the world's greatest cities—Alexandria. His return to Libya set his feet back on the ground in Africa before he took on the immense challenge of Alexandria.

Note that Mark did not go from Rome directly to Egypt proper, but first back to his own messianic Jewish people in Libya. There he would be received as a Levite. The Pentapolis of Libya was viewed as a vital culture of North Africa, west of Egypt, and at the time as a satellite within Alexandria's orbit. (See table 1 for chronology.)

In the African narrative, Mark is remembered as having first planted the apostolic seeds of Christianity among his countrymen, the faithful Jews of Libya (Sawirus, *HP*, 141-42; *Martyrium Marci* 1). To say "first" does not need to preempt the well-known testimony that even before Mark's missionary journeys there were those at Pentecost speaking in Libyan and Nilotic languages (Acts 2:10), as I mentioned. If the original participants in Pentecost other than Mark were the first to bring the good news to Africa, it still could be held that Mark was the first apostolically sent missionary to Africa. I leave it to further historical study to inquire into whether there is sufficient evidence that any of the Cyrenians at Pentecost actually returned to Cyrene, but it should not be ruled out.

The common African narrative of his itinerary is this: Mark goes from Rome back to Cyrene in Upper Libya where he preaches to the Jewish and Gentile populace where he grew up. His ministry is blessed with signs and wonders (*Martyrium Marci* 1-2). There he receives many believers into the growing African community of faith. If so, it is proper to say that African Christianity did not begin in Egypt but in the unlikely region of Libya.

The chronology of his leadership in Cyrenaica and Alexandria is variously remembered. One standard Coptic account of the traditional narrative states the chronology in this way:

> The spread of Christianity must have been quite remarkable because pagans were furious and fought St. Mark everywhere. Smelling the danger, the Apostle ordained a bishop (Anianos), three priests and seven deacons to look after the congregation if anything befell him. He left Alexandria to Berce, then to Rome, where he met St. Peter and St. Paul and remained there until their martyrdom in 64 A.D. Upon returning to Alexandria in 65 A.D., St. Mark found his people firm in faith and thus decided to visit the Pentapolis. There, he spent two years preaching and performing miracles, ordaining bishops and priests, and winning more converts. Finally he returned to Alexandria and was overjoyed to find that Christians had multiplied so much that they were able to build a considerable church in the suburban district of Baucalis.[2]

Note the synaxary sequence of Mark's travels after Rome: Alexandria to Berce in the Libyan Pentapolis, Rome and the death of Peter and Paul, Alexandria, Pentapolis, Alexandria and the death of Mark.

Here is how Sawirus, the classic Coptic historian, summarized the story:

> When St. Mark returned from Rome, he went first to the five cities [of Cyrenaic Pentapolis] and preached the Word of God. He showed them many miracles, the sick were cured, those with leprosy were cleansed and those with evil spirits were freed from them. Many believed in Lord Christ and broke down their idols. He baptized them in the name of the Father, the Son and the Holy Spirit. (Sawirus as quoted in Shenouda III, 38; cf. Father Paul Cheneau: *Les Saints d'Egypte* 1.494-510).

In this version the sequence is Rome, Pentapolis, Alexandria, and later again to Pentapolis and back to his death in Alexandria.

---

[2]Coptic Orthodox Diocese of the Southern United States; http://suscopts.org/coptic-orthodox/church/saint-mark/suscopts.org.

Contrary to the common assumption that Christianity was very late coming to Libya, we get the impression that Libyan Christianity emerged at the very outset of the history of early African Christianity. Mark "was the first who preached in the province of Egypt, and Africa, and Pentapolis, *and all those regions*" (Sawirus, *HP*, 141, emphasis added). The worshiping community in Cyrenaica and the worshiping community in Alexandria appear to be planted and growing almost simultaneously under the first generation leadership of Mark. If Mark preached, healed and ministered to *all* the districts of the Pentapolis, as Sawirus reports, that would surely have included not only Cyrene, but also Ptolemais (Barca), Hesperides (Benghazi, Bernike) and Teuchira. While in Libya he ordained bishops and clerics not only for the five cities but for the whole Libyan region (Sawirus, *HP*, 145; *Martyrium Marci* 6-10).

If so, this would have serious implications for the entire history of early Christianity in Libya and all of North Africa. If so, the first Christian teaching in Africa would have begun in Libya before reaching either Egypt or Carthage.[3] This sequence might be proven false, but lacking proof to the contrary, it can be viewed as a hypothesis to be further investigated. Even the claim is surprising—that Libyan Christianity emerged so very early in the sequence of African Christian communities, if not the earliest. Yet there has been no serious study of this premise.

In the land of his boyhood, Mark labored as a converted Christian adult (*Martyrium Marci* 6-10), where he ordained church leaders for the whole Pentapolis region. It was not until he had regained his footing in his native Libya that he was called to Alexandria. This was revealed to him in the course of his African ministry. The Spirit was "making the way easy," as Isaiah had promised, and would continue to do so from the very moment he set foot in Alexandria. The transition from the Pentapolis to Alexandria cannot be rightly told without understanding the unfolding way in which the Spirit is said to have guided Mark. Two angelic visitation narratives may interweave here: (1) Peter's angelic

[3]See Thomas C. Oden, *Early Libyan Christianity* (Downers Grove, Ill.: IVP Academic, 2011).

messenger's command that Mark go to Alexandria, and (2) Mark's angelic call to go from Cyrene to Pharos in Alexandria. The latter is our present concern.

THE VISION LEADS TO THE GREAT CITY: ALEXANDRIA

Mark's Gospel narrative began with these words recalling the promise of the prophet Isaiah: "The good news of Jesus Christ—the Message!—begins here, following to the letter the scroll of the prophet Isaiah: 'Watch closely: I'm sending my preacher ahead of you. He'll *make the road smooth* for you'" (Mk 1:1-2 *The Message*, emphasis added). Ever thereafter Mark's name would be melded with the promise of Isaiah that the Spirit was making the road smooth.

Mark was prompted by the Spirit to remember this promise on three memorable occasions:

- the moment he first set out to write his Gospel
- again when he was instructed by the Spirit to go to Alexandria
- again when he arrived at the lighthouse of Pharos in Alexandria to meet Anianus

This was Mark's vocation: to receive the gift of the Spirit to help make the road smooth in all of the African continent for proclaiming the good news.

After leading many in Cyrenaica to faith, Mark proceeded to Alexandria in response to the angelic vision that called him to Egypt's greatest city. Mark was prompted by the Holy Spirit to proceed directly toward Pharos, the lighthouse in Alexandria (*Martyrium Marci* 2). Immediately, the next day after receiving the vision, Mark headed for Alexandria. The iconic image of Mark has had ever since, in the background of his face, is the colossal lighthouse of Pharos, the famous symbol of Ptolemaic Egyptian intellectual and architectural creativity. One tradition has him traveling by ship, another following the coastal road by land along the Mediterranean littoral to Alexandria. The latter route was possible on foot or on a beast of burden. The sea route is more likely. As he entered Alexandria, he came to the gate of a place called Mendion (=Bennidion, *Martyrium Marci* 3; cf. Sawirus, *HP*, 142). This place was later memorialized by the founding of an ancient Alexandrian church near Mendion Gate.

Here is the traditional narrative of the calling of Mark to Alexandria, according to Sawirus:

> Martyrdom of the holy Mark, and his preaching in the city of Alexandria. . . . It fell to the lot of Mark the evangelist to go to the province of Egypt, and the great city of Alexandria, by the command of the Holy Ghost, that he might cause the people to hear the words of the gospel of the Lord Christ, and confirm them therein. (Sawirus, *HP*, 141)

The calling of Mark is reported as a singular work of the Spirit:

> And so the Holy Ghost appeared to him, and said to him: "Rise and go to the city of Alexandria, to sow there the good seed which is the word of God." So the disciple of Christ arose and set out, being strengthened by the Holy Ghost, like a combatant in war; and he saluted the brethren, and took leave of them and said to them: "The Lord Jesus Christ will make my road easy, that I may go to Alexandria and preach his holy gospel there." Then he prayed and said: "O Lord strengthen the brethren who have known thy holy name that I may return to them rejoicing in them." Then the brethren bade him farewell. (Sawirus, *HP*, 142)

Mark may have been already apprised of the nascent proto-Christian forms of expectation in Alexandria. He could have conceivably heard of the community that had taught Apollos or with some similar Jewish messianic communities described by Philo. Though not yet enjoying the fullness of Christian teaching or the work of the Holy Spirit, some in Alexandria were already in a state of readiness to hear the gospel.

Luke had written that Apollos was "a learned man" from Alexandria with "a thorough knowledge of Scripture" (referring to Torah and the prophets), who had been "instructed in the way of the Lord, and spoke with great fervor and taught about Jesus accurately, though he knew only the baptism of John" (Acts 18:24). The implication was that Apollos was a native of Alexandria and that he had been taught the Hebrew Scriptures in his native country.

It would not be surprising if Mark made immediate contact with messianic Jews in Alexandria when he arrived. These could have been Jews similar to Apollos. Many messianic Jews were resident in Alexandria when Mark arrived there. The texts are silent as to the possible chronological correlation of Apollos in Ephesus and Mark in Alexandria. What is clear is that Apollos was a coworker of Paul's in Ephesus and Corinth who provides a glimpse into what was going on among Alexandrian Jews probably in the A.D. 40s or 50s.

Does this mean that by the late 40s, there were proto-Christians in Alexandria? Unlikely, but there almost certainly were Jewish messianic believers who apparently had received some word concerning Jesus that was sufficient to prompt them to go all the way to Ephesus to witness. According to Helmut Koester, the mission of Apollos of Alexandria to Ephesus may even predate Paul's mission there.[4]

The previous narratives of the flight of the Holy Family, Simon of Cyrene, the Ethiopian eunuch and Apollos show early signs of Christianity on the African continent. Mark's arrival, however, signaled the beginning of the apostolic mission in Africa. We continue with the story as reported in African saint narratives.

ANIANUS

The promise of the vision that God will "make my road easy" was made known to Mark before he left the Pentapolis for Alexandria. It was awesomely confirmed upon his first hour of arrival in Alexandria, in his providential meeting with Anianus (or Anianos). We are now working from three analogous narratives, one early, one continuing in many editions and one late—namely, (1) the pre-Eusebian *Martyrium Marci*, which is the basic pattern for Sawirus, (2) the synaxary versions that continue over the centuries but which lack early extant versions, and (3) the late first millennium, longer narrative of Sawirus. All of them begin with a broken shoe strap.

This is the story learned by almost every child in Coptic Christianity: "So Mark journeyed to the city of Alexandria," coming from Libya. "And when he entered in at the gate," at a place called Mendion or Ben-

[4]Helmut Koester, *Introduction to the New Testament*, 2 vols., 2nd ed. (New York: Walter de Gruyter, 2000), 2:122.

nidion, "the strap of his [Mark's] shoe broke. And when he saw this, he thought: 'Now I know that the Lord has made my way easy'" (Sawirus, *HP*, 142). At the first gate leading into the city, he immediately "turned, and saw a cobbler there, went to him and gave him the shoe that he might mend it. And when the cobbler received it, and took the awl to work upon it, the awl pierced his hand."

Each step of the narrative that follows is regarded as providentially ordered, as is typical of early Christian narratives of the saints. Mark asked the cobbler to mend the broken strap of his sandal. The cobbler accidentally cut his finger and cried aloud in Greek, *"Heis ho Theos,"* that is, "God is One" (Sawirus, *HP*, 142; *Martyrium Marci* 3). Mark was filled with great joy upon hearing this, since it confirmed that the simple cobbler believed in one God within a pagan world. This confession of God as one signaled to Mark that the cobbler either had likely been educated as a Jew, or knew enough of monotheistic teaching, perhaps from Alexandrian Jews, that he had been taught this crucial expression and used it spontaneously. Out of this simple exclamation emerged the long history of Christianity in Africa.

Mark took these words as a signal that he had come to the right place, prepared by divine providence. He immediately prayed and healed the cobbler's hand. This opened the door for conversing with him about the New Reign of God revealed in Jesus.

The longer version of Sawirus:

> So he said: "Heis ho Theos," the interpretation of which is, "God is One." And, when the holy Mark heard him mention the name of God, he rejoiced greatly, and turned his face to the East and said: "O my Lord Jesus, it is thou that makest my road easy in every place." Then he spat on the ground and took from it clay, and put it on the place where the awl had pierced the cobbler's hand, saying: "In the name of the Father and the Son and the Holy Ghost, the One living and eternal God, may the hand of this man be healed at this moment, that thy holy name may be glorified." Then his hand at once became whole. (Sawirus, *HP*, 142-43)

By healing the cobler's hand Mark was participating in the messianic healing ministry of Jesus, who had promised that his disciples would do "greater things." By "turning his face to the East," Mark was remembering Isaiah's ancient promise echoing from the lands to the East: the way would be made easy.

In Alexandria Anianus was surrounded by images of Greco-Roman and Egyptian deities. Immediately the harder question concerning idolatry is put candidly by Mark:

> The holy Mark said to him: "If thou knowest that God is one, why dost thou serve these many gods?" The cobbler answered him: "We mention God with our mouths, but that is all; for we know not who he is." (Sawirus, *HP*, 143)

This portrays Mark as direct and guileless. So he is found to be direct in his Gospel. So is the cobbler direct and honest. He assumes that honest people do not pretend to know God in the same way that other finite realities are known. The straightforward response of Anianus anticipates a great tradition of reflection on the knowledge of God by means of "not knowing." It points toward the "negative way" of knowing God, namely, that we cannot point to God as if he were a finite object. To speak of God we must speak of that One who is not finite, not measurable, not temporal. We speak by negation.

This is the crucial beginning point for African Christianity. If God is One, then the worship of multiple gods must be intrinsically false. To assert many gods is to assert a self-contradiction. For if God is One, as the Jews had taught for centuries, then to assert that there are many gods, each of whom may represent this oneness, is to assert that God is not One, that there is not a Sovereign who rules over all, and knows all in a way that the gods cannot know all. Excepting the Jews, the presenting problem of popular Alexandrian forms of religious practice was idolatry. The whole continent and not Egypt alone appeared to be "sunk in the service of idols, and in the worship of the creature instead of the Creator. And they had many temples to their contemptible gods, whom they ministered to in every place, and served with every iniquity and magical art, and to whom they offered sacrifices among themselves" (Sawirus, *HP*, 141). This is a familiar theme found in the Hebrew prophets and in Paul and Peter, but it took special force in Alexandria, where the size and scale and crassness of idolatrous practices were evident.

Mark was grounded in the Hebrew memory: "Hear, O Israel, the Lord our God, the Lord is one" (Deut 6:4). Early African Christian writers would make clear why polytheistic conceptions of God by definition are inadequate: There is no other "god" to which God can be compared.[5] In Mark 12:29 Jesus affirms the ancient prayer of Israel from Deutronomy 6:4. Mark had served with Paul who wrote: "For us there is one God, the Father, from whom all things came, and for whom we live" (1 Cor 8:6). A statue or graven image of God must not be made within the covenant community. For God cannot be reduced to creaturely matter, even though God's glory may shine through creaturely beings. "If there are many Gods, how can one maintain that God is uncircumscribed? For where the one would be, the other could not be" (John of Damascus, *OF* 1.5).

Notice the conversational approach to witness embodied by Mark:

> And the cobbler remained astonished at the power of God which descended upon the holy Mark, and said to him: "I pray thee, O man of God, to come to the dwelling of thy servant, to rest and eat bread, for I find that to-day thou hast conferred a benefit upon me." Then the holy Mark replied with joy: "May the Lord give thee the bread of life in heaven!" And he went with him to his house. And when he entered his dwelling, he said, "May the blessing of God be in this house!" and he uttered a prayer. (Sawirus, *HP*, 143)

Note on each occasion that Mark responded precisely to what Anianus had himself said. It was not a conversation imposed as if from without. That is still essential to the good news mission today. Having been invited to eat at the table of Anianus, Mark said: You speak of bread, and I will speak of the Bread of life.

> After they had eaten, the cobbler said to him: "O my father, I beg thee to make known to me who thou art who hast worked this great miracle." Then the saint answered him: "I serve Jesus Christ, the Son of the ever living God." (Sawirus, *HP*, 143)

[5]Origen of Alexandria, *On First Principles* 1.1; cf. Tertullian of Carthage, *Against Hermogenes* 3; Arnobius of Sicca, *Against the Heathen* 3.

Only when asked about the source of his healing power did Mark witness overtly to Jesus Christ, Son of Man, Son of God, of whom the prophets had spoken. He found a spontaneous way, within a plausibly unfolding personal encounter, to express the good news of God's coming in Jesus (Sawirus, *HP*, 143). This would become the pattern of personal evangelization in Africa and elsewhere.

> The cobbler exclaimed: "I would that I could see him." The holy Mark said to him: "I will cause thee to behold him." (Sawirus, *HP*, 143)

The next step in Mark's way of communicating the good news: Enable the hearer to realize his need to hear more about the source of this miraculous power that had been already demonstrated. The cobbler recognizes his need, his hidden wish to encounter this One who is the source of mighty works. Mark does not point to himself, but to the triune God who has made himself known in this concrete history of Jesus. The evangelist's task is to enable the hearer to behold the Lord, even as Mark himself beheld the Lord in the flesh. The beholder of God through his prayer and the power of the Holy Spirit was able to convey the Lord's personal presence and power as if present. This is what changed the cobbler and his whole family.

FROM PROCLAMATION TO TEACHING

At this point the narrative of Sawirus moves from preaching the kerygma to teaching its truthfulness. This points to the beginnings of catechetics as early as Mark's first Alexandrian conversation:

> Then he began to *teach* him the gospel of good tidings, and the *doctrine* of the glory and power and dominion which belong to God from the beginning, and exhorted him with many exhortations and instructions, of which his history bears witness. (Sawirus, *HP*, 143-44, emphasis added)

The teaching is about a history. Mark is prepared to communicate that history just as he had seen it unfold. From the outset, African Christian teaching is grounded in a history—the specific history of the personal coming of the Messianic Servant promised by Isaiah. Mark then proceeded to explain the meaning of that history:

> [He] ended by saying to him: "The Lord Christ in the last times became incarnate of the Virgin Mary, and came into the world, and saved us from our sins." And he explained to him what the prophets prophesied of him, passage by passage. (Sawirus, *HP*, 144)

This teaching is related to a long history preceding it: the history of the Jews, the Egyptian exodus, the prophetic witnesses, and the coming of the Lord in person. Mark went directly to the Hebrew Scripture to point to its fulfillment in the risen Lord. He set forth the incarnation and resurrection as personally significant events.

> Then the cobbler said to him: "I have never heard at all of these books which thou speakest of; but the books of the Greek philosophers are what men teach their children here, and so do the Egyptians." So the holy Mark said to him: "The wisdom of the philosophers of this world is vanity before God." (Sawirus, *HP*, 144)

From the outset the question was raised of the relation of Greek philosophy so prevalent in Alexandria, even among Jews, to the history of Jesus.

> Then when the cobbler had heard wisdom and the words of the Scriptures from the holy Mark, together with the great miracle which he had seen him work upon his hand, his heart inclined towards him, and he believed in the Lord, and was baptised, he and all the people of his house, and all his neighbors. And his name was Annianus [Anianus]. (Sawirus, *HP*, 144)

In this way the first stone was laid in the foundation of Egyptian Christianity. The apostolic message had arrived healthily in Alexandria, the greatest city in Africa. Anianus repented, believed and was baptized into the new family of God in Africa. The cobbler and his family began a new life. Others in this neighborhood were converted (*Martyrium Marci* 4). There followed others who heard, believed and were baptized. The faithful soon multiplied in the great international city. Anianus himself began preaching and became Mark's helper and later successor as leader of the Alexandrian church (Sawirus, *HP*, 144-45).

ESCAPE TO PENTAPOLIS

The more Mark challenged the local forms of idolatry, the more furious was the resistance he received. Economic interests clouded reason. Anger turned to outrage. Mark's direct challenge to idolatry led to the continent's first Christian martyrdom (Sawirus, *HP*, 145; *Martyrium Marci* 5). Aware that his mission in Alexandria was in jeopardy, yet sensing the extreme volatility of the resistance, Mark exercised careful judgment on behalf of the survival of the new family of God in Africa. He determined temporarily to leave Alexandria for Cyrene, where he let things settle down in Alexandria while he tended to his former ministry in the Pentapolis.

The plan of Mark for a succession of leadership both in Libya and Egypt followed the pattern set by Paul: Due to the vulnerability of Christian leadership in persecution, the apostolic shepherd of the flock (who in the continent of Africa was Mark) prepared for conditions in which he would no longer be able to lead. With the consent of the community of believers, and under clear and present danger, Mark chose Anianus as his successor. This followed the precedent that both Peter and Paul had practiced in their mission to the north. This provided a core of indigenous leadership for the church in Egypt for decades to come.

Mark had already arranged for the ordination of Anianus as succeeding bishop (Sawirus, *HP*, 144; *Martyrium Marci* 5). He also ordained a team of leadership that would succeed Anianus if he could not serve. He ordained three others as presbyters: Malchus, Sabinus and Cerdo (or Milaios, Sabinos and Kerdos), plus seven deacons for ecclesiastical service (*Martyrium Marci* 5). These were commissioned to watch over the spiritual welfare of the growing congregations in case anything befell him. Cerdo would later succeed Mark as shepherd of the church of Alexandria and be remembered in the patriarchal histories as "father" (papa, later called patriarch) of the Coptic churches.

> So when the holy Mark knew that they were conspiring together, he ordained Annianus bishop of Alexandria, and also ordained three priests and seven deacons, and appointed these eleven to serve and to comfort the faithful brethren. (Sawirus, *HP*, 144-45)

Under these conditions of extreme threat, Mark ordained these eleven to serve in Alexandria. When he came back to Alexandria after his Libyan ministry he found the church flourishing.

> But he himself departed from among them, and went to Pentapolis, and remained there two years, *preaching and appointing* bishops and priests and deacons in all their districts. (Sawirus, *HP*, 145, emphasis added; cf. *Martyrium Marci* 5)

The apostle departed; the ordained leadership remained. This is the same pattern we find in Paul's ministry as witnessed in the Pastoral Epistles. This was not an act of fear but an act of prudence, to preserve the apostolic leadership of the community of faith under threat. This exercise of prudent discretion enabled his ministry in Africa to continue in both places. This would set the pattern for a long series of debates in African Christianity about when to seek a safe haven from danger and when to lay one's life on the line. Cyprian and Athanasius would face the same question later, and would both follow the pattern from preaching to temporary sanctuary to martyrdom that Mark had set. In this way the church in Africa was from the outset prepared and specifically organized for the contingency of the leader's death, so as to sustain the continuity of apostolic leadership in Africa, both in Egypt and Libya.

It was intrinsic to Mark's assignment to appoint apostolic leadership in Africa. The same pattern was occurring about the same time both in Alexandria with Mark and in Rome with Peter, who according to Tertullian and Epiphanius was followed by Linus, Anaclet and Clement of Rome. Within a short time frame after Mark's departure from Rome, there appears to be an active church already alive in both Libya and Alexandria.

By his life and death, Mark showed that under conditions of persecution, the flight to safety in order to serve the church another day could be a reasonable, prudent and providential action. Later he would freely give his life in martyrdom. For now he saw the greater need to shepherd the church from afar by trustworthy leadership and by correspondence. Thus a suicidal fixation on self-chosen martyrdom was never contemplated and never viewed as orthodox teaching consensually. The martyr's death may come unavoidably, but not by direct intention. In most cases of subsequent persecution, the civil authorities were requiring torture that sought to prevent death, then death when the torture did not produce the intended result. The African prototype of both flight from persecution and martyrdom, which was so widely emulated elsewhere, was John Mark.

Life is not undervalued in martyrdom if the witness of martyrdom is the only way open to preserve the continuing life of the worshiping community. Mark's behavior shows that the martyr concedes the necessity of martyrdom only when no other options are open. The choice to suffer in a necessary witness to the risen Lord is not a death wish. It is participation in the death and risen life of Jesus. It is a once-for-all occasion of witness, powerful to all who remembered. In this important precedent, as embodied by Mark, martyrdom was the ultimate testimony—hence the weighty word *martyria* (witness). The willingness to die when no other options are left is not inconsistent with the proper valuing and protecting of the human body as God's creation intended for service.

BACK TO ALEXANDRIA

After this period of service in the Pentapolis, Mark returned to Alexandria regardless of the dangers and resumed his work there, out of hope, not in desperation. The work in Africa began in a cow pasture:

> [Mark] returned to Alexandria, and found that the brethren had been strengthened in the faith, and had multiplied by the grace of God, and had found means to build a church in a place called the Cattle-pasture [Ta Boukolou], near the sea, beside a rock from which stone is hewn. (Sawirus, *HP*, 145)

The continuity of the church in Alexandria despite the absence of Mark and its survival of the first onslaught of the fury of idolatry were celebrated upon Mark's return.

> So the holy Mark greatly rejoiced at this; and he fell upon his knees, and blessed God for confirming the servants of the faith, whom he had

> himself instructed in the doctrines of the Lord Christ, and because they had *turned away from the service of idols*. (Sawirus, *HP*, 145, emphasis added)

There had been many riots and persecutions of Jews in North Africa before any Christians arrived. At the time when Mark came to Alexandria, thoughts of an anxious populace under distant Roman governance turned toward a fear of revolution. The worshipers of pagan deities saw in Mark a renewed threat to their gods. The messianic wing of the Jewish population of Alexandria was increasing in size and exuberance during the mid-first century. It was the miracles of ordinary believers that aroused the most suspicion both among Jews and Gentiles. Here is the build-up of anxiety as described by Sawirus:

> But when those unbelievers learned that the holy Mark had returned to Alexandria, they were filled with fury on account of the works which the believers in Christ wrought, such as healing the sick, and driving out devils, and loosing the tongues of the dumb, and opening the ears of the deaf, and cleansing the lepers. They sought out the holy Mark with great fury, but did not find him. They gnashed against him with their teeth in their temples and places of their idols, in wrath, saying: "Do you not see the wickedness of this sorcerer?" (Sawirus, *HP*, 145)

Word must have spread quickly that a Christian leader close to the heart of the new messianic Jewish movement was known to be back in the city. It was imagined that activists such as Mark might be preparing for a violent overturning of the idols in Alexandria. Out of this anxiety over civic disorder, the populous became furious that Mark was perceived to be threatening their social order, as evidenced by their anger preceding his earlier departure from Alexandria:

> And when those that believed in the Lord were multiplied, and the people of the city heard that a man who was a Jew and a Galilean [follower of Jesus] had entered the city, wishing to overthrow the worship of the idols, their gods, and had persuaded many to abstain from serving them, they sought him everywhere; and they appointed men to watch for him. (Sawirus, *HP*, 144)

From the time of Mark's first arrival in Alexandria, these rumors had been circulating. The fear was that messianic believers might threaten to deface and damage the ancient pagan deities and vilify them. The Alexandrian mob feared the potential political instability of their civic order that might follow from Mark's preaching and teaching. This dread apparently provoked the rage of the Alexandrian populace that ended in Mark's martyrdom (Sawirus, *HP*, 145; *Martyrium Marci* 6).

THE MOB

Other martyr locations than Mendion and the Cow Pastures were established in due time as recorded in the various narratives (synaxaries, *Martyrium Marci* and Sawirus). The most important was the nearby Serapeum (the temple of Serapis). All of these sites would be honored as martyr sites: the Serapeum in Rhakotis where Mark was seized, the Bucalis to which he was reportedly dragged and buried in the Jewish quarter near the shore, and the community near the Mendion Gate (see map 4 for their locations within Alexandria).

This anxiety provoked by Mark came to a head during a pagan festival held at the same time as the Christian celebration of the resurrection (Easter). The church was meeting near the Serapeum (Greek Serapion). It was the Paschal season among Jews in Rhakotis. Mark was celebrating the communion of believers with their risen Lord at their specific gathering place (Sawirus, *HP*, 145-46). The seizure of Mark occurred during a special celebration that created a unique series of events, at a particular place and in a particular kairos: (1) the Paschal Feast for Alexandrian Jews, (2) the feast of the resurrection for Christians and (3) the Festival of Serapis for pagan Alexandrians. The conditions turned out to be inflammatory.

This location can still be visited in the area of Alexandria near the highest point in the city. The location of an early church site is still marked at the ruins of the Serapeum. There was a community of faith in the area of the Serapeum as well as another community in Bucalis in the Jewish section near the shore (see map 3, *REC*, 112). The mob had gathered in front of the temple dedicated to Serapis. The enraged mob threatened Mark while he was presiding over the resurrection service of the house church gathered in the vicinity of the Serapeum. The mob forced its way into the congregation and seized the apostle. They put a rope around his neck. The crowd shouted: "Drag the boubalos through the Boukolou," that is, "Drag the buffalo [Mark] into the field of Boukolou where cows graze" (Sawirus, *HP*, 146; *Martyrium Marci* 7). Mark was seized by a crowd at the Serapeum in the midst of the service. They dragged Mark through the streets of Alexandria, apparently to Bucalis.

Centuries later, Sawirus recalled the same tradition that had left its bloody memories on Alexandrian streets for almost a millennium:

> And on the first day of the week, the day of the Easter festival of the Lord Christ, which fell that year on the 29th [or 30th] of Barmudah, when the festival of the idolatrous unbelievers also took place, they sought him with zeal, and found him in the sanctuary. So they rushed forward and seized him, and fastened a rope round his throat, and dragged him along the ground, saying: "Drag the [buffalo] through the cattle-yard! *[Syrōmen ton boubalon en tois Boukolou!]*" (Sawirus, *HP*, 145-46)

The last sentence especially has a ring of primitive authenticity, and may have been the core of the historic memory. It serves to connect the two sites together: The torture occurred from the Serapeum to Bucalis.

THE TORTURE OF MARK BY THE MOB

Jesus had been executed in the most humiliating way by the torture of crucifixion. Similarly Mark was executed by torture and public humiliation by being dragged through the streets. Sawirus reports Mark's response:

> But the saint, while they dragged him, kept praising God and saying: "Thanks be to thee, O Lord, because thou hast made me worthy to suffer for thy holy name." And his flesh was lacerated, and clove to the stones of the streets; and his blood ran over the ground. (Sawirus, *HP*, 146)

Just as the cross became a symbol of Jesus' self-sacrifice, so did the rope with horses become the symbol of Mark's sacrifice (see the cover illustration of this book). A dragging death was intended to be a slow and tortuous death. This form of torture was public and prolonged,

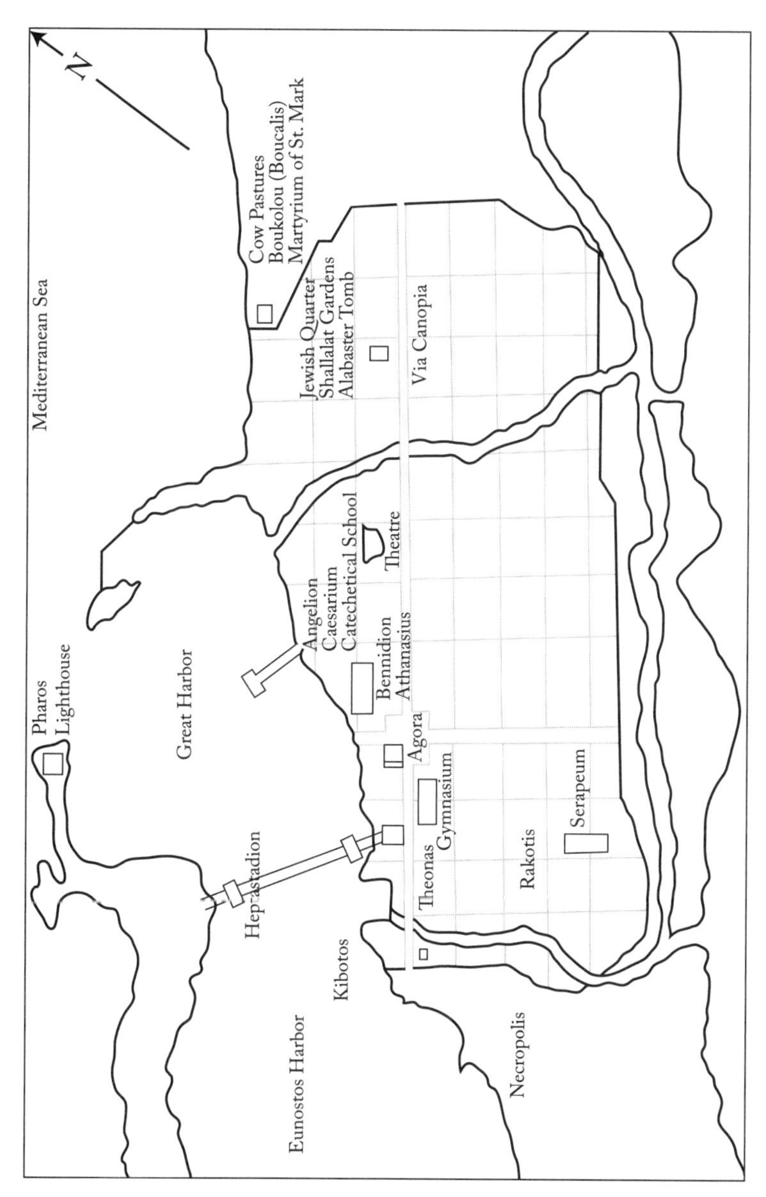

Map 4. Church locations in Alexandria recalling events of Mark's ministry and death
Each church site here commemorates some episode in the Alexandrian recollection of St. Mark: his arrival (the Bennidion), the conversion of Anianus (near Theonas), the Shallalat Gardens in the Jewish Quarter, the arrest (Serapeum), the dragging (Rakotis to the Cow Pastures, Boukolou), the attempt to burn the saint (Angelion) and the burial of Mark (Boukolou).

similar to crucifixion. Mark's life prefigured his death. His life had been lived in a wide orbit of transit. His death was required when he had at last come back to the continent on which he was born.

After his seizure, dragging and public humiliation, Mark was thrown into prison half alive. Then the narrative reports that there was an earthquake. The earth shook as if in revulsion against the treatment of Mark. Sawirus wrote:

> So when evening came, they took him to the prison, that they might take counsel how they should put him to death. And at midnight, the doors of the prison being shut, and the [jailers] asleep at the doors, behold there was a great earthquake and a mighty tumult. (Sawirus, *HP*, 146)

During this night when Mark was in jail, an angelic visitor comforted him, telling him to fear nothing at all. *Martyrium Marci* relates the visit:

> And the angel of the Lord descended from heaven, touched him and said: "O Mark, servant of God, . . . behold, your name has been written in the book of eternal life and you have been counted among the holy apostles; behold your memory will not ever be forsaken." (*Martyrium Marci* 8)

It was revealed that he was participating in the suffering and death of the Lord in whose resurrection he would soon be glorified. The angelic messenger was preparing him for the martyr's crown. The angel revealed to him that his name is written in the book of life, that he had proved worthy of bearing apostolic authority and that his death would not be in vain.

Whether this narrative of earthquake and miracle occurred as an actual historical event or as a later legend did not need to be dealt with in the story of the saint. Regardless of how modern observers answer that question, clearly this event has been remembered and celebrated for two millennia in Africa, especially in Nilotic languages, as an actual event manifesting an episode in the history of salvation. Whether history or not in the modern sense, it at least calls for a hearing, if not as demonstrable event at least as a picture of God's saving action that has shaped the African Christian mind from its beginnings.

MARK'S DEATH

The narrative of Sawirus continues:

> And when he awoke from his sleep he raised his eyes to heaven, and said: "I thank thee, O my Lord Jesus Christ, and pray thee to receive me to thyself, that I may be happy in thy goodness." And when he had finished these words, he slept again; and the Lord Christ appeared to him in the form in which the disciples knew him, and said to him: "Hail Mark, the evangelist and chosen one!" So the saint said to him: "I thank thee, O my Saviour Jesus Christ, because thou hast made me worthy to suffer for thy holy name." And the Lord and Saviour gave him his salutation, and disappeared from him. (Sawirus, *HP*, 146-47)

Mark was called the beholder of God. This could be a reference to his own eyewitness to the events of the last week in Jerusalem, or it could have been a reference to the resurrection appearance of the Lord in Mark's prison cell.

Mark was dragged again over the cobbled roads of Alexandria, his body battered, this time dragged to his death. The mob was determined to torture him again before his death. He was dragged back to the Serapeum. His blood was spilt on the streets of Alexandria until he at last died a tortured martyr's death. His blood attested the blood of the Son of God.

Sawirus concludes the martyr narrative: "And they drew the saint along the ground, while he gave thanks to the Lord Christ, and glorified him, saying: 'I render my spirit into thy hands, O my God!'" After saying these words, the saint gave up the ghost (Sawirus, *HP*, 147).

Mark's torn and broken body was to be burned on a pyre. This was intended to end all thought of remembering him in the future or celebrating his martyred body. But a heavy storm arose suddenly.

Sawirus reports:

> Then the ministers of the unclean idols collected much wood in a place called *Angelion*, that they might burn the body of the saint there. But by the command of God there was a thick mist and a strong wind, so that the earth trembled; and much rain fell, and many of the people died of

> fear and terror; and they said: "Verily, Serapis, the idol, has come to seek the man who has been killed this day" (Sawirus, *HP*, 147)

This "place called *Angelion*" would be remembered. A church would later be built there where the angels quenched the fire and saved Mark's body from destruction.

Amid the confusion, faithful believers removed the body of the saint and secretly buried him. His body was secreted out by his disciples and taken back to Bucalis, where a church would grow. His body was placed in a tomb in the eastern part of the city that had been carved in the rock.

> Then the faithful brethren assembled, and took the body of the holy Saint Mark from the ashes; and nothing in it had been changed. And they carried it to the church in which they used to celebrate the Liturgy; and they enshrouded it, and prayed over it according to the established rites. And they dug a place for him, and buried his body there; that they might preserve his memory at all times with joy and supplication, and benediction, on account of the grace which the Lord Christ gave them by his means in the city of Alexandria. And they placed him in the eastern part of the church, on the day on which his martyrdom was accomplished (he being the first of the Galileans to be martyred for the name of the Lord Jesus Christ in Alexandria), namely the last day of Barmudah according to the reckoning of the Egyptians, which is equivalent to the 8th day before the kalends of May among the months of the Romans, and the 24th of Nisan among the months of the Hebrews. (Sawirus, *HP*, 147-48)

The burial site was the same cow pasture (*boukolos*) where Mark had first nurtured the worshiping community following his meeting with Anianus. Mark was slaughtered like a cow. Cattle were among those animals most frequently chosen for sacrifice. Bucalis was the place of his burial and of the church that would continue there. It is within this rock nearby the sea and near a rock quarry that African tradition holds that the body of Mark was buried. These two places, the Serapeum and Bucalis, are identified locations in Alexandria today. They elicited two different early martyr oratories where the faithful came to pray. These two and several other martyr locations and memorials of Mark's death were celebrated in those parts of Alexandria where various events of his martyrdom occurred. Thus believers of successive centuries had a record in rock of Mark's coming to die in Alexandria. Nearly two-and-a-half centuries later, in 311, Bishop Peter of Alexandria would be martyred at the same tomb.

9

MARK'S MARTYRDOM SITES IN ALEXANDRIA

Mark's martyrdom reportedly occurred in Alexandria where his body was buried and a memorial oratory established to recall his dying sacrifice. We have inferential evidence that there was not just one martyrium to Mark in Alexandria but many. There were several corollary sites that correspond to various distinguishable times and places associated with Mark's ministry and death. These were linked with a common memory that was durable enough that churches were in due time built at the places where these events occurred.

Does that prove that the events occurred? It at least goes part way toward a plausible premise pointing toward their historical reality, which may remain forever debatable. If these sites were dependent upon a legend crassly invented out of thin air centuries after the attested events, how could they have been received consensually worldwide without a whisper of any debate. How could so many be fooled for so many centuries? It would not speak well for common sense. Why would many African women and men who were ready to offer up their lives in similar witness during the Diocletian persecution return to pray at these very sites? By A.D. 300 Bucalis (Boukolou) had been long attested. How long? Likely since the dragging of Mark occurred ca. A.D. 68.

We have not only traditional recollections but scattered archaeological inferences and evidences that point to the location of these earliest martyria in Alexandria.[1] They are in the heart of ancient Alexandria, however deeply their unexcavated ruins may have been buried under the modern city. All of these churches and sites named below refer their location to the arrival, life, ministry and martyrdom of Mark in Alexandria. Among these are:

- Serapeum (Serapium), the place of Mark's arrest during the Festival of the Cult of the God Serapis
- the church of the Angeloi where his body was planned to be burned but a miracle intervened
- the Bennidion (or Mendion) near where Mark arrived and healed Anianus
- the Shallalat Gardens north of Horriya St. where Christians in the Jewish quarter lived
- St. Theonas, where Mark arrived from Cyrene
- the ancient streets underneath now downtown Alexandria where he was dragged
- Boukolou (Bucalis), the Cow Pastures to which Mark was dragged and later buried in a rock tomb by the sea

The locations of the remains of the earliest known Christian sites in Alexandria correspond closely with literary recollections found in the accounts of Mark's martyrdom. It seems plausible to infer that the location of the events created the location of the churches. The less plausible hypothesis is that the first ones to "remember" these locations manufactured the events out of pure fantasy or economic interest centuries later. That hypothesis is crass and insensitive. Reasonable archaeological evidences point to these several places in early Alexandria that refer their location to the ministry of Mark. Though much more archaeological work is needed in early Christian Alexandria, it appears that among the earliest churches in Alexandria were the following.[2]

[1]For background discussion of the history and archaeology of Alexandria, see works in the bibliography by Charles Kannengiesser, Richard Layton, Fr. Tadros Y. Malaty, John McGuckin, Judith McKenzie, Tito Orlandi, C. H. Roberts and Barbara Tkaczow.

[2]For recent general discussion of Egyptian and Coptic archaeology impinging on Alexandrian

CHURCH LOCATIONS IN ALEXANDRIA

The "Cow Pastures" (Bucalis, Boukolou). When Mark returned to Alexandria, he found that the Christian community he had initiated was flourishing "in the grace and the faith of God." The most important church location in Alexandria was called Boukolou (Cow Pastures), a place of grazing near the seashore (Sawirus, *HP*, 145; *Martyrium Marci* 5), often spelled Bucalis (Boucalis), a location that once was known, but now is not visible, and may be under the sea. It appears that this community of faith emerged quickly after Mark's first arrival in Alexandria. It is the likely place where the earliest Christians in Alexandria worshiped (Sawirus, *HP*, 145; *Martyrium Marci* 7-10).

It was remembered in the Diocletian period as the location of the martyr's rock tomb on the (then) "outskirts of the city." It was the buffalo place or "cow pasture" in the eastern district, "beside the sea, beneath the cliffs" (Sawirus, *HP*, 145; *Martyrium Marci* 5, 10). The church was probably named after the event of Mark's death, not vice versa. Though the sea has now encroached upon this seaside area, the location was clearly identified and publicly known before Constantine. They "built a church for themselves at Boukolou (Bucalis) near the sea."[3] It is here that Mark was buried.

The Angelion. The Angelion, or the Church of St. Mark at al-Mualaqa in Alexandria, is revered as the place where the attempt was made to burn Mark's body but a miracle of storm intervened. Angelion, or the Church of the Angels, Angeloi, was founded on the site of "a temple built by Cleopatra in Alexandria. It was later converted to a church by the name of Archangel Michael" (Shenouda III, 17). Earlier known as al-Caisaron, it was later rebuilt and named after St. Mark. Usually referred to as the Angelion (or al-Caisaron; cf. Habib Guirgis, *St. Mark the Apostle*) or later as the Church of Constantine or Caisaria

archaeology, see works in the bibliography by Alexander Badawy, Roger S. Bagnall, Wolfgang Boochs, Christian Cannuyer, David Frankfurter, Albert Gehards and Heinzgerd Brakmann, and Winifred Kammerer.

[3]Sawirus, *HP*, 147-48; *Martyrium Marci* 7, 10; Birger A. Pearson, "Ancient Alexandria in the 'Acts of Mark,' " in *Gnosticism and Christianity in Roman and Coptic Egypt* (New York: T & T Clark, 2004), pp. 100-113; cf. M. Chaine, "L'Église de Saint-Marc à Alexandrie construite par le patriarche Jean de Samanoud," *Revue de l'oriente Chrétien* 4, no. 3 (1924): 372-86.

Church (Shenouda III, 121-22), or sometimes referred to as al-Kamha Church. Since before Constantine, it has honored the treasured memories of the martyrdom of Mark. It is the site of the sixth-century church of St. John the Baptist, built later, but recalling the martyrdom of both the Baptizer and the Evangelist, who both must have been prominent in its iconostasis during Byzantine times.

The Angelion and the catechetical school were likely located in the Greek area of Alexandria, the Bruchium (or Pyroucheion, *REC*, 151). "The place of the church was easily recognized by Butler because of its two [huge stone] needles. One of these needles was sent to London in A.D. 1877 and the other has been in Central Park in New York since 1879. We can locate its place in Alexandria which would be the right side of the end of al-Nabi Daniel Street, between the sea and Sultan Heissin and Safia Zaghlol Streets."[4]

The Angelion was still standing at the beginning of the Arab conquest but was burned during the conflict. It was built on the wall of the city near one of its towers.[5] The head of St. Mark was reportedly kept there after A.D. 644.[6] The body of St. Mark was stolen by Venetians in A.D. 828. The church was destroyed, again rebuilt and once again ruined during the French invasion in 1798. Its priceless library (as heir of the catechetical school) and many precious objects were removed to Rosetta during the French invasion. Some of these items wound up in the Coptic Museum.

The Bennidion. The Bennidion (variously Mendion or Mendidiou) is the place where Mark is remembered as having first met the cobbler Anianus, near the first-century gates of the city. In the Acts of St. Mark he went to a place called Bennidion or Mendion. It may correspond to the site of the Mosque of the Souq al-Attarin, demolished in 1830.[7]

St. Theonas Church. St. Theonas Church was in the far western part

---

[4]Nabih Kamel Dawoud, "Churches and Antiquities Carrying the Name of 'Mark,'" in Shenouda III, pp. 119-41.

[5]Alfred J. Butler, *The Arab Conquest of Egypt and the Last Thirty Years of the Roman Dominion*, 2nd ed. (Oxford: Clarendon, 1978), pp. 323-25.

[6]As noted by al-Maqrizi, medieval Muslim historian of A.D. 1441; see *Kawl Al Eprizi Lil Alama Al Maqrizi* (1898), p. 44; cf. Shenouda III, p. 122.

[7]Judith McKenzie, *The Architecture of Alexandria and Egypt, 300 B.C. to A.D. 700* (New Haven, Conn.: Yale University Press, 2007), p. 408n.

of Alexandria, south of Pharos, immediately south of the Kibotos Harbor in the Delta section. This is near the isle of Pharos, location of the famed lighthouse. This island was the traditional site of translation of the Septuagint, and the site of an annual Jewish festival commemorating the Septuagint. The Holy Spirit in Mark's calling had instructed him to go from Cyrene directly to Pharos.

The four churches discussed thus far are known by their lengthy history as firmly or proximately located places in Alexandria today. Coptic Patriarch Shenouda III has gathered a summary, assisted by Nabih Kamel Dawoud, of the evidences of other churches in Alexandria memorializing the martyrdom of Mark (Shenouda III, 124-26).

Shallalat Gardens and other locations. In addition there was also early Christian presence nearby the great synagogue (*REC,* 154). This is in the city near the main Jewish quarter north of Via Canopica in eastern Alexandria. Quoting Pearson and Goehring: "As to the area of Alexandria where the main first-century Jewish quarter was located, no systematic archaeological excavations have been done there," but it probably was the Shallalat Gardens north of Horriya St, or around ancient Via Canopica, or north of Latin cemetery where an Alabaster Tomb was found (*REC,* 154-56). More precise identification of this site would establish where Christians were living in the Jewish quarter near Canopica, but its likely neighborhood is known.

Other houses of prayer were in due time built on the sites of events of Mark's ministry and last days to venerate the major locations of his arrest, torture, suffering and death. Here both the archaeological and literary evidences appear to converge. A number of churches once existing, according to ancient literary evidence, are now buried under the multilayered pavements of the city. Some of these were referenced as early as the medieval accounts of Abu al-Makarem (A.D. 1208) and by al-Maqrizi (A.D. 1441).

The dangling question: If there are so many sites in Alexandria that recall Mark, his ministry, his arrest, his death, his attempted burning and his burial, why are they there in Alexandria if he never was in Alexandria? These martyr locations celebrated Mark: the place of his first conversion, his torture, his being dragged, his martyrdom, the martyrium built in his memory, a subsequent church and the lighthouse that reportedly guided Mark to Alexandria. What accounts for the antiquity and persistence of martyr sites that correspond to the literary records, if they were mere fantasy?

WHAT WE CAN LEARN FROM THESE EVIDENCES

Why are these physical locations pertinent to the history of Mark in Africa? These are likely the places of the earliest meeting places or churches to be identified or established in all of Africa. The ancient working hypothesis of the African memory of Mark is that *Alexandria's earliest known church locations were intentionally identified by and named after events specifically connected with Mark's name and history.* Each of these sites is important in itself, but taken together they form a cohesive Gestalt of evidence that cannot be ignored. These archaeological remains bear reasonable correspondence with key elements of the standard African narrative.[8]

These are good reasons to reevaluate the conclusion so rashly made by Westerners that Mark never arrived in Alexandria. They call for more archaeological investigation than has been possible under present circumstances.

Even before the reign of Constantine and before the writings of Eusebius, a martyrium was built at Bucalis on the site of Mark's grave. The martyrdom of Peter of Alexandria occurred on November 21, A.D. 311. Just before his death, Peter, the bishop of Alexandria prayed at the tomb of St. Mark at Boukolou. This was just before he joined Mark among the martyrs at that very location. Peter was beheaded. Mark was dragged to death. Thus before Constantine, still during the Diocletian persecution, the location of Mark's burial place was already a matter of consensual memory and public record.

The synchrony of the picture is poignant: Peter of Alexandria became the "*last martyr of Egypt*" before the peace of Constantine. Peter's last act was to pray at the tomb of the *first martyr of Egypt.* It is likely that Eusebius himself would have visited and physically seen Mark's

[8]Pearson, "Ancient Alexandria," pp. 100-113.

tomb before he wrote his history of martyrdom.

Some suppose that the record of Mark's tomb in Alexandria goes back no further than to the sixth century. But this ignores the attestation of A.D. 311 that Peter prayed at the tomb of Mark in Boukolou and the literary evidences we will present from Clement a century before Peter. The circumstantial evidence is strong that the martyrium predates Peter's dramatic visit, for why else would Peter go to what he and the worshiping community had always heard and believed was the tomb of Mark? Peter's prayer before his beheading makes little sense unless he was indeed standing at the grave of Mark.

But for how long had this tomb been there? Since A.D. 68 or some later point? If Mark's tomb was moved from its original location, surely that anomaly would have been preserved somewhere in the literature, but there is no evidence of this. Hence in my view the evidence weighs on the side of the assumption that the tomb of Mark had been in the same place 243 years at the time Peter prayed before his death.

Among leading skeptics about the death of Mark in Alexandria are Adolf von Harnack, Walter Bauer and Hans Lietzmann. This skepticism has become so normative for Western Markan studies that the African narrative is almost never mentioned. But in order to deny or even ignore the burial of Mark in Alexandria a long string of dubious conclusions must be drawn. To make the skeptical argument work, it is necessary to avoid numerous absurdities:

1. The skeptic must provide some plausible hypothesis as to why Peter of Alexandria would have sought out the tomb of Mark just before his death.
2. One must imagine that Eusebius was unaware of Mark's tomb, which had long existed and been revered as a sacred site by Christians in Alexandria when he visited Egypt.
3. One must imagine that the narrative of Mark's appearance in Alexandria was a fantasy invented out of whole cloth by someone with deceptive motives. Could it have been invented by people solemnly sworn to tell the truth: godly pastors and courageous bishops willing to die for the faith? The inventor of the hoax would then have had

the burden of convincing the whole laity in Egypt and elsewhere of the falsity of the consensus that had prevailed over many generations. The laity were not that easily hoodwinked.

4. The doubter must imagine that this deception could be sustained for a very long time—between A.D. 68 and 311—that is, over two-and-a-half centuries between the burial of Mark and the prayer at his grave of Peter of Alexandria.
5. One must then resort to an incomplete and awkward argument from silence. It is not reasonable to insist, based on arguments from silence, that Mark *never could have* been in Africa.

I am determined to proceed with high respect for modern Western historical criteria melded with what can be learned from the ancient narrative common to early African Christians. I ask only that the African narrative be given a hearing and not ruled out peremptorily. At issue: What would explain that there would be so many martyrial locations dedicated to Mark in Alexandria if Mark had never been to Alexandria?

In the years following Peter of Alexandria, Mark's burial place was attested repeatedly: In the early fifth century Philoromus, presbyter from Galatia, visited Alexandria and prayed at the Martyrion of Mark as attested by Palladius (*Lausaic History* 45). Other attestations appear liturgically in the Coptic Synaxary. Only much later was the narrative put in its definitive form collected by Sawirus, based on the widest range of previous sources surviving into the tenth century.

Birger Pearson sums up: "The historicity of this tradition, though unprovable, should not be ruled out. Indeed the tradition of the preaching of Mark in Alexandria may antedate the acceptance of the canonical Gospel of Mark in the Alexandrian church" (*REC,* 144-45). This is a significant conclusion: If Mark was already preaching in Alexandria even before the canonical Gospel of Mark was received in the Alexandrian church, as Pearson suggests, this turns on its head the prevailing and common chronologies of New Testament scholars, and places Mark in Egypt possibly at a very early date, just as the Coptic chronology suggests.

The most popular (and cynical) modern hypothesis for explaining the supposed lateness of testimony to Mark in Alexandria is that the patriarchate was invented before the martyr sites. It was the patriarchate that so desperately needed legitimation that it lied about times, places and events. It supposedly needed an explanation of why it was so important. But this leaves unexplained the prior question of why it was indeed so important, virtually equal in importance with Rome, and likely founded at almost precisely the same time as the church of Rome.

The lacuna of explicit timely written documents that would incontestably establish Mark's death in Alexandria is due to the massive destruction of long-guarded ecclesiastical and historical documents from the Diocletian period to the Arab onslaught. Silence, however, cannot stand as a decisive argument against the veracity of the longstanding consensual traditions.

The decisive question here is whether Mark was martyred in Africa. We are not able to say with absolute certainty that we know precisely what happened with Mark in Africa. But no one can doubt that there are few events of two millennia ago that are still remembered by millions, even if they do not conform to absolute demonstration according to Western historians. We cannot say with unerring confidence that Mark was the first African martyr, but there is a strong claim of social tradition and of the major martyr locations in Alexandria that Mark was martyred there. The fair assessment of scientific evidence depends especially on how martyr locations are weighed in historical assessments and how much weight may be given to a multigenerational Gestalt of circumstantial evidence. Even though this evidence may be vulnerable to lapses or to serious questions, or to the burning or destruction of hard documentation, the remnants of evidence cannot be dismissed. A very heavy weight of oral tradition and a shared African memory have survived. Together they make a compelling argument for Mark's enduring stamp upon Africa.

It did not take long for this memory to take root all over the continent, and indeed all over the universal church, as a firm consensual conclusion. Its details were remembered. Its locations were revered. This constitutes a kind of evidence, but one written in blood. Though this African narrative is typically discounted by modern historians, insufficient reason exists to deny it altogether. Meanwhile today, the African memory is not only surviving but reawakening in its twenty-first century of recollection.

To all these real and circumstantial evidences we can add a sad and almost comic postscript: This is not, strictly speaking, an argument, but intuitively it is to me one of the most persuasive indicators that Mark was in Alexandria. It comes from art history and is especially well told in Deborah Howard's wonderful *Venice and the East.*[9]

The Venetians, being savvy, shrewd and no-nonsense traders, were not a people to be easily fooled. I doubt that it was something other than Mark's body that was transported to Venice to become that city's chief martyrium: the Cathedral of San Marco. I do not think the Venetians would be hoodwinked. It is more likely than not that they knew exactly what they were getting when they stole the body of Mark. I do not know, nor does anyone, just how they knew, but my intuition says: They knew.

Venice ever thereafter was emulating Alexandria as a great city, comparable to Rome and Constantinople. The mosaics and symbols of Venice at San Marco Square reek with pride over their greatest conquest: the body of Mark.

THE HEIRS OF MARK

The mission of Mark in Africa rests upon a very old tradition. It is recalled most conspicuously by Eusebius (*CH* 2.16), though the tradition precedes Eusebius. It was linked with the pre-Eusebian Urtext of *Martyrium Marci.*[10] Much later Sawirus would rely without significant divergence upon this long tradition already established before Diocletian. It tells of a series of Mark's earliest disciples named Anianas/Anianus (A.D. 68), Milaios/Malchus, Sabinos/Sabinus and Kerdon/Cerdo, following Mark's martyrdom. They presided over the church of Alexandria from about A.D. 68 to 109, recording forty years of leadership in

[9]Deborah Howard, *Venice and the East: The Impact of the Islamic World on Venetian Architecture 1100–1500* (New Haven, Conn.: Yale University Press, 2000).
[10]PG 115: cols. 167-70.

Egyptian Christianity following Mark's death. All major centers of Christianity were morally bound to keep records validating their historic succession from the apostles, as we see in Ignatius. The written records were harder to protect in Egypt than in Rome or Antioch.

By the third and fourth centuries this account was a received, trusted and established ecumenical tradition. The same genre of references is found in texts of the fourth century (Paulinus of Nola) and continue to the seventh century in the *Chronicon Paschale*.[11]

Various intrepid leaders followed in Mark's footsteps. The martyrs of Scilli and Carthage came later—more than a century—*following* the pattern of Mark, linking the beginning of the Numidian, Carthaginian and Egyptian church with the apostles. Cyprian, bishop in Carthage, was willing, like Mark, to yield up his body as an unflinching witness to the risen Lord. Cyprian honored Mark as his predecessor. Mark was dragged to death; Cyprian was beheaded.

Mark's martyrdom placed an indelible stamp upon the embryonic beginning of the African church. Later the martyrs of Mauretania and Nubia and Libya proved also, if necessary, willing to sacrifice their bodies to witness to Christ. Who knows how many other unknown martyrs there may have been between Mark's death and the death of the Scilli martyrs (between A.D. 68 and 180)? Among other important African leaders who followed Mark to martyrdom were Origen's father, Leonides, Peter of Alexandria and Catherine of Alexandria.

What sort of evidence do we have to link Mark with his successors from Demetrius to Peter? We have the standard form of evidence that prevailed in the early centuries of Christianity—the carefully preserved and guarded lists of Mark's episcopal successors. This is the common way by which the apostolic tradition in all regions showed evidence of its continuity, succession and hence trustability. The apostolic pattern itself follows a common cultural pattern of establishing noble dynasties by preserving lists of the dates, names and continuities of noble or royal families. But this kingdom is not of this world.

---

[11]E.g., *Chronicon Paschale,* ed. L. Dindorf, Corpus scriptorum historiae byzantinae (Bonn: E. Weber, 1832). They are also found in a Coptic papyrus fragment Amherst-Morgan 15 which can be found in W. E. Crum, *Theological Texts from Coptic Papyri* (Oxford: 1913), pp. 65-68.

Apostolic validation is more than a cultural fantasy or social legitimation. It is grounded in a form of argument that had a scriptural and theological base resisted by modern historians. It was based on a mandate of the covenant community. The Hebraic view of God's revelation is intrinsically bound to a real history, not an imaginary one. The history of Jesus is a historical event. It is not a myth. That requires that its history be presented by eyewitnesses and preserved in continuity with the original eyewitnesses. That is what apostolic succession means. It is a form of historical evidence.

Between the eighth year of Nero (A.D. 62) and tenth year of Commodus (A.D. 189), there were reportedly ten bishops of Alexandria—from Mark to Demetrius, according to highly revered Coptic liturgical celebrations. These were confirmed in Eusebius. What do we know about these earliest Christian leaders on the African continent? They all understood themselves as successors of St. Mark. Since the palpable records were destroyed by centuries of war, persecution and conflict, we depend upon circumstantial evidence, unless we want to discard the African memory altogether. The surviving information in some cases is only the names of the saints and martyrs and their dates and locations of death. In other cases we have corroborating evidence in court records, letters, liturgy and in some cases in stone inscriptions.

Does this debatable evidence imply they were later invented? The argument from silence says yes. Measured historical judgment says no. The broad base of general lay consent says no.

If there were indeed ten bishops of Alexandria before Demetrius, it is likely that these would have been carefully documented in their own time and vigilantly preserved due to their importance. The African narrative assumes that there were such documents, even if they have not survived until today. But it is absurd to think that burnable evidence would have survived through three centuries of intense persecution and two tumultuous millennia of subsequent harassment.

The study of ancient history is replete with many figures known to exist, but about which we have only their names. Knowing only their names does not imply they did not exist. Why did their names survive? Not because they were made up or invented. This common leap of logic is often prejudicially applied to selective cases such as saints and holy men and women. It signals a subtle narrow-mindedness, a philosophical predisposition to disbelieve all events of sacred texts, all reports of miracle or supernatural references, since they are *prima facie* assumed to be false and misleading.

It is not an incidental question that Mark was succeeded by Anianus (62–85), and Anianus by Avilius (85–98), Avilius by Cerdo (98–109), Cerdo by Primus (109–122), and the line then continues as a direct succession: from Primus through Justus (122–130), Eumenes (130–142), Marcianus/Mark II (143–154), Celadion (157–167), Agrippinus (167–180) and Julian (180–189) before you get to the great Demetrius (189–231). They continue to Dionysius (247–264) and on eventually to Athanasius (326–373) and Cyril (412–444). The implication: Believers could therefore trust that their apostolic teachings were reliably remembered and faithfully transmitted.[12]

The whole of Africa today is the heir to bold witnesses and martyrs, both men and women. They left behind them some fragile documentary evidence, but more firm than stone was the consensual memory of the laity. This is sociological evidence, not documentary or literary evidence. Churches that followed them all over Africa were drenched in the blood of the martyrs. This is evident from visiting martyr sites from Tipasa in Algeria to St. Frumentius of Ethiopia.

These African martyrs received the apostolic vision from the beginning through Mark. They learned that the truth of the gospel is worth dying for. If the apostolate had become costly, it was worth it, promising eternal life with God. They had known their episcopal leaders personally before they buried them. Their bodies had been baptized by them. Their heads had been touched by their ordinations. They were not prone to forget where they buried them.

Is it possible that the death of Mark could have been invented out of phantasms or manufactured by mythmakers centuries later? To me it appears more likely that the mythmakers are those of nineteenth-

---

[12]Stephen J. Davis provides the fullest rendering of this succession in *The Early Coptic Papacy: The Egyptian Church and Its Leadership in Late Antiquity,* (New York and Cairo: American University in Cairo Press, 2004).

century historicism. It is demeaning to the original confessors to assume that these pilgrimage sites are bogus.

HOW DID THE MARTYRDOM NARRATIVE GAIN ANCIENT ECUMENICAL CONSENT?

There is no extant record of ancient inquiry about whether Mark actually died in Alexandria. The only memory is that of true martyrdom in a conspicuous city. If the ecumenical consensus were debated on this point, wouldn't there be some residue of literature about it? But there is none. The ecumenical consensus did not confirm the African memory of Mark by accident or without wide consent. Eventually it enjoyed virtually universal consent *until* the nineteenth century. Then the modern inventors of myth saw a target of opportunity in the saints themselves. Then the reductionist philosophers from Marx to Nietzsche to Freud worked their magic, and the saints disappeared from the universities.

Viewed from ecumenical Christianity, the story of Mark was remembered in virtually the same way by both great Sees of Rome and Alexandria. These were steadily corroborated by the faithful of Jerusalem, Antioch, Constantinople and Kiev. Ultimately the ecumenical consensus received the core of the narrative we have been describing, with few exceptions. This consensus stands as telling evidence of trust in the authenticity of a narrative that might otherwise seem improbable. It was received in widely varied cultural settings speaking many of the world's remote languages.

Such a coup would have been extremely hard to fake. However rashly or ignorantly the case against Alexandria is asserted by skeptical Western critics, they have not prevailed, except among a small coterie of academics. Those who reject the gravitas of this historic consent fail to make an alternative case convincingly. To do so, they must find some way of countering the weight of historic ecumenical consent. This has not happened.

On empirical grounds, Irenaeus expressed confidence in the classic Christian tradition of appealing to apostolic consensus. Around A.D. 180 he said of these carefully preserved lists of predecessors: "It is within the power of all, therefore, in every Church, who may wish to see the truth, to contemplate clearly the tradition of the apostles manifested throughout the whole world; and we are in a position to reckon up those who were by the apostles instituted bishops in the Churches, and [to demonstrate] the succession of these men to our own times" (*Against Heresies* 3.3.1).

The nonconsensual followers of Valentinus and Marcion and Basilides also attempted to gain legitimacy through ecumenical consent. They too made the futile attempt to show that they could trace their apostolic connections back to Paul and the apostles. They too compiled lists of preceding teachers attempting to gain intergenerational and international consent. But these alternative gospels and their noncanonical texts were never affirmed for very long by the laity worldwide, even if they might have been on a very small scale locally and for a very short length of time. What they lacked was long-term lay consensual confirmation sustained over many highly varied languages, centuries and cultures. That is what ecumenical consent uniquely possesses. The Gnostic lists were flatly rejected by the East-West consensus.

This consensus upheld lists of successors of the bishops of Jerusalem, Antioch, Rome and Alexandria. These successions were carefully preserved by centrist writers such as Irenaeus, Eusebius, Athanasius, Jerome and Augustine. This consensus still can be trusted. What other institution can list a leadership succession over two thousand years? The succession following Mark was evidently established as early in Alexandria as the succession of Peter was in Rome. These two great apostolic sees likely were established almost simultaneously.

The hard physical evidence of Peter in Rome is no more compelling than of Mark in Alexandria. Both hinge on epigraphic residues and martyr memorials as well as literary recollections. Both arguments are based on large accumulations of circumstantial evidence. Why then is the authenticity of Peter's story so often assumed and Mark's so often denied? My hunch is that it is a Eurocentric predisposition that wishes to be regarded as valid scientific evidence. That hunch may be argued, challenged or supported, like any other historical hypothesis, by examining the evidence, including sociological, circumstantial and inferential evidence.

CONVERGING FORMS OF EVIDENCE

Thus we have presented both internal and external evidences, both textual and archaeological, that point to an Alexandrian location for the martyrdom of Mark. According to most Africans over two thousand years, the bones of Mark are the palpable evidence of Mark's death in Alexandria. This "hagiography"—usually a term of dismissal—is precisely the same kind of oral tradition that has been thought so intriguing to the imagination of so many European historical scholars of the last century.

Unfortunately their interest did not reach as far away as Africa. It is only when they were trying to establish Christian origins in Rome or Corinth or Philippi or Tarsus that the form critics and redaction critics have made an academic industry out of oral tradition. A parade of speculative suppositions have gained excited academic recognition for a short time. Careers were built on these suppositions. But these same scholars did not exercise the same due diligence in searching for the hypothetical Urtexts of the Markan narrative. It was left virtually untouched as a problem of the transmission of oral tradition.

Africans have concluded from this that if a document comes from northern climes they have been found interesting for Western academic speculation. But if a document comes from Africa—well, let's not rush to conclusions.

An oral tradition that was filled with shared living memories of a well-attested martyrdom would surely have been written down within a generation after the martyrdom. Within days it would have become known to virtually every believer in its local area. Whatever documents were written down by eyewitnesses would likely have been carefully stored in church crypts or martyria. Some could have survived. Only a few of them survived the many phases of persecution that followed. But most did not. Many of those early Christian martyr documents and recollections that likely survived the Diocletian persecution must have been later burned or destroyed in the Arab sweep of North Africa. But some remnants and papyri and epigraphy actually did survive. This is what we must live with—the fragments of historical memory. Some may still remain hidden and may yet be unearthed.

Mark was the first of the eyewitnesses to the history of Jesus to preach the good news in a continent that now has almost a half billion believers. He was the first of untold numbers of Africans to give his life for the faith, the first to live out his baptism of fire on the African continent, and likely the first apostle to be buried in African soil. The story that began in Libyan Cyrene would echo throughout both Asia and Europe. From the greatest intellectual center of Africa, Alexandria, would come the landmark intellectual tradition of Christian thought with unparalleled and lasting contributions to the history of education. From that intellectual tradition has come a steady flow of brilliant literature that equals anything produced in Christianity's earliest centuries. Today the good news of Jesus is still being told all over Africa. An African-born Libyan was its first conveyor and servant. This narrative was learned and remembered all over the Africa of antiquity, south to Ethiopia and Nubia and as far west and south as Mauritania and the ancient kingdom of Ghana. Most believers in Africa of the first millennium knew of Mark as the first martyr of Christ in Africa.

DATING THE CHAIN OF EVENTS

All attempts at precisely dating ancient documents and events are tenuous, but that does not make the effort futile. I have used here as a norm of the African memory the Coptic Synaxarion (Baramouda [Ethiopic-Amharic Miyazia] 30) which concludes: "On this day, which coincided with the 26th of April 68 A.D., the great apostle St. Mark, the evangelist of the land of Egypt, was martyred." This is a fairly stable point of consensual reference. But we will compare this with other evidence.

Paul's reference to Mark in 2 Timothy indicates that Mark was still alive at that time: "Get Mark and bring him with you; for he is very useful in serving me" (2 Tim 4:11 RSV). That would likely put Mark's death sometime after A.D. 66. The ecumenical consensus remained firm after Eusebius, but its chronological details continue to be disputed.

- In his work *Lives of Illustrious Men* (*Lives* 8, PL 23:654), Jerome assigns the date of Mark's death to the eighth year of Nero (A.D. 62–63), "Mortuus est autem octavo Neronis anno et sepultus Alexandriæ." This may have been an inference from the statement of Eusebius (*CH* 2.24) that in that same year Anianus presumably succeeded Mark as bishop of Alexandria.

- The *Chronicon Paschale* fixes the date of Mark in Alexandria as two years before the reign of Claudius (about A.D. 39).
- The Coptic-Arabic history of Sawirus ibn al-Muqaffa, weighing all known accounts, assumed the date of Mark in Alexandria was in "the 15th year after the ascension of Christ" which could be between A.D. 40 and 48, depending on other chronological factors.
- Eutychius of Alexandria placed it in the ninth year of Claudius (A.D. 49–50).
- John Chrysostom argued that Mark wrote or revised his Gospel in Egypt (*Hom. Matt.* 1).

The range of these estimates tends toward earlier dates than most modern chronologies. Though varied, these are not more diffuse than many comparable estimates of dates in the ancient world, such as those disputed dates of important figures such as Clement, Pachomius, Menas and Dionysius the Areopagite.

It was the notion of the steady continuity with the apostolic witness that held together the manifold testimonies of witnesses of widely different cultures, languages and physical locations. More amazing than its diversity is its fundamental unity. This unity depends upon a theological premise: that the Spirit intends to elicit unity in the body of Christ. The argument is pneumatological, not historical; that means it hinges on the work of the Spirit, not physical or historical evidence. But it has many historical consequences. This form of continuity is based on a hermeneutical commitment seldom shared by modern historians, namely, that the Holy Spirit guaranteed the sufficient transmission of the sacred text through the hazardous conditions of human history.

Various ancient commentators have attempted to put a date upon the arrival of Mark in Alexandria ranging from A.D 39 to 66. The important feature of these reports and calculations is not their failure to agree, but the overwhelming fact that there was a *persistent effort to specify* the beginning and ending dates of Mark's mission in Africa and to view it as a specific apostolic mission to the continent. They agreed that whatever the date, it was worth debating factually, based on the available evidence at that time. That there are different dates does not mean that this was from the outset a hotly contested matter. It means rather that it was important enough to a number of different writers at different times to try to nail down the date. This attempt to be specific about the date of Mark's arrival in Alexandria would continue until the tenth century when it became more firmly fixed in the official history of the Coptic patriarchate.

Most probably Mark wrote or revised his Gospel at some time between Peter's ministry in Rome and Mark's period of residence in Alexandria. His recollections of the gospel narrative were coordinated closely with Peter's memory of them. Mark was an articulate and forceful communicator, fully capable of translating and interpreting the Aramaic of Peter into Koine Greek for the Greek-speaking ordinary folk of Alexandria. If the African picture of Mark is correct, this would have not been a difficult task for one raised in Cyrene who had resided with his mother in Jerusalem for some time. It is possible that Mark's Gospel was being read in Alexandria as early as the 50s or 60s of the first century.

The narrative of Mark's origin and ministry in Cyrene is not fanciful or completely impossible. Given the weight of its memory in Africa, it is plausible, even if unprovable by modern historical criteria. It is more than simply possible in my view that his life ended in Alexandria. If the Gestalt of circumstantial evidence is admitted, it comes close to fulfilling reasonable criteria for historical truth. If his body and likely his manuscripts were turned over to the patrimony of the Alexandrian church, as reported in the Letter to Theodore, his presence in Alexandria is virtually assured. Yet we have become accustomed to hearing nothing but skepticism. Western historians would be in a stronger and more principled position to dismiss the African memory of Mark if they had in fact examined all of the above documentation and evidence.

Recall that speculation on oral tradition has been absolutely essential to the methods of Western scholars. This has been the heart of the growth industry in standard university departments of religious studies for decades. Meanwhile oral traditions from Africa that support traditional claims have often been peremptorily dismissed. Given the increased interest in oral tradition since the 1920s, it is now time to ponder and reexamine wide-ranging social and circumstantial evidence.

My interest in the question of Mark in Africa has been recently reactivated by conversations among African historians on my study *How Africa Shaped the Christian Mind.* This book is the second in a series that includes that book, this study on Mark and a forthcoming sequel on early Libyan Christianity. From there all roads lead back to Mark. If Mark indeed brought Christianity to Africa, and if that datum is ignored by the non-African world, then scholars need to try to understand why.

REPRISE OF PART THREE

The core of this reasoning is best stated modestly:

1. All these efforts take seriously the durability and resilience of the narrative tradition that Mark was born in Cyrene and returned to Cyrene and Alexandria.
2. For several years I have felt a detective's premonition that the African story makes common sense when compared to the missing pieces of the puzzle seen from a Eurocentric perspective.
3. This is not to claim that the African narrative is provably "historical" on the same evidentiary level as vetted contemporary documentary evidence, but that it is a plausible tradition that has been too long ignored or prematurely dismissed.
4. Whatever one thinks of its historicity, the African narrative has in fact exercised a strong influence on the actual history of Christianity in Africa. The children of Mark have populated the African tradition.
5. The core of the Markan narrative that achieved consensuality in the early fourth century was grounded in events of the first century. This historical judgment is due to be examined not just as a matter of African curiosity but of composite evidence.

PART FOUR

Mark in the Historical Record

10

MARK'S AFRICAN IDENTITY VIEWED HISTORICALLY

There can be little doubt that an ecumenical consensus was established prior to the time of Eusebius which held that Mark died in Alexandria. In this chapter I will show textually how it developed prior to A.D. 325 and was reported as a long-standing consensus by Eusebius. Whether or not modern scholars agree with that consensus, virtually all commentators recognize that it prevailed with ample documentation from Eusebius to Jerome to John Chrysostom to Augustine and following, deep into the late nineteenth century, as reflected, for example, in the work of Henry Barclay Swete.[1] For scholars of classic Christianity, this consensus has survived twenty centuries. Modern skepticism about it has lasted for little more than a single century.

The challenge to the ecumenical consensus came primarily in the work of Adolf von Harnack. His view has prevailed in the modern period of scholarship. But will it continue? Harnack begins his tendentious history by dismissing the hagiographical tradition as altogether worthless, using these words: "The worthless character of this history is now recognised. . . . Whatever item from the apocryphal Acts, the local and provincial legends of the church, the episcopal lists, and the Acts of the martyrs, has not been inserted or noticed in these pages, has been delib-

[1]Henry Barclay Swete, *The Gospel According to St. Mark,* 1st ed. (London: Macmillan, 1898); 3rd ed. (London: Macmillan, 1927).

erately omitted as useless."[2] This leaves a huge hole that has affected the historical study of Christianity since Harnack. Echoing Harnack, Bauer condescendingly wonders in amazement "why they [the Alexandrian tradition] should be content with a figure of the second rank [Mark] instead of choosing someone else from that illustrious band of Jesus' closest friends."[3] Walter Völker's stinging critique of Bauer in 1935 is belatedly gaining acceptance, that Bauer arrived at his conclusions "by frequent use of the argument from silence, by bold combinations, by unsupportable conjectures which themselves are reused as a precarious foundation for further conjectures, by inferences drawn from later periods. . . . I cannot believe that such a reconstruction of history has prospects of becoming accepted."[4] Regrettably, Harnack and Bauer have taken such root in Western academia that this oversight is hard to root out. Recent inquires into the African memory of Mark, however, may point toward the beginning of a long-delayed unwinding of the Harnack-Bauer constrictions and their accompanying speculations.

Polycarp, Ignatius, Irenaeus and virtually all classic Christian writers who followed them thought that heresy arises from distortions of previous and original apostolic teaching. Tertullian made this argument in strong terms against Marcion. If we are to challenge the last century with the consensual evidences of the previous twenty, this requires a carefully unpacking of the documentary evidence of Mark in Africa from the ancient presbyters to Eusebius. Clifton Black has made a useful attempt to present this history, but without sufficient attentiveness to the African memory of Mark.[5]

Meanwhile few leading Euro-American historians have been dealing seriously with the arguments we have been reviewing. Especially

---

[2]From the preface to the first German edition, 1902, Adolf von Harnack, *The Mission and Expansion of Christianity in the First Three Centuries*, trans. James Moffatt (New York: Harper, 1962), p. xii.

[3]From first German edition, 1934, Walter Bauer, *Orthodoxy and Heresy in Earliest Christianity*, trans. Robert A. Kraft, Gerhard Kroedel et al. from the 2nd German ed. (Philadelphia: Fortress, 1971).

[4]Walter Völker, review of Walter Bauer's *Rechtgläubigkeit und Ketzerei im ältesten Christentum*, in *Zeitschrift für Kirchengeschichte* 54 (1935): 628-31, as quoted and translated in *Orthodoxy and Heresy*, p. 291.

[5]C. Clifton Black, *Mark: Images of an Apostolic Interpreter*, Studies on Personalities of the New Testament (Columbia: University of South Carolina Press, 1994).

ignored are the Coptic liturgical tradition and early Arabic sources. Until recently, few have been prepared to subject the assumptions of Adolf von Harnack and Walter Bauer to rigorous reexamination.

Birger Pearson wisely remarked: "If Walter Bauer and others can extrapolate backward in time from such early second-century Gnostic teachers as Basilides, Carpocrates and Valentinus, it is equally valid to extrapolate into the first century other varieties of Christianity, including more 'orthodox' ones, such as are represented in other early second century literature" (*REC*, 139). Among these were the *Teachings of Silvanus* and *Epistle of Barnabas*, and the *Gospel of the Hebrews* which was addressed to Jewish Christians of Alexandria, and the *Gospel of the Egyptians*, compiled for the Egyptians who were living in the Rhakotis district of Alexandria, as well as the *Gospel of Thomas*, which may have been a source used by some of the above. "The Epistle of Barnabas . . . is almost certainly of Alexandrian origin" (*REC*, 151). It is commonly dated about the time of Jewish revolt under Trajan (A.D. 115–117). All of these writings shared in common Jewish and Christian traditions in second-century Alexandria.[6]

The formation of the ecumenical consensus on Mark in Alexandria is often mistakenly ascribed to Eusebius. It is crucial to the African memory of Mark to show evidence of precisely how it was liturgically and typologically formed much earlier than Eusebius, and likely by the generation immediately following Mark's death. They honored with martyr sites the memory of his death and burial from the outset. The earliest core of testimony had formed prior to Papias (120–130). This previous tradition of the elders was reported by Papias. The bridge between Papias and Clement of Alexandria must be carefully reviewed in order to show the textual validity of this transition.

There are several landmarks along this road:

- The first to attest Mark's close relation with Peter were John the Elder and Aristion who were sources for Papias.
- The first to place Peter in Rome with Mark was Papias.

[6]Birger A. Pearson, *Gnosticism and Christianity in Roman and Coptic Egypt* (New York: T & T Clark, 2004); Helmut Koester, *Introduction to the New Testament,* 2 vols., 2nd ed. (New York: Walter de Gruyter, 1995), 1:229.

- The first to attest Mark's martyrdom in Africa is commonly thought to be Eusebius, but I will show the evidences for pre-Eusebian sources of this memory. Eusebius learned this from a previous continuing apostolic tradition which goes back to the "ancient presbyters," as attested by Clement of Alexandria.
- The first to attest Mark's birth in Libya were pre-Constantinian sources upon which the Synaxarion depended, likely from third- or early fourth-century sources such as the *Martyrium Marci* upon whose Urtext Eusebius also likely depended.

Only modest critical work has been done to uncover many of these connections. Much more is needed.

THE AFRICAN NARRATIVE OF MARK FROM JOHN THE ELDER TO IRENAEUS

The first writers or witnesses known specifically to attest Mark's identity and importance to early Christianity were Peter, Paul, Luke and John the Elder of Ephesus:

- Peter called him "my son Mark" (1 Pet 5:13).
- Paul called him "useful to me in my ministry" (2 Tim 4:11), "my fellow worker" (Philem 24), "the cousin of Barnabas" (Col 4:10).
- Luke records Mark as accompanying Paul and Barnabas, together and separately, as a coworker (Acts 12:25; 15:39).
- John the Elder in his remarks on Mark appealed to the ancient presbyters.

Mark's Gospel is most closely intertwined with Peter's perspective on the assumption that Mark was writing what Peter was preaching. After the New Testament period when there were no more living eyewitnesses, there remained actual or implied testimonies of Aristion, John the Elder, Papias, Clement of Alexandria, Origen and others who wrote before Eusebius.[7] (Once again table 1 supplies a possible

[7]For penetrating discussions of the African fathers of the church, see works in the bibliography by Angelo Di Berardino and Basil Studer, Charles Kannengiesser, Salvatore R. C. Lilla, John A. McGuckin, Tito Orlandi, Eric Osborn, G. A. Oshitelu, Norman Russell, Manlio Simonetti and Francis M. Young.

chronology concerning the evidence.)

John the Elder. The source of the earliest judgments about Mark come from John the Elder and perhaps Aristion (probably first bishop of Smyrna) as reported by Papias. It was on the authority of a well-known and esteemed elder, familiarly called "the elder," that Papias passed on the apostolic tradition that Mark's voice was on behalf of Peter. "Elder" implied a highly esteemed older man whom all younger associates would know. Though unnamed, the elder is most often thought to be John the apostle, the author of the fourth Gospel, and the disciple who was traditionally remembered as the one who cared for Mary, the mother of Jesus, in Ephesus.

But John the Elder could have been a contemporary of John the apostle, distinguishable by the name John the Elder. Whether apostle or distinguished elder or both, this pivotal figure was a principal bridge on the pathway between Mark himself and Papias. His judgments were entirely trusted by Papias and by the earliest forms of postapostolic consensus. Though John the Elder was sharply distinguished by Eusebius from John the apostle, he is often viewed at least as a close disciple of John the apostle, and perhaps the author of some of the Johannine writings. In any case he was among the "elders from the beginning" who passed along the original apostolic testimony. Prevailing early ecumenical tradition most often attributed all the Johannine books to a single author, the apostle John, author of the fourth Gospel.

"The elders from the beginning." Clement of Alexandria mentions as his source not any single written authority but "the elders from the beginning" (*tōn anekathen presbyterōn*—as quoted by Eusebius, *CH* 6.14). This suggests that Clement, writing ca. A.D. 180–215, had access in Alexandria to early manuscripts in the school of catechesis. These manuscripts likely preserved the consensus of the eyewitness apostles as the definitive authorities on the history of Jesus. Those authorities could include original autographs by Mark himself. If the Letter to Theodore is reliable, that *could* would read *must*.

Who were these elders? They were of the generation immediately following the apostles. They overlapped with those who "beheld his glory." They included not only Mark himself, but also John the Elder,

Aristion, Polycarp and Ignatius. Though Clement did not explicitly name them, he clearly knew of them and of their trusted antiquity. Whether or not Clement had documentation is less crucial than that they were commonly known in the *oikoumenē* to be reliable and consensually received before the generation of Clement.

Was the documentation on Mark's identity as apostle known as far south as the middle of the Nile Valley? Was Mark being read as a trustworthy voice of the apostolic tradition in second-century Egypt? The earliest papyri of the New Testament were discovered not in Rome or Antioch but in the Middle Nile Valley at an ancient library at Oxyrhynchus. They contained fragments from Logia that are thought to be identical with passages from Mark's Gospel. This tends to confirm its astonishingly early date for the reading of Mark in deep remote inland Egypt.

Aristion. We know little about Aristion (Ariston) except that he was regarded as having some personal knowledge of the apostles. He was considered a first-hand hearer of the eyewitness apostles. He was likely from Smyrna and was reputed to be the bishop of Smyrna. Aristion and John the Elder have been most often viewed not as themselves eyewitnesses to the Lord but reporters of eyewitnesses.

Jerome in discussing Papias remarked about Aristion: "It appears through this catalogue of names that the John who is placed among the disciples is not the same as the elder John whom he places *after Aristion* in his enumeration" (Jerome, *Lives* 18, emphasis added). Since Aristion was listed prior to John the Elder in some sources to which Jerome had access, he may have preceded him either in age or gravitas.

Papias of Hieropolis. Papias, Irenaeus and Clement of Alexandria all appealed to these named and unnamed "ancient presbyters"—second generation disciples of the eyewitnesses to Jesus. They were the source of information about the transmission of the apostolic tradition from the first to the second century. The earliest quoted documentation indicating the authorship and date of Mark comes from the period immediately after the New Testament documents were written—early second century. The first of these appeared about A.D. 100 to 130 in the writings of Papias, bishop of a crossroads center in Phrygia in western Anatolia, not far from Ephesus. Papias lived about A.D. 60–130, and had personal conversations with John the Elder. Between A.D. 95 and 110 he wrote a five-volume commentary on the "Interpretation of our Lord's Sayings." Irenaeus also mentions Papias as "John's hearer and the associate of Polycarp, an ancient writer, who mentions them in the fourth book of his works" (Irenaeus, quoted in Eusebius, *CH* 3.39.1).

Papias based his view not on his own opinion but on the authority of an "early elder" widely held to be the presbyter John or perhaps the apostle John. Papias served nearby Ephesus where John was thought to have spent his later years. If not the apostle John, it would likely be some elder in the province of Asia who was a younger contemporary of the first eyewitnesses. Papias wrote early enough in the second century to have had direct interaction with eyewitnesses to Jesus.

Though the main multivolume work of Papias, bishop of Hierapolis, on the Interpretation of the Sayings of the Lord is lost, portions have survived in fragments quoted by Irenaeus of Lyons (d. 202) and Eusebius (d. 339):

> But I shall not be unwilling to put down, along with my interpretations, whatsoever instructions I received with care at any time from the elders, and stored up with care in my memory, assuring you at the same time of their truth. (*CH* 3.39.3)

Note that these instructions were stored with care in sacred memory by Papias, who personally attests their truth.

> For I did not, like the multitude, take pleasure in those who spoke much, but in those who taught the truth; nor in those who related strange commandments, but in those who rehearsed the commandments given by the Lord to faith, and proceeding from truth itself. (*CH* 3.39.3)

Two main roads crossed at Hieropolis. Papias deliberately searched for the most authentic testimony to the history of Jesus. He was personally instructed by the first generation after the eyewitness apostles:

> And if anyone happened to come who had actually been a follower of the elders, I would inquire about the sayings of the elders. What did Andrew or Peter say? What about Philip or Thomas or James? What about John or Matthew or any of the other disciples of the Lord? And

> the things that Aristion and John the elder say, who were also disciples of the Lord? For I thought that things from books did not benefit me as much as the sayings of a living and abiding voice. (*CH* 3.39.4)

Papias was attentive to authoritative personal voices more than written words. What mattered is how early and reliable was their testimony. Words alone were treated as a step away from the immediacy of the personal relation of Jesus with the original apostles themselves. Some have taken this passage to suggest that Papias distrusted books and have drawn the conclusion that Papias may have been an unreliable reporter, since he did not focus on written testimony. But the phrase attests precisely what it says: Papias did not benefit from books *as much as* the living voices of the apostles, without demeaning rigorous scholarly study. He himself was the author of many books.

Papias was passing along the previous tradition he had received from the most reliable witnesses who had personal knowledge of the eyewitnesses. They said that Mark had served as the interpreter (*hermēneutēs*) of Peter. He wrote down accurately, though not necessarily in order, the teaching of Peter.

> Mark indeed, since he was the interpreter of Peter, wrote accurately, but not in order, the things either said or done by the Lord as much as he remembered. For he neither heard the Lord nor followed him, but afterwards, as I have said, [heard and followed] Peter, who fitted his discourses to the needs [of his hearers] but not as if making a narrative of the Lord's sayings; consequently, Mark, writing down some things just as he remembered, erred in nothing; for he was careful of one thing—not to omit anything of the things he heard or to falsify anything in them. (*CH* 3.39.15, ca. A.D. 311)

It is thus clear from his method that Papias did not invent this out of his own imagination, but received it from the most authoritative sources of the worshiping communities: the earliest elders and, particularly in this case, Peter. This confirms the tenacity of the clear memory that Mark preached and wrote down the same Gospel that Peter had attested. Mark's apostolicity is thus validated in second-generation sources by Peter's apostolicity.

Though in the African memory, Mark is often portrayed as an eyewitness—as indeed "the beholder of God"—Papias of Hieropolis held that Mark "neither heard the Lord nor traveled alongside him." Eusebius (*Demonstration of the Gospel* 3.5) and Jerome (*Comm. Matt.* Prol. 18), as well as the fourth-century *Dialogue of Adamantius* appear to follow Papias on this point. Papias in Western Asia may not have known of the conviction widely received in Egypt, that Mark was a direct eyewitness to Jesus (Shenouda III).

The description of Mark by Papias as Peter's interpreter was assumed by subsequent classic interpreters of Mark. Origen confirmed that Mark had written as Peter had directed him. Tertullian (ca. 150–220) also argued that "the Gospel which Mark published [edited] is affirmed to be Peter's, whose interpreter Mark was" (*Marc.* 4.5).

Justin Martyr. Justin Martyr, writing in the mid-second century (ca. 150–155) reports that Mark's Gospel was written as the "memoirs" of Peter (*Dial.* 106.3). Since Justin was martyred in Rome under Marcus Aurelius when Junius Rusticus was prefect (between 162 and 168), it is reasonable to view Justin's testimony as prior to that of Irenaeus and of early African writers such as Tertullian and Clement.

Mark's Gospel might have been known as the Gospel According to Peter if Peter alone had been its author. On a matter of such importance to apostolic tradition, it surely would have been mentioned if there was controversy or doubt. All the early writers who expressed an opinion attributed to Mark the authorship of our present Gospel.

To these earliest postapostolic sources from Africa may be added, from Italy, the Muratorian Fragment (A.D. 170). In its first line it alludes to Mark's presence at Peter's discourses and his composition of the Gospel. From about the same time (A.D. 160–180) an Old Latin manuscript contains a preface attached to the Gospel of Mark, now called the "Anti-Marcionite Prologue." It describes Mark as "Peter's interpreter. After the death of Peter himself he wrote down this same gospel in the regions of Italy."[8]

---

[8]E. Earle Ellis, *The Making of the New Testament Documents,* Biblical Interpretation Series 39 (Atlanta: Society of Biblical Literature, 1999), p. 359; William L. Lane, *The Gospel According to Mark: The English Text with Introduction, Exposition, and Notes,* The New International Com-

Irenaeus of Lyons. Irenaeus, a native of Asia Minor and a disciple of Polycarp of Smyrna (who was a disciple of the apostle John) became bishop of Lyons in 177, after having spent substantial time in Rome during about the same period that Justin was there. He regarded the Church of Rome as the most ancient church, since it was founded by Peter and Paul (*Against Heresies* 3.3). His arguments against the heretics are bolstered by the fact that an earlier tradition, that of the earliest apostolate in Rome, disproves them.

Irenaeus adds to the picture of the author of the Gospel of Mark that was handed on to Papias by "the elder" and remembered as the memoirs of Peter by Justin. The same tradition that is reported by Papias of Mark's special relation with Peter was repeated by Irenaeus in Gaul writing around A.D. 180. Irenaeus identified Mark as "the disciple and interpreter of Peter himself," who "also handed down to us in written form the things that had been preached by Peter" (*Against Heresies* 3.1.1; 3.10.6). "And Papias, who was John's auditor and Polycarp's companion, a man of the earliest era, also attests these things in writing the fourth of his books. For there are five books composed by him [Papias]" (*Against Heresies* 5.33.4). If Papias was "John's auditor," and he interrogated the earliest elders around John and Polycarp as thoroughly as he says, and wrote down only what he heard from them directly, then we can conclude that the identity of Mark was clearly established and consistently remembered in the early second century. We can locate Mark somewhere within the arena in which Peter served in Rome just before Peter's martyrdom. In his *Letter to Florinus*, which survives as a fragment, Irenaeus spoke of "Polycarp having thus received [the truth] from the eye witnesses of the Word of life" and of John as "that blessed and apostolical presbyter." The connection of Mark with Peter holds firm throughout the course of the second century, with no known dissenting opinion.

CLEMENT OF ALEXANDRIA

It is useful to identify early African recollections of the identity of John

mentary on the New Testament (Grand Rapids: Eerdmans, 1974), p. 9.

Mark during the period immediately following the earliest known comments on Mark by John the Elder, Papias, Aristion and Irenaeus. The next major figure was the most eminent Christian teacher on the African continent after Mark—Clement of Alexandria. When I speak of early African commentators on the identity of Mark, none is earlier than Clement (ca. A.D. 150 to 215), the teacher of Origen and a contemporary of Irenaeus.

From Clement we glean only a few glimpses, but they are sufficient to suggest Clement's understanding of Mark's Alexandrian history. It is likely that Clement knew of Mark's martyrdom in the very city in which he was then living and writing. Clement of Alexandria (150–215) in fragments of the eighth book of his *Hypotyposeis* indicates that Mark relied on the ancient "tradition of the elders" in writing his Gospel. Eusebius had a source, likely from Clement himself, that suggested that Mark wrote his Gospel at the request of believers in Rome (*CH* 2.15.2; cf. 6.14.6-7). Clement writes: "This Mark was the first that was sent to Egypt." This is none other than he who "first established churches in Alexandria" (*Hypotyposeis* 8, quoted in Eusebius *CH* 2.16.1). This means that as early as A.D. 200 there was testimony from Clement that Mark was *sent* to Egypt, that Mark was the first *apostle* to be sent to Egypt, that Mark was the first to *establish churches* in Egypt, and that these churches were first established by Mark in *Alexandria*.

Thus likely from Clement's own hand we have the strongest early literary evidence of Mark in Alexandria. Drawing these and other early observations together we may derive several gleanings, even if approached hypothetically. It appears that:

- Mark was in Rome with Peter, as viewed by the Alexandrian Christians
- Mark wrote his Gospel in response to a request
- the request to Mark came from the multitude of hearers, that is, likely from the whole laity of Rome, especially the equestrian officers, and not merely their leaders
- Mark had "followed [Peter] for a long time"

- Peter's virtual son Mark was providing assistance to him under conditions of threat
- the threat was imprisonment, so Peter and Mark had to be in a safe place at a distance from Palestine
- Mark wrote what Peter preached

These findings all confirm that Clement stood in the same stream of testimony of the previous writers—John the Elder, Papias, Aristion and Irenaeus. More telling, however, is a phrase easily missed in the *Hypotyposeis*. The fragment of the multivolume work as quoted by Eusebius says plainly that Mark had accompanied Peter "for a long time," or as some Coptic sources say, "on *all* his journeys." But note the implications of "for a long time":

- If it means Mark accompanied Peter for a long time, then that tends to confirm two points crucial to the African hagiographical imagination that already places Mark under Peter's care and pedagogy, and in the Judean desert with his father as a youth.
- If Mark accompanied Peter on *most*, or even *many*, of his journeys, this tends to confirm the African memory's hypothesis that Mark may have been a relative of Peter's, and perhaps known him from his childhood or youth, as the African narrative of Mark in Capernaum indicates.
- Even more surprising, it suggests that Mark may well have been with Peter when he wrote his first letter. Where was that? According to the letter, Peter said he and Mark were "at Babylon." I have shown already that there are good reasons to reconsider the identification of this site as "Babylon of Egypt," the likely site of the gathering of refugees at a crucial military and trade location marking the dispersal of the Nile into the wide stretch of the Delta region.
- Even if "for a long time" doesn't mean that Mark was *always* with Peter, it still leaves the question of whether Mark knew Peter in Capernaum and "at Babylon" open for further investigation. These hypotheses are no more speculative than redaction-critical hypotheses common within Western New Testament scholarship.

Second, Clement says frequently that he is not relying on his opinion or his own way of thinking but upon the "earliest presbyters" (*CH* 6.14.5). Who were these "earliest presbyters" whom Clement says instructed him and guided his judgments? They could have been:

- the commonly received writings of the eyewitness apostles themselves that were destined to become canonical Scripture
- reliable records of those who personally knew the eyewitnesses, whose opinion was received as reliable everywhere the church emerged
- those resident in the church of Alexandria who had a reliable intergenerational memory of the eyewitnesses, and who had carefully passed on their memory to Clement's generation

Whichever level of meaning is given to "earliest presbyters," it is clear that the tradition Clement transmitted is not his own speculation or invention, since Clement insists that he was passing along the previous long-standing "*tradition* of the elders" with regard to the Gospel writers. This is the tradition he had likely learned previously in Alexandria under Pantaneus who presumably served as head of the Alexandrian School. It is reasonable to conclude that Clement would not have appealed to these "earliest presbyters" if he had no documents or reliable records on which to base his appeal.

Clement's Comment on 1 Peter 5:13. A translation of Clement's Adumbrations appears in English translation in the Ante-Nicene Fathers (ANF 2:571-87). The following quotation is from the Latin of Cassiodorus as modified by Clifton Black:

> Mark, Peter's follower *[sectator]* while Peter was preaching *[praedicante]* publicly the Gospel at Rome in the presence of certain of Caesar's equestrians [*equitubus*, i.e., members of the equestrian order] and was putting forward many testimonies concerning Christ, being requested *[petitus]* by them that they might be able to commit to memory the things that were being spoken, wrote from the things that were spoken by Peter the Gospel that is called, "According to Mark."[9]

Here crucial information emerges from Clement's hand. It is offered

[9]Black, *Mark,* p. 139.

in addition to what we have already gleaned from Papias and Irenaeus. It suggests that:

- Mark was thought to have physically accompanied Peter in Rome
- Mark was present to hear Peter on a unique occasion: his preaching in the presence of high Roman military officials
- these Roman military officers were so impressed by what Peter was saying that they wanted to memorize it
- Mark was requested by high authorities to write down Peter's preaching
- this writing became later received by all as the Gospel According to Mark
- these comments were made in connection with 1 Peter 5:13

Clement could not have written this about Mark unless he had had some plausible documentation before him in Alexandria on the context in which Mark was with Peter. This is unique information acquired from no other earlier source that we have independent access to. Hence Clement apparently had records or documents in the huge libraries of Alexandria, especially that of the bishop, of highly specific information on Mark's regular accompaniment of Peter.

More important is the special context in which this comment was made. It was an adumbration by Clement on the passage in 1 Peter 5:13 in which Peter greets distant believers in Anatolia. It appears that Peter at the time was being accompanied by Mark personally. There Peter, under conditions of dire threat, makes clear that he views Mark as "my son."

Why would Peter be greeting the believers in Anatolia with the conjoined greeting from Mark who is with him "at Babylon"? Did Babylon refer to Rome or the Egyptian Babylon? There are no firm indicators, unless the text is conjoined with Acts 12:17 where Peter is found dazed on the doorstep of the house of Mary the mother of Mark, and immediately after Peter departs and goes to "another place." As discussed earlier, suppose that Peter's more urgent motive in coming to the house of Mary was to pick up her son Mark to accompany him and assist him to another safer place. In this case the trajectory could have been toward Babylon of Egypt (now Old Cairo). Why Babylon of Egypt? Because it was a well-known route of refugees from Palestine to Africa, the major point of the division of the waters of the Nile into the Delta.

Already in chapter seven we examined 1 Peter 5:13, but now we can see the passage in the light of Clement's *Hypotyposeis* which reports that Mark accompanied Peter "for a long time" or on "many of his journeys." (Some Coptic sources prefer the translation "on *all* his journeys.")

If Clement had concluded on the basis of documentation not available to us today that Mark was with Peter in Old Cairo (Babylon), then that would explain the preoccupation of much Coptic interest in 1 Peter 5:13. It would help explain why the See of St. Mark would later be located in Babylon of Egypt and why the Coptic Museum is still located there. This view could have come from Clement himself, or it could have come from some documentary source that was available in Alexandria to Clement.

Sources available to Clement. Alexandria was the center of intellectual formation of the Roman world during Clement's time. Clement was living amid the vortex of that center of Christian intellectual life. Clement was consensually remembered as one who served in a key role in the founding and teaching of the catechetical school of Alexandria. Thus it is unlikely that he would have forgotten or misrepresented these earliest presbyters or whatever sources to which he may have had access.

The sources available to him in the city with the best libraries in the world could easily have included the texts of the pre-Eusebian testimony of John the Elder and Aristion or similar sources now destroyed and unknown, but well known in Clement's time. The appeal to these earliest presbyters reflected Clement's confidence in the reliability of the transmission of the consensual early tradition. These ancient presbyters who instructed Clement may have been the primary source of the prized Alexandrian list of the apostolic succession following Mark. This list would form the spine of the narrative assembled later by Sawirus.

Summing up the argument embedded in Clement's own writings: Clement must have had access in Alexandria to sources not now extant that point toward *Mark's accompaniment of Peter in Egypt.* How do I derive that conclusion? (1) Mark had long followed Peter according to Clement's sources. (2) Peter journeyed to Egypt, as African memory suggests. (3) Clement had sources we do not have that reflected the views of "the earliest presbyters."

All three of these conclusions are further reinforced by the alleged letter of Clement "To Theodore," which I will discuss straight ahead, but before that I will discuss the residence of Clement in Africa. Admittedly, there is no clear record of the birthplace of Clement. What is clear is that during the period of his extant writing he was residing in Alexandria. He was among the leading Christian intellects of his time. This would be discernable from his writings. This is so whether he was associated loosely or closely with the catechetical school of Alexandria in the period between his teacher Pantaenus and his pupil Origen. The fact remains that Clement is unanimously celebrated in the Christian tradition as Clement of Alexandria; no ancient source called him Clement of Athens. This is a datum that runs counter to the common speculation that he may have been born in Athens.

Regardless of whether Clement was born in Africa, there is no doubt that he wrote in Africa. The criterion for the arena I am calling the African memory of Mark includes all documents written on the continent of Africa in reference to Mark. All major writings from Clement appear to be written on the continent of Africa. Clement passed on to the churches and candidates for baptism "what he had received" concerning Mark. According to the Letter to Theodore which I will next examine, Mark's papers had been left to the church of Alexandria, to which Clement himself must have had full access in whatever form they survived after the Severan persecution. If he was the head of the Catechetical School of Alexandria, as so frequently reported in Egyptian tradition, he must have had full access to documents in the patriarchal library.

THE LETTER TO THEODORE

The more controversial source connected with Clement is his alleged Mar Saba "Letter to Theodore." Naming this document objectively as "Letter to Theodore" is in my view greatly to be preferred, rather than tendentiously as "Secret Gospel of Mark," which limits attention only to one portion of the letter, and is not in fact its most crucial historical contribution—which is *the pre-Eusebian testimony to Mark in Africa.* The text of the letter expresses historical and theological concerns of equal or greater importance than an alleged secret Gospel corrupted by heretics.

Here we enter into highly controverted territory: The text of the purported letter from Clement was found handwritten into the end-papers of Isaac Vossius's 1646 printed edition of the works of Ignatius of Antioch. The scarcity of paper in Palestine in the mid 1700s explains why the original version of the letter, presumably in the Mar Saba library, was copied on to a free sheet of paper of a book already located in the library.

The letter is addressed to an unknown recipient named Theodore. He had asked Clement to comment on an unusual, noncanonical version of Mark. Clement was familiar with this version, as well as the canonical version accepted for reading in the churches. Two excerpts are quoted by Clement in his critique of the noncanonical version. We are now working from photographs (made earlier by Morton Smith and later by the Jerusalem monastic librarian), since the original document remains either purposely hidden from public view, or misplaced, or lost, or for whatever reason inaccessible.

Morton Smith published a portion of this purported letter from Clement under the title *Clement of Alexandria and a Secret Gospel of Mark.*[10] Smith presents the Greek text with a critical commentary. It tells of the 1958 discovery in Mar Saba Monastery in Palestine of a letter that according to Smith was written by Clement of Alexandra. Its genuineness has been argued on the basis of language idiosyncrasies, Clementine style and intellectual content.

Why it should not be prematurely dismissed. Distinguished patristic scholars have examined the language of the letter for its literary and stylistic correspondence with other extant writings of Clement. Included among them are Werner Jaeger, Cyril C. Richardson, W. H. C.

[10]Morton Smith, *Clement of Alexandria and a Secret Gospel of Mark* (Cambridge, Mass.: Harvard University Press, 1973).

Frend, R. P. C. Hanson, Robert M. Grant, Guy G. Strousma, Annewies van den Hoek, Scott G. Brown and Judith L. Kovacs. However different their perspectives may be, they have on the whole found it hard to believe that it was crassly counterfeited. Since the arguments on behalf of Clement's authorship of the Mar Saba Letter to Theodore have been thoroughly explored in the literature, I will not here repeat those arguments.

Despite fierce episodes of controversy, many leading Clement experts agree that the letter could have been written by Clement. It corresponds with the style and content of Clement's other writings. Stephen Patterson, in 1994, wrote, "The handwriting can be dated to around 1750. Smith published the letter in 1973. Early discussion of it was marred by accusations of forgery and fraud, no doubt owing in part to its controversial comments. Today, however, there is almost unanimous agreement among Clementine scholars that the letter is authentic."[11]

More recently that evidence has been exhaustively reviewed by Scott G. Brown, in *Mark's Other Gospel: Rethinking Morton Smith's Controversial Discovery,*[12] with positive conclusions about the authenticity of the attribution of authorship to Clement. An even more recent and somewhat tendentious study by Peter Jeffery, *The Secret Gospel of Mark Unveiled,*[13] has focused so narrowly on sexuality issues that the more consequential questions relating to the African memory of Mark have been left unattended.

Some of the attacks on the authenticity of the letter are exaggerated and at times a bit hysterical. What follows will be regarded by some as speculative, but it is far less speculative than the conjectures of the detractors of Morton Smith. References to Clement below should be qualified, since I am referring to the Clement as portrayed in the Letter to Theodore.

---

[11]Stephen Patterson, "The Secret Gospel of Mark: Introduction," in *The Complete Gospels: Annotated Scholars Version,* ed. Robert J. Miller (San Francisco: HarperSanFrancisco, 1994), p. 408.

[12]Scott G. Brown, *Mark's Other Gospel: Rethinking Morton Smith's Controversial Discovery* (Waterloo, Ont.: Wilfrid Laurier University Press, 2005).

[13]Peter Jeffery, *The Secret Gospel of Mark Unveiled* (New Haven, Conn.: Yale University Press, 2007).

Bart Ehrman, writing before Jeffery and Brown published their books but having reviewed previous arguments pro and con, noted "it would be well nigh impossible to imagine someone other than Clement being able to write it."[14] Birger Pearson, who had earlier accepted the authenticity of the Clement fragment, has expressed more recently his dissatisfaction with some of Morton Smith's theories of the Secret Gospel of Mark or the verifiability of the document.[15]

Stephen Davis writes: "The previous tradition of historical scholarship epitomized by Harnack did not have access to this previously unknown letter attributed to Clement."[16] Much historical scholarship in the long trail from Harnack to Bauer has prematurely dismissed the ecumenical consensus concerning Mark in Alexandria as unreliable, viewing it merely as an attempt at legitimation. Hence the question must be reopened on the basis of more recent studies from Colin Roberts to Stephen Davis.

Clement was clarifying to Theodore that Mark had expanded his earlier Gospel with his own and Peter's memory to produce "a more spiritual Gospel." The pertinent point here: Clement was assuming that Mark was present in Alexandria, and that this assumption was regarded by Clement as passed on to him by the "earliest presbyters," of which he had adequate documentation. The author of the letter is affirming that the presence of Mark in Africa had been received consensually long before Eusebius, who would echo it a century later.

A portion of this Letter to Theodore needs to be quoted in full:

> As for Mark, then, during Peter's stay in Rome he wrote an account of the Lord's doings, not, however, declaring all of them, nor yet hinting at the secret ones, but selecting what he thought most useful for increasing the faith of those who were being instructed. *But when Peter died a martyr, Mark came over to Alexandria, bringing both his own notes and those of Peter, from which he transferred to his former books the things suitable*

[14]Bart D. Ehrman, *Lost Christianities: The Battles for Scripture and the Faiths We Never Knew* (Oxford: Oxford University Press, 2003), p. 79.

[15]Birger Pearson, *REC*, p. 138, cf. J. E. Sanzo, "The Secret Gospel of St. Mark: Find or Forgery? Panel Discussion Review," *St. Shenouda Coptic Quarterly* 4, nos. 1-2 (2007–2008): 8-14.

[16]Stephen J. Davis, *The Early Coptic Papacy: The Egyptian Church and Its Leadership in Late Antiquity* (Cairo: American University in Cairo Press, 2004), p. 8.

> *to whatever makes for progress toward knowledge.* Thus he composed a more spiritual Gospel for the use of those who were being perfected. Nevertheless, he yet did not divulge the things not to be uttered, nor did he write down the hierophantic teaching of the Lord, but to the stories already written he added yet others and, moreover, brought in certain sayings of which he knew the interpretation would, as a mystagogue, lead the hearers into the innermost sanctuary of that truth hidden by seven veils. (emphasis added)

If genuine, the Letter to Theodore confirms textually that:

- Mark came to Alexandria.
- Mark left his writings to the archives of the church of Alexandria.
- Mark brought with him to Alexandria his notes from Peter which served as the basis for the canonical Mark and perhaps for a more spiritual version intended for those Alexandrians who were seeking the higher Christian life. Some were heterodox.
- Mark was noticeably attentive to the special needs and competencies of his Christian audience in Alexandria.
- If the letter is reliable, we have learned from these sentences more than we have ever known about the status of Mark's martyr tradition that preceded the early years of the catechetical school.

After Mark was martyred, what did the church of Alexandria do with his literary remains? The only evidence we have is from the Letter to Theodore, but it is quite clear and specific:

> Thus, in sum, he prepared matters, neither grudgingly nor incautiously, in my opinion, and, dying, *he left his composition to the church in Alexandria, where it even yet is most carefully guarded, being read only to those who are being initiated into the great mysteries.* (Letter to Theodore, Morton Smith translation, emphasis added)

If Clement left this manuscript in the archives of the church of Alexandria, it is likely that he would also have left other remaining manuscripts to the same archive. The time frame of preservation would be from about A.D. 68 to about 190, that is, about 120 years, or about four generations. It is plausible that within this rather brief and manageable time frame, the ancient sources could have safely preserved Mark's own autographs, as the Letter to Theodore indicates. In Clement's view they had been, due to their apostolic importance.

Most of the controversy over the letter has been engendered not by theological historians but by New Testament scholars. Some have shown eagerness to make their mark either by supposedly discovering alternative texts of Mark or by derogating such discoveries. That way of putting the question is not the major concern of the African narrative of Mark. It remains a question of relatively minimal interest in the larger battle today over the legitimacy of early African Christianity. The more pressing issue is not whether Clement thought Mark actually lived in Alexandria. Rather the decisive issue here is focused on clarifying how the martyrdom of Mark in Alexandria occurred and became known, whether it was rightly preserved, and how early.

The Letter to Theodore answers these issues in two phrases (see italicized above). These two sentences have been almost completely neglected in the controversy over a supposed alternative text of a so-called Secret Gospel of Mark. In these two phrases, the Letter to Theodore answers this question so crucial for the evidentiary presentation of the connection between Mark and Alexandria.

The first phrase provides evidence that:

- Mark's Gospel as accepted for public use (later canonical Mark) was written in Rome with Peter's blessing
- after Peter's death Mark came to Alexandria
- Mark brought his own notes to Alexandria
- Mark also brought Peter's notes to Alexandria
- Mark transferred from his earlier writings in Rome to his Alexandria audience "*the things suitable to whatever makes for progress toward knowledge*"
- his criterion for writing further: a selection fitting to the context of his Alexandrian hearers
- for the unique conditions of those hearers seeking special mystical

knowledge of the history of Jesus, he wrote a supplement that was never intended for public use in the church or liturgy

With all the pushing and pulling of the "secret text" controversy, this larger context has been neglected.

In the second phrase noted above, the evidence is further provided that (1) Mark himself left his manuscripts in Alexandria at the time of his death, ca. A.D. 68, and (2) the original manuscripts remained under the guardianship of the church of Alexandria at the time when Clement examined them carefully in the 190s.

Since Mark was in Alexandria to the end, he wanted his body of written work to be safeguarded by the great church he was nurturing on the continent of Africa. So "*he left his composition to the church in Alexandria.*" Where better to safeguard them than in the greatest academic center in the known world? He left them not to any particular individual but to the actual worshiping community to be shepherded by his successor bishops. He had already ordained its leadership. This is an immensely important datum of information left largely unnoticed by most commentators on Morton Smith.

Mark's martyrdom in Alexandria had been partially anticipated. The rumblings had already been increasing before the mob seized him. It was likely that Mark himself made his own deliberate decision: Protect the literary body of work he had produced, of whatever size. He protected his own writings by passing them along to the succeeding church of Alexandria. If so, this preserving act of Mark would presumably constitute the very beginning of the Christian library that would later become the growing archive of the patriarchate of Alexandria accessible to the catechetical school.

These books and manuscript of Mark's were to be "*most carefully guarded.*" They have, according to the Letter to Theodore, remained carefully guarded "*even yet*"—that is, even until Clement's time. According to the letter, Mark himself made this proviso in advance of his death. What was the time frame of the phrase "even yet"? What period are we in? The date of Clement's report of this would be around A.D. 190, and no later than 215.

This evidence helps us understand the bridge between Mark and Eusebius. It accounts for the lacuna of documents about Mark in Alexandria in Eusebius spanning the years between A.D. 68 and 320. It is this lacuna upon which liberal German historical scholarship since Harnack has depended so heavily, and judged so harshly.

If the Letter to Theodore is authentic we have a glimpse into the established tradition recalled in Alexandria around A.D. 190 concerning Mark in Africa. Many of the most intractable puzzles regarding Mark's identity would be solved by this remarkable document. Survey the puzzles resolved:

- The *date* of Mark's preaching in Africa is directly associated with the time shortly after the death of Peter in Rome.
- Clement had *documentary access* to what he regarded as a dependable memory of Mark that places Mark clearly in Alexandria in Egypt on the African continent. This was at the time when Mark's canonical Gospel was perhaps being further edited for the special needs of a small number of Alexandrian Christian perfectionists, after the body of the Gospel had been written in Rome.
- Clement knows about a secreted version of Mark, but strongly disputes its consensual acceptance. This means that Clement was *aware of alternative versions of* Mark, likely stored in the catechetical library.
- One of these versions Clement regards as corrupted, hence inauthentic, because it had been stolen and *tampered with* by a sect Clement calls the Carpocratians—a group with an alleged reputation for licentiousness.[17]
- At his death, Mark *left his writing to the safekeeping of the church of Alexandria.* If so, Mark would likely have been dwelling in Alexandria at the time he left his writings to their safekeeping.
- Clement knows that Mark died in Alexandria.
- Clement argued that the Carpocratians made their own dubious additions to the Markan text, so their version was corrupted and

[17]Smith, *Clement and Secret Gospel,* p. 15; Davis, *Early Coptic Papacy,* p. 8.

not fit for circulation. Clement warned that "a certain presbyter of the church in Alexandria . . . got from him [Carpocrates] a copy of the secret Gospel, which he both interpreted according to his blasphemous and carnal doctrine and, moreover, polluted, mixing with the spotless and holy words utterly shameless lies. From this mixture is drawn off the teaching of the Carpocratians."[18] This *corruption* of the original occurred in Alexandria within or before Clement's time.

- Clement argued that the secret version especially must be "carefully guarded," due to its high *susceptibility to misinterpretation*. This information was so carefully protected in Clement's time that only those who had been initiated into the sacred mysteries were allowed even to hear about it, much less to see it or study it as a heresy.
- Clement knew that Mark had written a second secret or mystical version of his Gospel *for "those being perfected."*
- Clement responded by advising Theodore to keep it quiet that this secret Gospel existed. Why? Because it is heretically dangerous, and therefore should *not be circulated* for general consumption. This implies that though it existed *sub rosa,* it should not become public or become an occasion for detracting from or demeaning the accepted Gospel of Mark already known and familiar to the liturgy and teaching of the church of Alexandria and elsewhere.
- Clement *did not ask Theodore to lie* or dissemble about the other version of Mark, but to keep it confidential on behalf of the peace of the church. It is for this same reason that the literary guardians of the Letter to Theodore were keeping it in tow. Hence the librarians at Alexandria, Mar Saba, and later the Jerusalem patriarchate refused to release it.
- Even if the Letter to Theodore is shown to be spurious, the case for the African memory of Mark is not dependent on this one controversial source. As we have seen, the case for the African memory of Mark depends on many *other factors* totally unrelated to the debat-

[18]Letter to Theodore, Smith translation.

able assessment of the authenticity of one particular document.

The reason I have given so much attention to the Letter to Theodore is that, if reliable, it resolves these enigmas that are otherwise left unresolved in the vast Western literature on Mark. Hence it is a useful corroboratory link in the long line of other arguments.

Clement was not embarrassed by the fact that some texts are best reserved for those who can properly and reasonably assess them. Some of these have remained a secret tradition. In Clement's time they were still held in a guarded status. Since some disputed texts are prone to becoming polemical instruments against consensual Christian teaching, there is good reason to limit their access. Clement believed Christianity to be the pure representative of God's true mysteries which others, such as the Carpocratians, had stolen and corrupted. Clement's purpose was to resist distortions of Mark's Gospel. He did not support the public use of a document that at best was intended only for those who would be spiritually prepared to exercise caution in approaching it.

Thus there were three versions: canonical Mark, a spiritual Mark, and a Carpocratian distortion of the spiritual Mark. Clement rejects the last, accepts the first, and comments on the second. If the letter is authentic, the arguments made in this letter establish Clement as a plausible source for Eusebius's view that Mark died in Alexandria. Recall that Clement, born about A.D. 150, wrote before Tertullian and Origen, and a half century before Cyprian. This places Clement about a century after Mark and a century before Eusebius. Thus Clement becomes the crucial bridge between Mark and Eusebius. If these considerations are taken seriously, Mark is attested as being in Alexandria not only by his likely literary remains but also by prolonged African liturgical memory. It is the *conjunction of these two streams*, literary and hagiographical, that strengthen the case for Mark in Alexandria, and not one stream alone.

How did Eusebius know of Mark's African martyrdom? Eusebius could easily have learned it from Clement, whom he highly respected, or from Origen, who likely would have followed his teacher Clement in these matters. Origen, in fact, could have been one of those seeking spiritual perfection about whose spiritual welfare Clement was concerned. Whatever the source, Mark's mission to Alexandria was assumed as a reliable memory by the time of Clement, long before this was reported by Eusebius. From these sources there appears to be a correspondence between the apostle Peter's death, Mark's coming to Alexandria, bringing the preaching of Peter to a new audience in Africa, and immediately convincing many people of the truth of Christianity. This is precisely the view that was considered long-standing and accepted tradition by the time of Eusebius, whose views on the matter we next consider.

Whatever we make of the Letter to Theodore, the African memory of Mark has stood solidly without it for twenty centuries. Hence virtually all aspects of the African memory of Mark can be set forth without any reference whatever to the Letter to Theodore. The evidences attesting Mark's presence in Africa do not depend on Clement alone, but on the ancient apostolic tradition of the "earliest presbyters" attested by Clement. This tradition is continuous from Mark to Clement and is not based exclusively on Eusebius.

If the cumulative evidence of Mark in Alexandria referenced by Clement is reliable, this would constitute the most substantive surviving written attestation between the apostolic era and Eusebius confirming that Mark was physically in Alexandria. It comes from one who should know: the head of the Catechetical School at Alexandria run by the church of Alexandria under the direction of its bishop, Demetrius. Who is more likely to have had full access to the earliest documentation of Mark in Africa than Clement? Clement was probably teaching in Alexandria from about A.D. 190, and likely connected either by affection or official affiliation with the catechetical school under the ecclesiastical direction of Demetrius.

RECOLLECTIONS OF MARK'S AFRICAN MISSION IN EUSEBIUS

Eusebius of Caesarea wrote in the 320s: "*They say* that this Mark was *the first to have set out to Egypt to preach the gospel*, which he had already written down for himself, and the first to have organized churches in

Alexandria itself" (Eusebius, *CH* 2.16.1, emphasis added; see also 2.24). In this single sentence we learn that:

- Mark preached in Egypt (recall that Egypt in much ancient geography included the Pentapolis of Libya)
- Mark wrote his Gospel before his mission to Africa, likely in Italy
- Mark was the first to organize churches in Alexandria

This is the tradition that Eusebius had received from the "earliest presbyters"—those who had known the first generation of apostles. This is wrongly thought to be the first reference of a written source to Mark in Alexandria. As we have already shown, Eusebius comes at the end of a long line of reportage on Mark's mission, which in due course brought him to Africa and martyrdom.

Eusebius ascribed the beginning of Christianity in Africa to Mark. He did not have any difficulty finding precedent for this, as some suppose. The consensual reception of Mark in Africa was by the time of Eusebius already widespread, so general that it would have seemed repetitious to do so. Like Clement, the view of Eusebius was based on its traditional acceptance from the "earliest presbyters." In his history of the church, Eusebius continued the steadily received traditions that Papias had reported (about Mark's relation to Peter) and that Clement had received in Alexandria (that Mark came physically to Africa).

Eusebius was the most widely trusted early historian of Christianity of the time of Constantine. Eusebius is the only source for much of our specific information about the primitive church. What church historian is more widely quoted as authoritative than Eusebius? He has come to speak for the consensual tradition with few exceptions. Virtually all studies of the ancient church have had little choice but to take Eusebius's report as on the whole reliable, though unclear on specific points.[19] Eusebius was writing his history of the church in the period between A.D. 300 and 325. He watched the Diocletian persecution unfold, and the empire recover under Constantine.

[19]G. M. Lee, "Eusebius on St. Mark and the Beginnings of Christianity in Egypt," *Studia patristica 12: Papers Presented to the Sixth International Conference on Patristic Studies Held in Oxford 1971,* TUGAL 115 (Berlin: Akademie-Verlag, 1975), pp. 425-27.

The crucial words of Eusebius read: "*They say* that this Mark was *the first to have set out to Egypt to preach the gospel*" (*CH* 2.16.1). But who is the "*they*" in "they say"? "They" were the "earliest presbyters" upon whom Papias, Clement and Irenaeus relied for their information. There is no basis for imagining that Eusebius was wildly speculating on some undocumented hypothesis. His stated task was to draw together all the written testimony he could find on early Christian history. He was not without textual evidence. We do not know all their names, but we do know some of them (John the Elder, Aristion, Polycarp), since Eusebius states their names. They were listened to with great care by the times of Papias and Irenaeus. It is they, Eusebius says, that testified that Mark witnessed with his very lifeblood in Alexandria.

It is significant that Eusebius refers to his references in the *plural*, as "they," not in the singular. Therefore, he must have been referring to more than one of his sources. Since we know that one of his sources likely was Clement of Alexandria, who might the others have been? Morton Smith argued that "they say" referred specifically to Clement and Papias whom Eusebius has just before mentioned.[20] It could also refer to other authoritative postapostolic voices whom Eusebius considered reliable—writers that Eusebius himself knew but does not name. Even if we do not know specifically who all of them were, Eusebius certainly did know and trusted them.

But the standard trend of modern scholarship has been either to ignore or to discredit the whole lot of attestors to an African Mark, whether it be Papias or Eusebius or Clement, or more recently Smith. It makes us wonder: Where will such skepticism end except in doubting all sources altogether—the hermeneutic of suspicion on steroids—which finally brings all historical inquiry to a slow halt.

Eusebius was drawing upon many written records at his disposal, but which we cannot now adequately assess because portions of his library do not now exist. Eusebius thought that Mark brought some form of his already written Gospel with him to Alexandria. His Greek version of Peter's memories of Jesus, written by Mark himself, must have ful-

[20]Smith, *Clement and Secret Gospel*, p. 119.

filled its purpose well in a city where many languages were spoken, including Hebrew and Aramaic, but where the leading commercial and functional language was Greek. Many native Egyptians were living in Alexandria alongside Jews and Greeks in the early first century. Some spoke variants of traditional Egyptian Pharaonic proto-Coptic languages, in addition to Greek.

Until recently it was commonly thought that the story of Mark in Africa depended exclusively on the fragile testimony of Eusebius, who at times drew debatable conclusions. But Eusebius had in his possession an unsurpassed personal library of early Christian primary sources in Caesarea. Much of it had been inherited or copied from Origen's own extensive library and from the diocesan library in Caesarea, as well as distinguished private benefactors such as Pamphilus. Eusebius devoted a section of his church history to a closely-argued assessment of the writing of Mark's Gospel and how Christianity came to Alexandria.

It is not the case that the African writers accepted Eusebius into the stream of their recollection of Mark, as sometimes portrayed in the West. Rather it was Eusebius that accepted the African memory of Mark as received consensual ecumenical teaching. Note that this is not merely Eusebius's private opinion, but the chronology of the tradition Eusebius had received with extensive contemporary and historical documentation, documentation that existed in his time but not ours.

From whom did he receive it? From the consensually received sources that Eusebius reported as reliable for the whole international church to depend on. This is the stated purpose of Eusebius's history—not to invent theories or speculations, but to report the reliable facts of the tradition he had received based on written documents he had available to him in his library, supplemented by impressive libraries in Jerusalem and Antioch, and through his own personal observation in Egypt and elsewhere. Eusebius himself had one of the best libraries in the Near East—a legacy of the time when Origen was resident in Caesarea.

Despite the awkwardness of having to flow against the Western critical stream, a growing company of scholars from both Africa and the West are becoming more equipped to reexamine the African memory of Mark. This direction is summed up by the Egyptian historian,

Aziz Atiya, who wrote: "Indeed, the apostle of Egypt was a native Jew of Cyrene, St. Mark the evangelist, who came to Alexandria by way of the Pentapolis, and, after planting the new faith in Egypt, himself returned to Cyrene to work with his fellow citizens on more than one occasion."[21]

Eusebius has provided the first known specific dating of Mark in Africa. It is precise and to the point. This gives it weight that cannot be ignored. The probable date of Mark's arrival in Alexandria today remains highly controversial, but for Eusebius it was a known point in time. Eusebius specifically dates the *arrival* of Mark in Alexandria in such a precise way that it is hard to imagine that he had no reliable source for it. He fixes the date exactly, and very early: as the third year of the reign of the Roman emperor Claudius. That would be A.D. 43, considerably earlier than most Western chronologies, but still possible. This may add a bit more plausibility to the hypothesis already discussed, that Peter was with Mark at Babylon of Egypt.

The *Chronicle* of Eusebius assigns Mark's African arrival to the time of Claudius, and his *death* as the eighth year of Nero (the year that Mark was succeeded by Anianus as the bishop of Alexandria) which would be about A.D. 62. This would imply that Mark would have been the unique apostolic representative to Alexandria for a very long period—almost twenty years, though these could be intermittent years. There is some early evidence that Peter came to Rome in A.D. 42. If Mark accompanied him as his assistant (as Clement claims Mark does in all Peter's travels), Mark could have been sent directly from Rome to Alexandria around A.D. 43, just as the Eusebian narrative suggests.

The Eusebian chronology must answer a reasonable objection in any attempt to correlate it with the likely chronology of Acts, which reports that when Mark left Antioch and separated from Paul and Barnabas, he proceeded to Cyprus (Acts 15:39, which according to common chronologies would be around A.D. 49–50) and other locations, without

[21]Aziz S. Atiya, *A History of Eastern Christianity* (London: Methuen, 1968), p. 433.

mentioning Alexandria. Might Mark have secretly accompanied Peter to Babylon of Egypt even before he accompanied Barnabas and Saul to Cyprus and the Anatolian coast?

Mark could have been already serving as the apostolic herald to the church of Alexandria at the time when he was intermittently engaged in other ministries to the north as reported or implied in Acts. Joseph MacRory wrote wisely a century ago:

> There is nothing indeed to prove absolutely that all this is inconsistent with his being Bishop of Alexandria at the time, but seeing that the chronology of the Apostolic age is admittedly uncertain, and that we have no earlier authority than Eusebius for the date of the foundation of the Alexandrian Church, we may perhaps conclude with more probability that it was founded somewhat later. There is abundance of time between A.D. 50 and 60, a period during which the New Testament is silent in regard to St. Mark, for his activity in Egypt.[22]

There are several possible reasons why this could have happened:

- The busy missionaries to the north of Jerusalem could have been so distracted by their many challenges that they did not know of Mark in Egypt.
- They could have known and reported it, but the documents are lost.
- They could have known and not reported it.

None of these hypotheses are completely implausible. As stated before, if there had been serious doubt or debate on such an important point on which so much ecumenical consent would later depend (that Mark died in Alexandria as founder of the church of the African continent), surely there would be some residues of it in the literature, but none are found. All the evidence is on the side of Mark being in Africa for a significant amount of time.

---

[22]*The Catholic Encyclopedia*, ed. Charles George Herbermann et al. (New York: Encyclopedia Press, 1913–1914), vol. 9, s.v. "St. Mark." Apparently MacRory did not have opportunity to ponder all the evidence I have set forth above from John the Elder, the "earliest presbyters," Papias, Irenaeus and Clement; hence the phrase "no earlier authority than Eusebius." A major reason for this book is to set forth the complementarity of these witnesses, which could not be as plausibly correlated a hundred years ago.

THE SPECULATION OF EUSEBIUS ON PHILO'S THERAPEUTAE

A report by Eusebius on Philo touches indirectly upon Mark's chronology, but it is full of controversy. Eusebius correctly understood that Philo in Egypt (d. ca. A.D. 50) had carefully observed a vital community of believers. Philo "deemed their pastimes, gatherings, meals, and every other aspect of their lives worthy of being recorded in writing" (*CH* 2.16.1-2). Many scholars are quick to discredit Eusebius because historians now largely agree that Philo was not referring to Christians but most likely to a lively community of Jewish ascetics (Therapeutae, as described in Philo's *De vita contemplativa* VIII-XI [64-90]). This community could have been something like the kind of proto-Christian community that taught Apollos. Philo was not referring to Christians, but to a community of Jewish ascetics he called the Therapeutae—a healing, contemplative community that had a very close-knit and integral understanding of the life of prayer, of gathering and of having meals together. This was before Mark's arrival in Alexandria. Though Eusebius was obviously exaggerating when he connected Philo's Therapeutae with Christian converts, Philo "was right in stressing that the 'apostolic men' of the days of Philo and Mark were 'of Hebrew origin and thus still preserved most of the ancient customs in a strictly Jewish manner.'"[23] Hence the testimony of Eusebius should not be ruled out just because he misunderstood the precise chronology between Philo and Mark. If Mark's arrival in Alexandria was as early as Eusebius records it to be—the third year of Claudius, namely A.D 43—that would be earlier than most other reports and perhaps within Philo's lifetime.

Philo wrote his own account of the religious character of the ascetics in Egypt living in the desert south of Alexandria near Lake Mareotis. This would correspond roughly with the location of the beginnings of community monasticism in Scetis and Cellia. They represent an early sign of many characteristics of the primitive monastic traditions.

The times of Philo (ca. 20 B.C.–A.D. 50) may be precisely coordinated with those of the reign of Claudius. Philo visited Claudius in Rome

[23]Pearson in reference to Eusebius, *CH* 2.17.2.

together with a Jewish delegation from Alexandria in the year 42. They requested lenient treatment for their own Jewish Alexandrian community, which was under serious threat. Philo wanted the Jewish communities of Alexandria to be excused from the idolatrous act of venerating the imperial gods (*De vita contemplative* III [27]; *Quod omnis probus liber sit* XII [75-87]).

As noted earlier, Eusebius is not the only one who attempted to place a very early date on the arrival of Mark in Alexandria. Others range from A.D. 39 to 68. The official Coptic history assumes the date of Mark's arrival in Egypt was in "the 15th year after the ascension of Christ" which would be around A.D. 45. That could possibly place it before the Council of Jerusalem. The fact that there are different dates proposed does not necessary imply that it was at the time of Eusebius a hotly controverted issue. Rather the opposite: Eusebius was simply reporting the already established and received ecumenical tradition concerning Peter, Mark and Alexandria. The dating of Mark was consequential enough for several important early writers to try to be quite specific about it. Since the ecumenical consensus on Mark in Africa prevails after Clement and Eusebius, there is little need to go into detail in further setting it forth.

There can be little doubt that most classic ecumenical writers after Eusebius agreed that Mark was the first apostle to be sent to Africa. There are no competitors. Far from implying the priority of Rome to Alexandria, Eusebius was implicitly asserting the basic equality of Alexandria with Rome in the synchronicity and affinity of the founding of the churches of the two continents. Obviously the church of the East out of Antioch had preceded both. Alexandria had always had equal status with Rome, according to Eusebius, and should not be downgraded. After Clement and Eusebius, a continuous flow of consistent Markan memory has prevailed in Africa for two millennia.

POSTCRITICAL INTERLUDE

Settling this question may require what is becoming known as "postcritical" inquiry. Those who use the term *postcritical* ordinarily mean a method of taking into full consideration the compelling conclusions amassed for over two centuries of critical skepticism based on written documents, yet balancing them with other forms of literary, archaeological, exegetical and circumstantial evidence.

Postcritical here means an inquiry that can emerge with persuasive force only after the modern critics have done their work. It stands on the shoulders of modern criticism, but aware of the weakness of those shoulders. *Post* means "after"—after, that is, the prevailing modern forms of thinking.

No previous work of criticism is beyond criticism. This inquiry requires a critique of much previous criticism that is still sadly regarded as normative. Were it not for the weight of the societal consequences, the question of Mark's Africanness could be infinitely delayed. But the predispositions of the previous accepted critical view and the social importance of the question in Africa make it urgent today. Anyone who challenges standard criticism is understandably required to point out neglected facts. My task is something like a trial lawyer defending an already convicted client he knows is innocent but who has remained imprisoned without a voice or remedy for decades. The condemned defendant in this case is the African memory of Mark, and more generally African Christianity in the early patristic period. I hope the jury is composed of fair-minded observers.

PART FIVE

The Ubiquity Of Mark

11

THE PUZZLE OF MARK

The paradox of Mark is that he appears unexpectedly in so many crucial points of the New Testament, yet his personal identity remains obscure. It is the paradox of ubiquity and anonymity that begs for a solution. The close relation between Mark and the earliest apostles is not speculation. It is explicit in numerous New Testament texts and inferred from Mark's own text, as well as complemented and confirmed by occasional passages of Paul's letters, Luke-Acts and the Catholic Epistles. John Mark had a long-term, close working relationship with many of the most important figures in the earliest apostolic tradition: Simon Peter, Paul, Barnabas and Timothy, as we see from the variety of references to him.

ASSEMBLING THE PIECES OF THE PUZZLE

One persistent feature of the Mark's presence in the New Testament is how silently Mark appears at the most crucial times of the narrative. Nevertheless, Mark is among the most well-connected and seemingly ubiquitous of all the earliest Christian witnesses. He shows up constantly:

- Mark is among the disciples from the beginning with the church in Jerusalem (Acts 12:12).
- He is in Antioch (Acts 12:25–13:5) with the earliest Christian leaders and prophets.

- We find him present at the beginning of Paul's and Barnabas' first missionary journey (Acts 13:4-14).
- He is present in Cyprus with Barnabas (Acts 15:37-39) whose family offers sacrificial funding for the earliest Christian mission (Acts 4:36-37).
- The next we hear of Mark may come several years later, perhaps as long as a decade, in the references in Colossians 4:10 and Philemon 24. He is present with Paul (as implied in Colossians 4:10), the earlier breach having been healed. He is now considered loyal to Paul, honored as his fellow worker, and a great comfort to Paul. Paul sends greetings from Mark to Philemon, who must have known him as well. At this time Mark was apparently in Rome and had some intention of visiting Asia Minor.
- Mark appears as a close associate of Peter when he was at "Babylon," which could have referred to the refugee center in Babylon of Egypt, or perhaps with Peter in Rome. Peter speaks affectionately of Mark as "my son" in 1 Peter 5:13.
- Since 1 Peter was addressed to various churches of Asia Minor (1 Pet 1:1), we may conclude that Mark was personally known by Christians from Pontus, Galatia, Cappadocia, Asia and Bithynia, as implied in the salutation.
- Probably Mark was in Ephesus A.D. 54–55 (as implied in Helmut Koester's *New Testament Introduction* 2:104).
- At the crucial time when Paul was facing death in Rome, Paul wrote to Timothy at Ephesus asking him to pick up Mark from somewhere and bring him with him urgently to Rome, adding "for he is profitable to me for the ministry" (2 Tim 4:11).
- If Mark came to Rome at this time, he was probably there when St. Paul was martyred.
- Mark was also likely with or near Peter in Rome during his last days, according to both Roman and African memory.

If Mark appears so closely integrated into the leadership of the earliest Christian missionary activity, especially in relation with Peter and Paul, would not Mark be an obvious candidate to take on the next major unfinished objective of the Great Commission mandate? If the Great Commission is to all, to the ends of the earth, and if Africa is a major continent which prior to Mark had not received apostolic testimony, would it not be a natural assignment for Mark to return to his native continent? Would not Peter be the obvious one to make this assignment of this particular trusted "son" to this vast and important arena of witness?

Given these mostly known facts and added inferences, why would it not be consistent with all of the above to consider it plausible that Mark might have also been sent under Peter's direction, to Alexandria, the second largest city in the Empire? This is what Eusebius reports as a long standing tradition before Constantine on the basis of what the earliest presbyters say. This hunch must be validated by evidence, if it is to hold up to critical investigation.

While there is no explicit mention in the New Testament that Mark taught and died in Alexandria, the hypothesis that Mark did go to Alexandria has extraordinary inferential support:

- There are major obscurities in the New Testament narratives by and about Mark that are bridged and answered by the Alexandrian mission.
- The general consensual tradition stemming from the "earliest presbyters" who spoke with Papias were reflected by the writings of Clement and the Urtext of *Martyrium Marci*. This tradition was followed by Eusebius, Jerome and most leading ecumenical teachers after them. All signs point to Mark in Alexandria.
- The analogy between Alexandria and Rome as the two greatest cities of the time makes it imperative that someone would be sent to Alexandria earlier, not later.
- There are compelling reasons, which I will spell out, why Mark was the best choice for the mission to the continent of Africa.

The steady stream of testimony of the most reliable subsequent ancient Christian writers of the earliest Christian centuries becomes more compelling the closer we examine it.

The earliest textual sources that have survived are virtually unanimous: Mark was a major figure among the apostles. Tradition says that he was chosen to bring the gospel to Africa. This includes the earliest traditions from the Eastern Church, the Western Church, and the proto-Coptic Egyptian-Libyan tradition.

Every puzzle presents dilemmas that are not clear at first, but gradually become revealed. So with Mark. Most scholars agree that the other Synoptic Gospels were reliant on Mark. But few have entertained the imaginative African memory of Mark as actual history. This memory is viewed as unreliable hagiography, the mere study of saints, received with a yawn. Thus Mark appears as an unsolved identity within a complex detective story, an unplaced fragment of a large puzzle, a question in a riddle, a complex pattern of circumstantial evidence in a courtroom. These are complementary metaphors. My hope is that continuing scholarship will in due time better grasp an overall plausible *Gestalt* of this compelling circumstantial evidence. I have sought to make this plausible in the eyes of the jury (you, the reader). The task of the jury in a case of inferred evidence is the recognition of a compelling configuration or pattern of truth that makes sense.

The form of presentation of evidence is here more for the ordinary reader of the Gospel than the professional literary or historical critic. These pages bring together commonsense clues into a single pattern, which once it is grasped, brings many otherwise ambiguous factors into place. That is the nature of a Gestalt. Once you see it, you grasp it. You say, "Aha, I get it." You then feel a sense of relief and accomplishment. I am setting this Gestalt before you, but only your eyes can recognize it for yourself.

THREE KEY CLUES TO RECOGNITION OF THE GESTALT

In this section I am attempting a closing argument, like a defense attorney, based on all the above data. This requires putting together many elements of data and imagination in order to construct a uniting hypothesis in which all pieces of the puzzle fit. I believe this recognition cannot be fully plausible until these three elements are thoroughly understood and conjoined. All three focus on possible interpretations of New Testament passages which suggest that Mark's family stood in close relation to Peter's family.

The traditional narrative sees all three as conjoining indicators of an intimate, and perhaps even a familial, relation between Peter and Mark. All three have a textual basis in the New Testament, which must be viewed in their contexts. They beg to be fitted together.

These three scriptural testimonies are

- Peter called Mark "my son" (1 Pet 5:13)
- Peter in a daze escaped directly to the home of the mother of Mark (Acts 12:6-17)
- Mark reported explicit details of the healing of Peter's mother-in-law (Mk 1:29-31)

While all three have been explored already, they have not yet been conjoined in the plausible Gestalt that solves the puzzle. Each must be understood in relation to the other two. The Gestalt recognition depends upon careful exegesis of these three events and their relationship.

Crucial to the solving of the puzzle of Mark is this remarkable closeness of Mark to Peter, and perhaps Mark's family with Peter's family. First, why did Peter call Mark "my son"? Either the voice of Peter himself is echoed or at least the tradition of Peter is preserved in the first letter of Peter (1 Pet 5:13).

Varied standard interpretations of "my son" have included the following:

- Peter may have baptized Mark.
- Peter clearly regarded Mark as his close companion, assistant or protégé.
- Peter may have thought of Mark as a member of his own extended family in the Galilee.

The African hagiographical narrative combines all three of these interpretations into a single, simple Gestalt. Any or all of these degrees of intimacy (baptismal, collegial or familial) could have been signified by Peter's acknowledgment of Mark as "my son." An intriguing subplot hinges on traditional and quasi-textual arguments that Peter was physically with Mark in Old Cairo at the time referred to in 1 Peter 5:13. Later Mark appears to be either physically with or near Peter in his last days in Rome just before Mark was sent to Alexandria.

Does this unusual salutation indicate that Mark was with Peter in Egypt? This question is closely connected with how we may answer the already discussed hypothesis of "Babylon" as the Old Cairo refugee center. I cannot call this a probability, but I think it is an entirely plausible possibility that should not be arbitrarily ruled out. The claim of some African writers is that Peter wrote, or could have written or dictated to an amanuensis, his first letter from Babylon in Egypt where he was being accompanied by Mark, who would have known this culture and territory. This has seldom been examined in modern Western scholarship. But it has been argued by African sources (Atiya, Girgis, Shenouda III).

Whether or not there was a family relationship connection between Mark and the sons of Jonah, there are four ways in which it seems fitting to understand Mark as Peter's son in the faith.

- *Mark was Peter's son in his calling.* Mark was first to report Peter's calling by the Lord in Capernaum. In the African narrative, Peter was first to call Mark to faith and baptism.
- *Mark was Peter's son in his mission, his struggles, his journeys.* Peter likely commissioned Mark to go to Antioch. Mark accompanied Peter on many, if not most, of his journeys. Peter was the one who through angelic inspiration sent and encouraged Mark in his mission to Alexandria.
- *Mark was Peter's son in his preaching and writing.* Peter was an eyewitness to the whole narrative of Jesus' ministry. Peter had experienced it more directly and personally than any other. Mark was thoroughly aware of what had happened to Peter in the Lord's presence. At the end of his life, Peter deliberately selected Mark out of many others to interpret what he had been preaching throughout

his ministry. Mark remembered it just as Peter had narrated it.

- Add to these a possible fourth: *Mark was indeed a member of the same family as Peter of Capernaum, as held in the African memory,* though not in Scripture explicitly nor in Western history. This is why Mark knew exactly what happened in the healing of Peter's mother-in-law, who may have been one of his own relatives. For some combination of these reasons, Peter calls Mark his son.

This takes us back to the very beginning of the African narrative: Aristopolus was Mark's father who was converted by Mark in the Jordanian wilderness. He was the husband of the remarkable woman whom Jesus chose to prepare the feast for the first Eucharist. Mary of Cyrene, Aristopolus and Mark were close relatives to Barnabas who accompanied Paul on his first missionary journey with Mark part way.

Next our attention shifts to closer inspection of another already noticed scene of the narrative: How did Peter find his way to the home of the mother of Mark? This second episode is especially revealing in grasping the significance of Mark's relation to Peter. It may reinforce the familial relation. To recapitulate: When Peter was dazed and disoriented after being thrown in jail and miraculously released, the apostle fled as quickly as possible directly to the house of the family of Mark in Jerusalem. Note these details:

- Peter's own voice was instantly recognized from outside the wall of the house (Acts 12:14).
- Inside the house the disciples were at that very time earnestly praying for Peter and hoping for his safety (Acts 12:5, 12).
- When the maid saw Peter alive and free, she was so excited "in her joy she did not open the gate." She ran back to tell the intercessors that their prayers were being answered, all the while "Peter was standing at the gate" (Acts 12:14 RSV).
- The disciples tried to discern whether this could be so, or whether it was a deception or perhaps a supernatural visitation. Peter continued to knock. At that moment he was mortally vulnerable as an escaped prisoner outside the gate. He needed a safe house. "There was no

small stir among the soldiers over what had become of Peter" (Acts 12:18 RSV). The soldiers were actively and desperately searching for him. These very soldiers were killed by the order of Herod when they did not find Peter (Acts 12:19).

- The disciples were amazed when at last they saw Peter. He had no time for explanations. He motioned them with his hand to be silent. He had to flee. "Tell this to James," he said and immediately "went to another place" for safety (Acts 12:17 RSV).

He first reported to the gathered disciples in a place with which he was familiar, the home of John Mark and his mother which he considered a safe house. Then he "went to another place," perhaps depending upon Mark to take him there.

Thus Peter's release from prison raises the question: How did Peter know exactly where to go? Was Mark's house a continuing meeting place for the disciples—before the crucifixion, after Pentecost and in the earliest stages of international mission? The synaxary account of Mark draws the conclusion that all these location references point to the same place—the home of Mary the mother of John Mark.

But how can we rely upon the synaxary account? The story of Peter's dramatic escape from imprisonment is much better known than the episode about what happened to him after he escaped. This glimpse is revealing: Herod was arresting Christians. James, the brother of John, had been put to death by the sword. Herod "killed James, the brother of John with the sword; and when he saw that it pleased the Jews, he proceeded to arrest Peter also" (Acts 12:2-3). In prison, sentries stood guard at the entrance (Acts 12:6). While Peter was sleeping between two soldiers, bound in two separable chains, the nascent church was earnestly praying for his release (Acts 12:5). Where were they gathered? The house of the mother of Mark.

Stay closely with the narrative: An angel appeared in the prison cell. The angel said, "Follow me" (Acts 12:7-8). Peter's chains fell off. Stunned, Peter followed the mysterious guide out of the prison. But he had no clear idea what was really ahead (Acts 12:9).

- When the angelic visitor awakened him and told him to dress himself urgently, Peter followed his orders (Acts 12:7-9).

- Peter thought he was dreaming. He did not know that what was happening under the angel's guidance was real and thought instead that he was merely seeing a vision (Acts 12:9).
- It was not until he was past the iron gate and walked the length of one street that the angel departed and Peter began coming to his senses (Acts 12:10-11).
- Only after some time of dazed reflection, as he was grasping what had happened, did he regain his composure. When Peter came to himself, he realized he had been miraculously rescued from a prison under the highest level of security.

Where did Peter go? Luke's narrative in Acts is very specific: "*When this had dawned on him, he went to the house of Mary the mother of John, also called Mark*" where the disciples had already gathered to pray for him (Acts 12:12, emphasis added).

Even without the angelic guide, what premise could account for that inner gyroscopic memory that led him to the safe house of Mary? Perhaps some deep intuition or dream-state awareness enabled him to find Mark's mother's house, and hence presumably Mark's house. Or perhaps the disciples had met there so often it was habitual to return to it.

A standard Catholic account is similar: "Mark's mother was a prominent member of the infant Church at Jerusalem; it was to her house that Peter turned on his release from prison; the house was approached by a porch (*pulon*), there was a slave girl (*paidiske*), probably the portress, to open the door, and the house was a meeting-place for the brethren, 'many' of whom were praying there the night St. Peter arrived from prison (Acts 12:12-13)."[1]

The text reinforces the thought that Mark was very close to Peter. Several key events such as the Transfiguration were first noted in Mark where only Peter and James and John were present. Mark had to be privy to these events by report or personal knowledge. This suggests

[1]*The Catholic Encyclopedia,* ed. Charles George Herbermann et al. (New York: Encyclopedia Press, 1913-1914), vol. 9, s.v. "St. Mark."

that Mark had access to intimate firsthand knowledge, analogous to the kind of knowing that is closely held within a family.

The third test of Mark's familial affinity with Peter is the narrative of the healing of Peter's mother-in-law. The incident is reported near the very beginning of Mark's Gospel. The scene is Capernaum. The event is Jesus' first healing miracle. Capernaum appears frequently in the Gospels. Jesus was known to have worked and preached there in his earliest ministry. If Mark had a family connection in Capernaum, it might explain why the healing of Peter's mother-in-law appeared so early in Mark, indeed as the earliest of all Jesus' many healing miracles. He would likely have known firsthand of the events he reported and thus provided such explicit detail. Indeed he might have had eyewitness knowledge of this incident.

None of the archaeological evidence I will refer to later was known to those who first transmitted the proto-Coptic narrative. They knew only the text of Mark's first chapter, where Jesus, while in Capernaum, immediately "left the synagogue, and entered the house of Simon and Andrew, with James and John. Now Simon's mother-in-law lay sick with a fever, and immediately they told him of her. And he came and *took her by the hand and lifted her up*, and the fever left her; and she served them" (Mk 1:29-31, emphasis added).

There is little doubt that the event claimed a high priority in the sequence of Mark's narrative. But what is most exceptional in the narrative is how Mark could have known all these details. These details included:

- The personal names of those present
- Their family relationships
- The specific gestures in this act of healing

How could Mark have known these details? The conclusion of the African memory of Mark: Either Mark was there, or Peter's report of it to Mark had extraordinarily precise, personal detail. Mark was the first to report it in written form.

The question haunts the African memory: Was Peter's mother-in-law Mark's own relative? Was the earliest Christian church in Capernaum built on the site of Peter's house? Remarkably, here is where the literary and archaeological evidences begin to dovetail. Egeria (*Itinerarium Egeriae* 2.5.2, A.D. 381–384) indicates that according to Peter the Deacon (*De locis sanctis*, CCSL 175.98-99) the subsequent church at Capernaum was built on the site of Peter's house. Confirming an early Christian community there are rabbinic references to *minim* (heretics) at Capernaum, which seem "clearly to refer to Jewish Christians."[2]

As for archaeology, there is an early Christian place of worship in Capernaum, now popularly known as "Peter's House." This site has been carefully excavated. The reports indicate that the location was in the first century a domestic structure. It existed before A.D. 100. Significantly, it was converted to public and ecclesiastical use at a very early date—about A.D. 100. The excavations exposed an octagonal mid-fifth-century church built on top of the remains of the earlier domestic structure. The room contained within this octagonal shrine appears to be part of a complex of small single-story residential rooms and courtyards, possibly as a *domus ecclesia*, a private house used as a church, with the words "Jesus," "Lord," "Christ" and "Peter" appearing in Aramaic, Greek and Latin graffiti. If so, Christians appear to have been meeting and praying in that location during the first century, and perhaps not long after Mark's first report of this miracle.

All three crucial episodes pour into a single Gestalt, reflected in the hagiographical narratives. The more probable conclusion is that Peter referred to Mark as "my son" (1 Pet 5:13) since he was a relative; Peter in a daze escaped from prison directly to the home of his own relative in Jerusalem, the mother of Mark (Acts 12:6-17); Mark reported explicit details of the healing of Peter's mother-in-law at the beginning of his Gospel because it was a very dear experience in his own family's lore (Mk 1:29-31). The Synaxary version, either from then-existing historical sources or by intuitive inference, grasped this plausible three-point Gestalt. Non-African sources never grasped it.

---

[2]Roderic L. Mullen, following *Ecclesiastes Rabbah* 1.8.4; 7.26.3, *The Expansion of Christianity: A Gazetteer of Its First Three Centuries* (Leiden: Brill, 2004), p. 25.

WEIGHING ANCESTRAL AND FAMILIAL LINKS

This prompts the thought that Mark may have been to Capernaum earlier and known the very people of reported in the story. Such imaginative interpretation does not establish these family connections as historically reliable, but they add intriguing color and texture to the imaginative African mosaic.[3] Mark's narrative of the healing of Peter's mother-in-law became a focal point for proto-Coptic inferences about the relation of Mark and Peter.

We learn from Luke 1:36 that Mary the mother of Jesus was a relative or kinswoman (*syngenis*) of Elizabeth the mother of John the Baptist. The family of Jesus appears in many episodes of the New Testament. There are persistent suggestions in the African tradition of the holy family that two families intertwined: the extended family of Jesus in Nazareth and Jerusalem (son of Mary, who with Joseph fled to Egypt, according to Matthew 2:13-15) and the extended family of John Mark (by tradition from Cyrenaica, which was a part of Egypt).

Mark and his mother show up according to various Coptic sources at the wedding of Cana (associating Mark with one of the servants sent to fill the jars with water) along with Jesus and his mother (Jn 2:1-12). Was there an African Diaspora wing of the family of Peter in Capernaum? Westerners scoff at the lack of evidence. Africans are curious. They have long been intrigued over the mutual crossovers of populations and family between Palestine and Egypt. The distance is not great. The borders meet near Gaza.

This prompts another typological analogy that will be experienced as unlikely to those enthralled by narrow modern historical criticism. This analogy employs an ancient African method for interpreting sacred texts, one that virtually defines the heart of African exegesis—the anticipation of correspondence between types of biblical events and subsequent events in history. The focus is upon anticipative typological interpretation of prophetic events. Here we recall that a seemingly unrelated narrative impinges and almost intrudes upon this subject mat-

---

[3]For recent African discussions of tradition, ancestry and heritage, see works in the bibliography by Tokunboh Adeyemo, Ukachukwu Chris Manus, J. N. K. Mugambi, Charles Nyamiti, Lamin Sanneh and Josiah Ulysses Young III.

ter—the flight of the Holy Family to Egypt and Mark's family in flight from Africa.

As endangered Jews fled to Egypt, so did Joseph, Mary and Jesus, the incarnate Lord. Egypt was from time immemorial regarded as a valley of abundance and civil order where Jewish refugees sought safety (Mt 2:13-15). This epic narrative lives in the iconography all up and down the Nile valley. The African exegetes, especially Origen, shaped this insight. It was later treated in more detail by John Chrysostom, as well as Augustine and Cyril:

> But why was the Christ child sent into Egypt? The text makes this clear: he was to fulfill what the Lord had spoken by the prophet, "Out of Egypt have I called my son." From that point onward we see that the hope of salvation would be proclaimed to the whole world. Babylon and Egypt represent the whole world. Even when they were engulfed in ungodliness, God signified that he intended to correct and amend both Babylon and Egypt. God wanted humanity to expect his bounteous gifts the world over. So he called from Babylon the wise men and sent to Egypt the holy family.[4]

The Markan echo of this drama is the flight of Mark's family, under threat in Africa, to Jerusalem as a safe haven. The typic flight of the Holy Family to Africa is analogous to the flight of Mark's family to Jerusalem and to the flight of Peter and Mark to Egypt.

---

[4]John Chrysostom, *The Gospel of Matthew*, Homily 8.2 (ACCS NT 1:31).

12

WHEN THE JOHN MARK OF HISTORY MEETS THE ST. MARK OF MEMORY

For almost two thousand years, Christian memory and scholarship and exegesis from the Nile Valley, Libya, Ethiopia and the Maghreb have remembered Mark as native founder of African Christianity, as a son of Libya, as the first Christian martyr in Africa, and as *the apostolic father of every believing Christian in Africa, then and now.* No apostolic figure has made greater impact on African Christianity than John Mark. Even when the church at Carthage was most closely identified with Rome, there was no thought of questioning Mark as founder of Christianity on the African continent. Even the early liturgy of the Western church in North Africa honored and reflected the liturgy of St. Mark.

The positive examination of evidences of this traditional view is emerging gradually among a respected group of contemporary scholars. They are taking a new look at the *indigenous early African memory of Mark's martyrdom.* The evidence is stronger than is generally accredited by the older school of Euro-American historical interpreters and is ripe for a careful review. Many current scholars are now looking at this evidence in a different way from that of Harnack, Bauer and company.

In recent years the modern historical study of Mark has been almost completely inattentive to the traditional memory of Mark. Is this a case of excessive reaction? Surely there must be some way to bring the two perspectives back into a conversation and perhaps an integration. I have sought to prepare some way for that to improve, despite my limitations.

Modern scholarship has entertained many conjectures about Mark that have long cast a cloud of doubt that he might have had any connection whatever with Africa. Pearson notes, however, that the historicity of Mark's association with Alexandria "though unprovable should not be ruled out." (*REC*, 144). Even though resistant to absolute proof, the proximate forms of evidence need not be disregarded.

The definitive historical datum that would absolutely validate the historic truth of the birth and death of Mark may not come soon, but it will likely come eventually, especially when Alexandria is properly excavated. My conviction is that the truth lies in some position in between the Western and African views.[1] But even within Western premises, there is no compelling reason to rule out altogether the hypothesis that Mark came to Jerusalem from Cyrene in Africa and, having assisted Paul and Peter, returned to Alexandria where he was martyred.

Western textbooks hold that the African memory is a legend, an unreliable hagiographical oral tradition. The point is easily missed that an oral tradition could also have been a once-firm written tradition without ceasing to be later an oral and liturgical tradition. It is self-evident that all written traditions were oral traditions before they were written. At best, it is highly speculative when historians assume that they can identify with confidence the time or the date in which an oral tradition became written.

For many years I defended or tolerated an overall accommodation to modern Euro-American academic culture. This came at the cost of overlooking the African memory of Mark. I was all too ready to forego my better practical judgment. This happened especially with the Bultmannians and form critics with whom I was closely associated in my early writings.[2]

In the 1970s I was cast out of the garden of political correctness that

[1]For recent discussions of Mark's narrative from the point of view of African history and identity, see the works in the bibliography by Michael Kirwen, Laurenti Magesa and Thomas C. Oden.

[2]See Thomas C. Oden, *Radical Obedience: The Ethics of Rudolf Bultmann*, with a response by Rudolf Bultmann (Philadelphia: Westminster, 1964).

blossomed briefly in universities and religious circles. I put aside my Bultmannian fixation. It lies in my dusty attic along with a war-chest of avant-garde memorabilia, protest signs and Nehru jackets. Only gradually was I freed from the obsession with cultural accommodation. This happened more than thirty years ago during a time when I was laboring to produce the early drafts of *Agenda for Theology*.[3]

Every day since a wintry day in Algeria in January 2003, early African Christianity has stood at the head of my research interests. On that day I stood awed in the basin of the dusty baptistery of the ancient church of St. Augustine in Hippo. Since then I have been thinking of Africa. The privilege of examining, pondering and writing on the African memory of Mark has been the vocational exercise I have most valued in these years of my life since completing the Ancient Christian Commentary on Scripture.

The validation of the African memory of Mark is best seen as a *mosaic* of fine points viewed as a pattern of circumstantial evidence. Only then will it come to have the plausibility for Westerners that it has enjoyed for twenty centuries among Africans. A similar analogy comes from the technique of painting called *pointillism*. Small dots of color create the impression of larger patterns of color by optical blending. The task of the artist is to select the colors so the eye can blend them. The challenge of the beholder is to blend the colors into a recognizable pattern. This is best seen in the paintings of Georges Seurat. What I have sought to do is paint this picture very slowly by tiny points, hoping that the reader will grasp the pattern. The pattern in the case of St. Mark cannot be rightly assessed without assembling an extensive and plausible constellation of evidences. This has required a longer book than I intended to write, since my goal was to reach lay readers, not professionals alone.

WEIGHING THE ARGUMENTS

If the Markan story was invented as a hagiographical fantasy, what could have been the motivation for its invention? If legitimacy was the

---

[3]Thomas C. Oden, *Agenda for Theology* (New York: Harper & Row, 1979), rev. as *After Modernity—What?* (Grand Rapids: Zondervan, 1989).

inventors' aim, then surely they could have invented something more probable than a Libyan birth. The common Western assumption of this era has been that there is no evidence of Libyan Christians before the third century, and almost no Christians in Egypt before the second. It took a long period of contemplative inquiry for me to begin to risk questioning those fixed assumptions.

The notion that the memory of Mark's martyrdom was invented in fourth-century Alexandria simply to bolster the prestige of a shaky patriarchate is even more implausible. The documentation surrounding the history of the patriarchate of Alexandria shows that it has seldom thought of itself as wobbly, as if an endangered species. I have sought to show how the African memory, much older than modern skepticism, displays a pattern of highly plausible features.

Much historicist reasoning amounts to an argument from silence. What if that same rule were applied to other figures whose names we know but about whom we know nothing else in detail (Hittite and Pharaonic kings, or Buddha or Pythagorus, for example)? But in the case of Mark, we have much more data than merely his name. We have both his own writings and numerous reports about him, and large shelves of books full of interpretations of those reports. Anyone can test this out by going go to a well-fitted university or theological library, then go to the New Testament stacks and journals, and see firsthand the extensive number of Mark studies there. More quickly, go online. Compare the huge numbers of studies on Mark with those on Pythagoras, about whom we also can know very little at the level of absolute certainty. This does not establish the Africanness of Mark, but it does question the method of those who hold as suspect all other evidence than that which fits their reductionist-empiricist philosophical assumptions.

Among our best young historians on this subject is Stephen Davis of Yale. He has made a book-length study of the Coptic Papacy, treating it with great respect. Note how cautiously he states his view that we can talk with reliability only about "early Christian traditions recording Saint Mark's reputation as the founder of the church in Alexandria."[4]

[4]Stephen J. Davis, *The Early Coptic Papacy: The Egyptian Church and Its Leadership in Late Antiquity* (Cairo: American University in Cairo Press, 2004), p. 1.

The constraints of strict historical inquiry have compelled him to make such a careful disclaimer.

In this arena we are required to talk less about empirically verifiable historical data and more about the traditions reporting the events. If we take modern history to its extreme, we are not talking at all about Mark founding the church in Alexandria but merely about his somehow being recollected as its founder.

Professor Davis has shown that there are growing empirical evidences that these traditions are to be taken with much greater historical seriousness, even if we must properly qualify their veracity. This stands in tension with scholarship that has entirely stepped away from ascribing any historical credibility to these accounts of an African Mark.

AFRICAN HISTORY IN SEARCH OF ITS ROOTS

Regardless of what Euro-American historians may hypothesize on Mark, go to Africa—any part of it—and you will get a different story. In Africa it is widely held that the resistance to Mark's Africanness comes out of deep Eurocentric prejudice, to put it mildly. Premature Western dismissal has profound social consequences in Africa. It has been destructive to the self-esteem of Christians in sub-Saharan Africa. It has been an impediment for serious scholars in African studies. In much of the African academy there is often only the thinnest sense that there is or ever was a great and noble intellectual and textual tradition of early African Jews and Christians. That is because many of them have learned their African history from colonizing Euro-American academics who did not bother to inquire into the nineteen hundred years of that textual history. The wisdom of these texts beams magnificently from early Africa. The African continent in late antiquity produced a lasting and influential literary and intellectual tradition.

For many believers in sub-Saharan Africa who have learned history under conditions of colonialization, Christian history in Africa does not really even begin until the nineteenth century. This is reflected repeatedly in the theological literature. To verify this, go to the indexes of recent literature and see how few references there are to Cyprian, Origen and Augustine in comparison to the many references to Hegel, Marx,

Freud and Fanon. If they had been already deeply instructed by the texts and evidences of early African ecumenical Christian teaching, they would not be trapped in a syndrome of negative self-esteem. They would already have discovered that the great minds of the church of North Africa were long indigenized to African inland continental cultures and languages, and to local subcultures of the Nile and Maghreb.

If you take away orality from traditional African religion, you take away its beating heart. If you take away the relation of father and son, kinship relations, and distant ancestors, you take away its continuity with the past. Translated into classic Christian terms, the metaphor of ancestors points to the apostolic witnesses, as continued by the ancient Christian writers. Take that away and you rob African Christianity of its vital center.

This is exactly what Western historicism has inadvertently done by insisting on hard empirical evidence as the sole basis for validating the story of a saint. The story is what animates the perception of the saint, without diminishing facts. The story gives the facts a context. The story cannot be reduced to external evidence, since it is self-evidencing. In classic Christian doctrine, God the Spirit awakens the perception of the truth in the icon.

In Africa the story of Mark is the prototype that makes possible our remembering of all that follows in African Christianity. Mark is the father who brings the family the memory of God's own personal dwelling with humanity. Mark witnessed this event: God the Son among us in the flesh. His narrative is all about revealing that fleshly, historical narrative of the God-man, who was truly man and truly God, whose death and risen life fulfilled Hebraic messianic expectations. Only through this Spirit-led recognition do we get to the historicity of the holy life.

The roots of African Christianity are not fully revealed by presenting hard, ratifiable, objective evidence alone. That is the Western way, not the St. Mark story or the African apostolic imagination, which requires the telling of a story, the story of a saint. Mark is the apostle chosen by God under the guidance of Peter to first embody this story in Africa. He is the revered founder of the church of Africa not because he chose to be, but because he was transcendently elected and sent.

Speculations based on supposed or probable oral traditions are rife, endemic and ubiquitous within modern historical scholarship. This is particularly the case in the post-Bultmannian decades of the study of the New Testament, in which I was once an avid participant. So I am not treading upon grounds ruled out by critical scholars themselves. I am appealing to neglected African oral and written traditions using their own methods.[5]

Let us suppose hypothetically that this African oral tradition (that Mark died in Africa) might be able to be proved entirely wrong. Suppose it is utterly devastated by critical methods. Suppose it is judged worthless and of no use to future consensual Christian scholarship. Even then none of the skeptics could successfully deny that it has shaped the spirit of African Christianity for two thousand years. For that compelling reason alone it must be taken into account and not swept under the rug or lost in the fog of academic ideological warfare.

The pursuit of Mark has been an enduring preoccupation and privilege for me. I deliberately selected Mark as the first volume of the Ancient Christian Commentary on Scripture (ACCS). It was first because we had been warned that a patristic commentary on Mark could not be done, because it was thought that there would not be enough patristic material on Mark. We took that as a challenge. Along with my coeditor of the Mark volume, and associate editor of the entire twenty-nine-volume series—Chancellor Christopher Hall of Eastern University—we showed that it could be done and could have been done much earlier.

We gathered together by exhaustive digital searches, the history of early Christian comments on every verse in Mark in Greek, Latin, Syriac and Coptic. In doing so we investigated the literary-critical questions of Mark's narrative, authorship and date, especially as viewed by the early Christian writers.

But it was not central to our purpose in the ACCS to place Mark in an African context. It took many more visits to North Africa and lectures in Libya and meetings with historians and theologians in Ethio-

---

[5]For recent African discussions of New Testament interpretation, see the works in the bibliography by Byang Kato and John Mbiti.

pia, Kenya and French West Africa, and much reading, to shift my attention from Eurocentric to specifically African influences.

As a dustbowl child of the mid-American plains, the assertion that I might have a covert Afrocentric ethnic bias is hard for anyone to take seriously. That would be to misunderstand the ancient ecumenical teachers, where my heart lies, and more particularly the brilliance of its African teachers. My interest here is rather in the liturgical, architectural, epigraphic and textual evidences to corroborate the exegesis of the early African commentators on Mark's Gospel from Clement to Sawirus to Shenouda III. Were all of them simply ill-informed or ignorant? Were they naive to accept a thinly veiled fraud that claimed that Mark was the first apostolic voice in African Christianity? If they were naive, it would be hard to substantiate. Rather we have a brilliant African literary tradition from Mark to Clement and Origen to Cyril the Great and Augustine to today's Coptic scholars.

Is this endeavor Afrocentric? Yes, in the sense that it is addressed primarily to African scholars, and only secondarily to the West. But no, in the sense that the term *Afrocentrism* is typically used to refer to a biased fixation on African ideology and interests that distort historical sources. My resistance to ideological Afrocentrism as usually defined is that it tends to twist, bend and warp the facts of history on the basis of a predisposed ethnic or racial preference. The Ancient Christian Commentary inquired into the full range of consensual patristic sources of the first millennium, not into African sources alone. But in doing so, we discovered how decisive the African patristic writers have been for the intellectual life of all Christian communities. This is the passion that drives these pages. Our outrage has been intensified by the ugly fact that the African texts and narratives have been ignored in the West, most notably in studies on Mark.

Those who pursue the African memory of Mark will elicit resistance. The potential loss of credibility to the scholar in North America is real and undeniable. Even to enter this arena is to suffer that loss. Especially where questions of tenure and publication are at play, the cost for young scholars could be exceptionally high. Where ideological interests are strong and where faculties are overtenured and defensive, the cost of being rejected and shunned is especially wrenching. Young scholars competing for teaching positions, grants, appointments and publication opportunities will feel these costs in the most painful way.

Why then enter this arena? Our vocation is to tell the truth. In the decades ahead our partners in dialogue will be mostly in Africa, not North American elites, whose voices are subsiding. I have already enjoyed a long season of publication and teaching and lecturing in North America in significant universities and publishing houses—now is the time to give something back in return. I truly love the intellectual vitality of the early African Christian intellectual leadership, where my heart lies.

13

THE MARKAN NUCLEUS OF AFRICAN LITURGY AND CATECHESIS

Mark's most crucial contribution to early African Christianity may have been the planting of the original idea for the Catechetical School of Alexandria. Its core is seen already in his first conversation with Anianus. This teaching mission has proved exceptionally fruitful not only to North African Christianity but to higher education the world over. Anba Shenouda III writes of Mark's three leading accomplishments: "His individual great work was his Gospel, his Liturgy, and the establishment of the Theological School of Alexandria" (Shenouda III, 24).

Mark was from the outset a catechist, as we see from his Gospel and from his dialogue with Anianus. Preaching and teaching were his central purposes. Those who picture him in Alexandria will picture him teaching. In icons Mark is seldom without a book. Assuming his early teaching in Alexandria, it is likely that from the embryo of that teaching sprang the first catechetical school within Christian history.

The Alexandrian School is the first of its kind and a model for all subsequent expressions of Christian higher education. This school developed from humble origins to become the most emulated educational institution of the Christian world. Its patterns of exegesis were soon followed in Carthage (Tertullian), Caesarea (Origen), Cappadocia (Gregory of Nazianzus) and Rome (Gregory the Great). These patterns sought to ferret out the spiritual sense of a sacred text without losing touch with its plain or historical sense. This exegetical process would stand at the core of consensually held classic Christian teachings. Alexandrian exegesis was well established by the end of the second century (the 190s), and became ecumenically recognized long before Constantine. It was a mature method as early as the time of persecutions in Africa under Septimius Severus (202–210) and Valerian (253–258). These spiritual forms of exegesis would be spawned further in Antioch, Cappadocia, Syria and west all the way to Bede in Northumbria and Anselm in Canterbury.

The place of origin for this widespread practice was the school whose roots were in the tradition engendered by Mark in Alexandria, the catechetical school that was the hub of Christian intellectual and literary development and Christian preaching that was grounded in the Hebrew Scriptures. As we have seen, Coptic sources hold that it was Mark who started a catechetical system for the edification of the newly converted catechumens, who hungered for reliable understanding of the Hebrew Scriptures and the good news that illumined them. Traditionally, Mark is viewed as the first leader of the catechetical school of Alexandria. This is not to claim that Mark himself deliberately conceived or initiated the catechetical school in its mature form. But its core idea is consistent with the African memory of Mark. I am not suggesting that the institutions of Christian learning that would develop during the late second through fourth centuries were in full flower in the first century. Their nucleus in Alexandria had to grow over the centuries. But the bones of Mark in Bucalis surely must have resonated with the formation of a deep and thoughtful form of catechesis.

It is not inconceivable that their core method of transmission of gospel teaching may have been in some sense intuitively Markan in origin, since it was multicultural, multilingual, straightforward and evangelical. Evangelical and Catholic colleges and universities and seminaries should be looking at Mark's catechesis. Whatever might have been the historical connections, the subsequent leaders of the Alexandrian School thought that their teaching was derived from the nucleus of preaching established by Mark on the African continent. There he taught indigenous Africans. If he was himself an indigenous African, that would give added strength to this teaching.

SUCCESSION IN THE CATECHETICAL SCHOOL OF ALEXANDRIA

Note the leaders that were elected to head the patriarchate. Most often they exercised leadership in the catechetical school, and from there they were elevated to patriarchal leadership. This reflects the importance of catechesis in the Alexandrian church that was founded by Mark. No doubt this combined pattern of strong teaching and ecclesiastical leadership was earlier conceived by Peter and Paul, and subsequently practiced by Mark. This we see especially in the precedents that prevailed in the orderly transition of Paul's ministry to Timothy and Titus—by ordination.

The succession of key names of leadership in the Alexandria Catechetical School was carefully reported by Eusebius. After its embryonic founding presumably by Mark, its leadership passed from Pantaenus to Clement to Origen to Heraclas and on to others. Many of the early leaders of African Christianity had earlier served as head of the catechetical school. As Heraclas became bishop (231–247), he was followed by Dionysius (247–264). Both were elevated to the episcopal office from leadership of the Catechetical School. Later Peter of Alexandria would also serve as dean before becoming bishop. Those who were commissioned to become teachers of the Christian faith in Africa in the second and third century faced persecution, imprisonment, torture and death. They were often following precisely in the pattern of Mark. Just as all early bishops faced persecution, so did all the early catechists. To be a bishop in the African sense was to be a teacher, as we see in Cyprian, Peter of Alexandria, Athanasius and Cyril the Great.

Clement was thought to be a disciple of Pantaenus, who is traditionally regarded as the earliest formal head of the Alexandrian Catechetical School. Clement was harassed; Origen was imprisoned. In his *Stromata*, Clement writes: "Now these men, preserving the true tradition of the blessed teaching straight from the holy apostles Peter, James, John, and Paul, receiving as a son from a father . . . came with God, depositing those ancestral, apostolic seeds even up to our time" (*Stromata* 1.1.11.3).[1] Origen, who was the student of Clement, died as a result of torture after being imprisoned in Tyre. He was followed by Heraclas who was martyred.

From the very apostolic writers in whom believers most trusted—in Africa prototypically from Mark to Athanasius—the apostles deposited apostolic seeds that are even now still springing up. They continue to take root because the apostolic tradition always bears fruit. It bears fruit because the Spirit intends to offer the good news to all humanity.

Teachers in the apostolic tradition were ordained to tell the truth without flinching, in such a way that the DNA of the truth remains genetically unaltered, while yet discovering ever new forms of relating to evolving cultures and languages.

The school was known more for *unchanged* transmission of the apostolic faith than for presumptuous forms of *originality* or individual creativity. Origen, who headed the Catechetical School, is sometimes portrayed as the most original of the early African writers. But it was he who insisted that "the teaching of the church is preserved unaltered handed down in unbroken succession from the apostles and existing to this day in the churches" (*First Principles* Pref. 2).[2]

In African memory all along the Nile, from Thebes to Ethiopia and Nubia, the apostle Mark has been always viewed as the first teacher of African Christianity and revered ever thereafter as the exemplary head of the Great School of Catechesis. This may give reasons why, among the Coptic successors to Saint Mark, eight bore the name of Mark. Both John and Mark proved to be exceptionally frequent names among Libyan and Nilotic Christians, among both church leaders and laity.

The African church views itself as an apostolic church. This is not only because its founder is Mark the apostle, but also because he ordained bishops, priests and deacons to secure the continuity of apostolic ministry. It is not only because Mark was martyred and buried in Africa,

---

[1]Clement, quoted in Stephen J. Davis, *The Early Coptic Papacy: The Egyptian Church and Its Leadership in Late Antiquity* (Cairo: American University in Cairo Press, 2004), p. 20.

[2]Origen, *On First Principles: Being Koetschau's Text of the "De principiis,"* trans. G. W. Butterworth (New York: Harper & Row, 1966).

but also because his successors have been viewed as an unbroken chain of witnesses since the apostolic age (Shenouda III; Davis, *Early Coptic Papacy,* passim). In this direct way the African church preserves the apostolic teaching throughout her life, spirituality, liturgy and dogmas.

Among Africa's greatest needs is sustained attention to education. There was a time for Christians in Africa when education was at the top of their list of priorities. Christianity in Africa emerged in a city that put lifelong learning in the spotlight. The apostle Mark, as popularly remembered as honorary founder of the School of Alexandria, placed a high value on education. It could happen again. There is a steady stream of precedent from day one.

THE LITURGY OF ST. MARK

Iconic representations of Mark are innumerable in ancient Coptic churches throughout the Nile Valley and all over the Maghreb.[3] There is hardly a church in North Africa in which the name or icon of Saint Mark is not honored with the utmost respect, often visually and in a prominent place in common worship on the iconostasis. He is regarded as the founding apostle of all believers on the continent.

Images of Mark appear in the earliest African iconography and in illuminated ancient manuscripts preserved in Coptic archives and monastic libraries. Of the surviving early expressions of Mark's countenance, two thirteenth-century paintings may be traced in early codices, one dated 1220 at Dayr al-Suryan in Wadi al-Natrun (MS no. 21) and another dated 1291 in the Patriarchal Library in Alexandria (MS no. 5/196). Two earlier portrayals can be found in the cathedral church of Dayr al-Suryan dated 912 and 928. Another from the tenth century is in the Mu'allaqah Church of the Virgin in Old Cairo. Another thirteenth-century icon of Mark was discovered at the chapel of Saint Antony in Dayr Anba Antuniyus in the Eastern Desert dated 1233. These survived the iconoclastic destructions of the eighth century and following.

The prayer on the Coptic feast of St. Mark gives thanks for John Mark who was "an Apostle of Christ who learned from the pre-

[3]For discussions of Coptic liturgy and iconography, see works in the bibliography by Frank E. Brightman, O. H. E. (Khs-)Burmester and Peter Grossmann.

eminent Peter, and did shine like the sun upon the lands of the Alexandrians, being their adornment. Through thee was Egypt freed from deception . . . honoring thy memory, we keep splendid festival" (Feast of St. Mark Troparion). From what deception did Mark free Egypt? The illusions of the goodness of idolatry. From day one in Alexandria he was resisting the deceptions of some imagined center of value or god that is destined to disappoint. How is this to be weighted? On a scale of one to ten this seems to register somewhere around a minimal one or two in the modern Euro-American worldview. This is compared with something like the optimal nine or ten in classic Coptic memory. If there is a distinctly African memory of Mark, it may be lodged more in the liturgy expressed daily through acts of worship, than as a form of evidence admissible through the criteria of historiography.[4]

The Divine Liturgy of St. Mark remains even today at the heart of historic African spirituality. According to the liturgies common in Coptic, Ethiopic, Nubian and Libyan traditions, Mark composed the core of the first Eucharist to be confessed and repeatedly recited by the Coptic faithful in the ancient churches of the whole Nile basin.[5] The liturgy attributed to Mark constitutes the earliest form of Eucharistic offices in Africa and one of the earliest in the world.[6] The Markan Eucharist has been at the core of the central rite of African Christian worship from the outset, from which other liturgies (of Basil, Gregory and Cyril) presumably were derived. It has continued to be celebrated in diverse forms throughout Africa. Its antecedent is remembered as having been first celebrated in the house of Mary, the mother of Mark (Acts 12:1-17; cf. Mk 14:12-25), which was first reported by her son.

It is telling that the ancient Divine Liturgy of St. Mark was celebrated in the See of St. Mark centuries before it was celebrated in Canterbury or Paris or Cordova or Kiev. African based liturgies still heard today are derived from that ascribed to St. Mark. Major sections of the

[4]For recent African discussions of hermeneutics and historiography, see works in the bibliography by Ukachukwu Chrirs Manus, Dominic A. Nicoliello, Charles Nyamiti and Lamin Sanneh.

[5]Joseph Hanna, *Office of the Holy Communion According to the Usage of the Coptic Church in Egypt, from the Divine Liturgy of St. Mark the Evangelist* (New York, 1875).

[6]Archdale A. King, *Liturgies of the Past* (Milwaukee: Bruce, 1959).

Divine Liturgy of St. Mark have been preserved by the Ethiopians in their ancient Ge'ez liturgy, the archaic language of Ethiopia, which ceased to be a living language in the fourteenth century, but has been retained as the official and liturgical language of the Ethiopian Orthodox Church.

Portions of this Eucharistic service have been discovered on papyrus fragments from Nilotic and monastic libraries of the Justinian period. The Vatican Library contains extant manuscript copies of the ancient Markan liturgy among its thirteenth-century codices.[7] From the liturgy ascribed to Mark, many of the other major African liturgies were derived, not only of the Coptic, but also of Catholic and Orthodox traditions. This is so even if they became separated by language or governance into Copts, Melkites, Diophysites, Ethiopians or other cultural histories.

The Divine Liturgy of Cyril derives directly from the Divine Liturgy of St. Mark. It is the primitive and archetypal worship service of the Orthodox Church of Alexandria. The Divine Liturgy According to St. James the Apostle became the primordial model received by the early Apostolic Church in Jerusalem. Similarly the Divine Liturgy of St. Mark was thought to be the prototypical pattern for classic African liturgies. It is possible to some extent to reconstruct portions of the early history of the Liturgy of Mark by references from Clement of Alexandria (d. ca. 215) and Athanasius (d. 373), the Prayer Book of Serapion, and Pseudo-Dionysius (The Divine Hierarchy).

Today the Coptic Orthodox Church uses three Liturgies, all based on the Markan prototype: (1) The Divine Liturgy According to St. Basil, bishop of Caesarea, (2) The Divine Liturgy According to St. Gregory of Nazianzus, bishop of Constantinople, and (3) The Divine Liturgy According to St. Cyril I, the 24th Patriarch of the Coptic Orthodox Church. Cyril's Divine Liturgy is basically the same as the Di-

[7]Among the oldest that have survived: the Codex Rossanensis, Vatican Graeca 1970, the Rotulus Vaticanus, Vatican Graeca 2281, and the Rotulus Messanensis, Codex Messanensis Graeca 177. The *Missale Alexandrinum Sancti Marci* may be found in Giuseppe L. Assemani, *Codex liturgicus Ecclesiae Universae in XV libros distributus, in quo continentur libri rituals, missales, pontificales, officia, dypticha & Ecclesiarum Occidentis & Orientis*, 13 vols. (Rome: 1749–66), see esp. vol. 7, book 4, part 4, *Missale Alexandrinum sancti Marci in quo Eucharistiae liturgiae.*

vine Liturgy of St. Mark, edited and rearranged by Cyril, with litanies added. The Liturgy of Basil is used most of the year, Gregory's on feast days, and Cyril's version of the Markan liturgy is often used during Lent. Gorgias Press has recently reissued the English version of these primitive liturgies—*The Liturgies of Saints Mark, James, Clement, Chrysostomos, and Basil, and the Church of Malabar*—translated in the nineteenth century by John Neale.

THE SEE OF SAINT MARK

African Christianity has typically viewed its core legitimacy as closely related to its factual and historical founding by the apostle Mark. African preachers of early times appealed to the authority of Mark and prized their direct lineage from that apostolic succession. The Council of Nicaea in A.D. 325 decreed: "Let the ancient customs in Egypt, Libya and Pentapolis prevail, that the Bishop of Alexandria have jurisdiction in all these" (Canon 6).[8] There would flow a steady stream of leaders that were selected by an orderly due process and confirmed as the successors of Mark.

The unity of the body of Christ worldwide was taught by the earliest preaching traditions that would later become the New Testament (Jn 17; Eph 1–4; 1 Cor 12). By and large, the churches in Africa maintained this apostolic dedication to unity even under the harshest conditions of persecution. Though variously understood, Orthodox consciousness in Africa, whether Coptic, Greek, Melchite or Ethiopic, has always placed the highest importance on the apostolic continuity of African Christianity and the unity of believers in all cultures and continents. This is why an exaggerated Afrocentrism based exclusively on ethnicity has never adequately conveyed the depths of the African Christian tradition.

There was in early Africa no neglect of the apostolic witness. It became the ecumenical consensus of teaching all over the globe within

---

[8]NPNF 2 14:53; On the history of the Pentapolis, see Hassan Soliman, *Libya Between the Past and Present* (n.p., 1962), E. L. Butcher, *The Story of the Church of Egypt* (London: Smith, Elder and Company, 1897); Zaher Riad, *The Church of Alexandria in Africa* (Cairo: Coptic Orthodox Patriarchate, 1962).

worshiping communities of Christians. There was firm resistance to innovation that would pretend to have improved on the apostles' teaching. While modern culture remains captive to exaggerated progressive metaphors of development, improvement and change, early African Christianity steadily paid its highest attention to continuity with apostolic truth.

This was not just a matter of political interest or legitimacy. It was rather a question of truth. Was the truth of universal history revealed once for all in the history of Jesus? If so, the truth had to be told in the form of narrative based on observed events. This is what Mark did and was first to do. This hunger for apostolicity was not reducible to politically or culturally based reasoning. Rather it was a tested mode of historical reasoning whose main subject was the meaning of universal history. Key African exponents of the study of universal history were Origen, Arnobius of Sicca, Lactantius, Cyril and Augustine.

This is what is meant by exegesis in early African Christianity: examining the revealed Word in a way that is consistent with commonsense and truth-telling. It concerns the truth that has been passed on from the original apostolic testimony. This is not a passing sociological anomaly but a truth-driven theological commitment of African Christianity. This is a theme already present in Paul's preaching and in the Catholic epistles. It is deeply written into New Testament church order, with its emphasis on the faithful transmission of truth through time. If recaptured, it promises to restore depth to modern Christianity in Africa, which is sometimes described as a mile wide and an inch deep.

In early African Christianity, the list of bishops dating to the apostles was an expression of the concrete connection with the truth of the apostolic memory. This is why a linear list of witnesses faithful to the apostles appeared so early and so persistently in the first Christian centuries: to establish these lines of apostolic continuity to ensure true rather than false transmission. In the first and second centuries, anyone could examine the list of a region's bishops from apostolic times. These names could be objectively checked out and fairly assessed in relation to all claimants. Every well-informed believer would know the answer. This was never a secret list. It was always a matter of public identity.

The point was to identify with the earliest apostolic memory rather than the latest trend.

In Alexandria that connection was from the earliest times embodied by Mark. It was followed and validated by a carefully preserved list of successors to Mark. This procedure was not unique to Africa. It was happening all over the church throughout the known world. But in Africa it was especially clear and distinct with a rationale grounded in universal history as seen through Scripture.

Four lists in particular became crucial in the four earliest regions of Christian world mission: those of Jerusalem for Palestine, Antioch for Asia, Rome for the West, and Alexandria for Africa. Other local lists depended on their relation to one or more of these lists. The church in Alexandria is still referred to as the See of St. Mark, one of these earliest four Sees, or shepherds of responsibility. Most early African Christians would never have thought of asserting: "Look at us—we have recently discovered a better idea of Christianity than the earliest apostles had." That is strictly a modern idea. Such an assertion would invalidate the apostolic claim if made, as in the case of the novel ideas of Praxeas and Marcion. When their new views surfaced in Carthage as if they were in spirit and intent apostolic, they were actively contested by Tertullian and Cyprian.

These arguments were presented on historical grounds using historical evidence. Virtually all African teachers, excepting those who were blatantly nonconsensual, appealed to apostolic continuity by linear succession. These arguments were most notably stated by the most presbyterial of all early theologians, Tertullian and Jerome. They did not fall into this habit by listening to the later heretics that distorted the gospel. They learned it earlier from the apostles themselves. By this method they effectively resisted nonconsensual ideas of faith. This is why it was self-evidently necessary for Demetrius, when he was elected bishop of Alexandria in A.D. 189, to reestablish the same apostolic identity that his predecessors had guaranteed, just as others had done in Rome and Jerusalem and Antioch. On the African continent the earliest appeal was consistently linked with Mark. The goal was not to consolidate worldly political power. These were citizens of heaven who did not look finally to worldly power. Rather it was based on exegetical, liturgical and theological forms of historical reasoning, which many modern theologians have such a hard time understanding or crediting. This is what has temporarily immobilized recent theology in its accommodation to modern consciousness.

The reason for this apostolic appeal was this: the truth was revealed in an event, and the testimony to the event was the historical testimony of eyewitnesses. Classically, there are four marks of the church: it is one, holy, catholic and apostolic. If apostolicity is not there, the church's catholicity is questionable. Thus when a doctrine is under challenge, the African church has always shown that its teaching comes from the apostles not some source later than the apostles. For Africans this apostolic confidence derives in particular from the first of the African apostles, Africa's own John Mark. This was the intentional classic Christian method of showing the catholicity and apostolicity of Christian communities: by historical means—a succession of credible leaders willing to put their lives on the line to embody the truth they were teaching. Many were put to death.

Believers have a view of salvation history based on definite historical events. They are actual occurrences such as exodus, captivity, crucifixion and resurrection. If so, believers must be prepared to make fair historical judgments about its proper transmission through changing history. If the faithful lose their personal and historical grounding in the incarnation, crucifixion and resurrection, they misplace the historical nature of these events.[9] The truth is remembered through a history, the event of God's personal coming, born in time as the Son of God, the Word made flesh. This is the crucial fact that I could never have learned from Bultmann, as much as I studied him: The truth is embodied in a person with a real history that awakens the remembering community, not a remembering community that invents a history.

From the outset it has been necessary to demonstrate pastoral authori-

---

[9]For recent African discussions of these doctrines and points of theology, see works in the bibliography by Kwame Bediako, Bénézet Bujo, Kwesi Dickson, Byang Kato, John Mbiti, Takatso Mofokeng, J. N. K Mugambi, James Nkansah-Obrempong, John Pobee, Lamin Sanneh and Josiah Ulysses Young.

zation by teaching that unique faith taught by the apostles. This has been transmitted through time by the simple device of setting forth the succession of any given church's leaders from the apostles. This necessity grew deeper through the severe persecutions in Africa.[10] With each persecution the leadership was more determined to keep the succession intact. For this reason bishops and elders were the first to be tortured and killed, throughout the Severan persecution (202–206) and on to the Decian (249–251), through the Valerian, Galerian and to the Diocletian (303–311).

To establish the link between Mark and Athanasius and Frumentius, African Christianity relied on the same historical argument that the churches of Rome and Jerusalem and Antioch were developing about the same time as the church was being formed in Alexandria. African Orthodoxy relies on early lists of bishops who were consensually confirmed by laity and clergy in those locations. Their records were as carefully safeguarded and preserved as any documents in Christian history. The spiritual charisma of African Christianity could not have been borne out of phony witnesses or by those unfaithful to the original eyewitnesses or those unwilling to suffer for the truth. The leaders did not receive their legitimacy because they transmitted their own private views but the views of apostolic witnesses to the truth made known in history. It is this history that Mark was the first to report.

What remains clear is that the link with Mark was taken to be definitive for the identity of the church all over Africa. The authenticity of the African church looked to Mark to connect it directly with the earliest witnesses to the incarnate truth. The African church came to a firm conclusion quite early that the gist of the commonly held narrative of Mark in Africa was an entirely true historical version of real events. This awareness developed as resolutely in Africa as it did in Rome or Antioch.

---

[10]Davis, *Early Coptic Papacy*, pp. 21-42.

CONCLUSION

The most penetrating objection to the argument made in this book is that it requires too many hypotheticals to elicit a clear judgment. True, there are many factors that must come together in order to recognize this unique Gestalt. But that is the very nature of Gestalt-recognition. Thus in any court case involving circumstantial evidence, the task of argument is precisely to make all the elements plausible in such a way that the Gestalt can be grasped. The verdict sought is "not guilty." That means in this case that the African memory of Mark is not entirely false. There is not enough evidence against it to dismiss it as "a mere echo and a puff of smoke."[1] Unless there is compelling evidence to the contrary, it must be taken seriously (*REC*, 144; Davis, *Early Coptic Papacy*, 9).

To continue to neglect the African memory of Mark involves high costs:

- For Africans the price is an act of obliteration of memory, of blanking out from consciousness a major episode of African intellectual history that, if understood, would increase African self-esteem in a world that is inclined to demean it. For Africans to neglect Mark is analogous to European Christians forgetting Paul or Jews wondering who Jacob is.

[1]Walter Bauer, *Orthodoxy and Heresy in Earliest Christianity*, trans. Robert A. Kraft, Gerhard Kroedel et al. from the 2nd German ed. (Philadelphia: Fortress, 1971), p. 45.

- For Westerners the price is ignorance of a gift offered to the world from Africa: African Christianity as the seedbed of Western culture. Among the outpourings of this gift are the catechetical school of Alexandria, which nurtured the idea of a university and the vast contributions of Africa to the study of sacred texts.
- For global Christian believers the price is inattentiveness to (1) how providence provided a great soul for the early apostolic witness to Africa and (2) how Africa then became the source of great intellectual and spiritual wealth for the whole world. The price is the sacrifice of a saint whose sacrifices in Africa have shaped the entire Christian world. The price is the ignorance of the great gift of the beginning of Christianity on the one continent where Christian faith is growing exponentially and where today almost a half billion Christians live.
- For world peace, the cost is the intensification of the estrangement of Africa from the rest of the world.

The invention hypothesis posits the invention of a legend that is not based on historically verifiable fact. In the case of Mark it is the notion that the Alexandrian church needed an apostolic origin, and so the legend of Mark's martyrdom was invented. To those who insist on writing off all of the above patterns of evidence, I ask: What reasonable assumptions must you give up in order to do so? In order to pursue a consistently skeptical hypothesis against Mark in Africa historically, you have to play a very precarious game. The rules of the game go something like this:

Suppose that after Nicaea it became politically necessary to invent an apostolic authority for the church of Alexandria. By that time the church in Africa had already been living and dying for a dozen generations without any knowledge of an apostolic foundation. The next needed step, taken by Harnack and Bauer and company, is the hypothesis of a "creative act" of a falsely remembering community. By this means, the worshiping community is compelled to *invent* and perpetuate some story that is connected with some prestigious figure. So they chose Mark. Why Mark? It doesn't matter, since they made it up anyway. It is only fantasized as an event, according to the deception.

But this fantasy cannot explain why African believers were willing to die. They saw their own death as a refraction of what happened on the cross and in the lives of the martyr successors of Mark. The invention theory is made all the more implausible when we recall that the supposed invention of this myth of Mark would have had to occur extremely early, at least by the time of Clement (A.D. 190–215) and Peter of Alexandria (d. A.D. 311)—that is, well before the Council of Nicaea. Indeed given the further evidence I have set forth, it would have had to be well established before the liturgical recollection of Mark's martyrdom, death, burial and his consensual reception in Africa as a saint.

Even then the inventors would have a hard time finding a way to gain wide acceptance in Africa, much less ecumenical reception. How could such a flimsy invention be swallowed by serious African believers who by the time of Nicaea had already lived through a long history of brutal persecutions? They worshiped in the oratories of Mark's history. This invented premise is doubly implausible if you imagine that the manufacture of this fantasy would have had to await the writings of Eusebius—after the early 300s to be expressed clearly. Then it would have to be later analyzed by historical scholars not noted for their willingness to die for their convictions.

On the other hand, the events that must be plausibly established with reasonable historical certainty to counter this invention hypothesis are rather few in number:

- that Mark was once buried where he is consensually said to have been buried
- that there exists a paper trail of evidences of a sustained tradition following Mark in one city only—Alexandria
- that martyr memories would be hard to invent after the fact

If skeptics are determined to narrow down authentic Christianity only to that which can be indisputably proven by restrictive modern methods of assessing evidence, whom do they finally have as an audience? Well, first of all, not the church in Africa. Their largest potential audience is a tiny cluster of professional academics in the modern secular university.

The African memory of Mark's martyrdom was already firmly fixed in the mind and memory of the second and third centuries in reference to events that occurred in the first century. My purpose in this book has been to show the greater plausibility of the African memory of Mark than of its modern mythic alternatives. I have presented evidences and primary sources to challenge this modern myth. These include not only New Testament references but many second-century evidences from Papias, Irenaeus, Origen and Clement, and from there on to the fourth-century evidences from Eusebius, Chrysostom and Jerome. Far from being poisoned fonts of unreliable testimony, these are among the greatest minds of the earliest Christian centuries. They were reporting what they assumed had long before them been previously received from the "earliest presbyters" and the most ancient apostolic tradition. Africans have a right to retrieve what modern historicism has taken captive.

Treating as myth two thousand years of testimony is bad historical method. It displays moral callousness toward those who suffered torture and death on behalf of their conviction based on the truth they proclaimed. The invention hypothesis puts in bold display the temptations of the hermeneutics of suspicion. Such suspicion is today giving way to a greater respect for the stories of the saints. More readers are coming to realize that the church in Africa was founded on the blood of the martyrs after the pattern of Mark the apostle who was willing to die for the truth.

SELECT BIBLIOGRAPHY

To the Reader: The body of literature on Mark and that on African identity are each massive. I have selected those few that ordinary readers might wish to pursue and those that scholars of Mark would desire or need to know.

Abdel-Sayed, Edris. *Les Coptes d'Egypte: les premiers Chrétiens du Nil.* Paris: Publisud, 1992.

Abun-Nasr, Jamil. *A History of the Maghrib.* Cambridge: Cambridge University Press, 1971.

"Acts of Mark." In *Acta Apostolorum Apocrypha,* 2:431-53. Edited by R. A. Lipsius and M. Bonnet. 3 vols. 1891–1903. Reprint, Darmstadt: Wissenschaftliche Buchgesellschaft, 1959.

Adeyemo, Tokunboh. *Salvation in the African Tradition.* 2nd ed. Nairobi: Evangel, 1997.

Ameen, Hakim. "St. Mark in Africa." In *St. Mark and the Coptic Church.* Cairo: Coptic Orthodox Patiarchate, 1968.

Athanasius. *The Letters of Saint Athanasius Concerning the Holy Spirit.* Translated by C. R. B. Shapland. New York: The Philosophical Library, 1951.

Atiya, Aziz S. *A History of Eastern Christianity.* London: Methuen, 1968.

———, ed. *The Coptic Encyclopedia.* 8 vols. New York: Maxwell Macmillan International, 1991.

Badawy, Alexander. *Coptic Art and Archaeology: The Art of Christian Egyptians from the Late Antique to the Middle Ages.* Cambridge, Mass.: MIT Press, 1978.

Bagnall, Roger S. "Archaeological Work on Hellenistic and Roman Egypt, 1995–2000." *American Journal of Archaeology* 105 (2001): 227-43.

———. *Egypt in Late Antiquity.* Princeton: Princeton University Press, 1993.

———, and Dominic W. Rathbone. *Egypt from Alexander to the Copts—An Ar-*

chaeological and Historical Guide. London: The British Museum Press, 2004.

Barnard, L. W. "St. Mark and Alexandria." *Harvard Theological Review* 57 (1964): 145-50.

Basset, René M. J., ed. *Le synaxaire arabe jacobite (rédaction Copte). Texte arabe publié, traduit et annoté par R. Basset.* 6 vols. Patrologia Orientalis 1 (1907): 215-379; 3 (1909): 243-545; 11 (1915) 505-859; 16 (1922): 185-424; 17 (1923): 525-782; 20 (1929): 735-89.

Bauer, Walter. *Orthodoxy and Heresy in Earliest Christianity.* ET 1971. Reprint ed., Mifflintown, Penn.: Sigler Press, 1996.

Baumeister, Theofried. *Martyr invictus, der Martyrer als Sinnbild der Erlösung in der Legende und im Kult der frühen koptischen Kirche: Zur Kontinuität des ägyptischen Denkens.* Forschungen zur Volkskunde 46. Münster: Regensberg, 1972.

Bediako, Kwame. *Christianity in Africa: The Renewal of a Non-Western Religion.* Edinburgh: Edinburgh University Press, 1995.

———. *Theology and Identity: The Impact of Culture upon Christian Thought in the Second Century and in Modern Africa.* Oxford: Regnum, 1992.

Bell, H. I. *Jews and Christians in Egypt.* London: Oxford University Press, 1924.

Ben-Jochannan, Yosef, et al. *The Afrikan Origins of the Major World Religions.* Edited by Amon Saba Saakana. 2nd ed. London: Karnak House, 1991.

Best, Ernest E. *Mark: The Gospel as Story.* Rev. ed. Edinburgh: T & T Clark, 2000.

Boochs, Wolfgang, ed. *Geschichte und Geist der koptischen Kirche.* Langwaden: Bernardus-Verlag, 2004.

Bowers, Paul. "Nubian Christianity: The Neglected Heritage." *Africa Journal of Evangelical Theology* 4, no. 1 (1985): 3-23.

Boyd, Paul C. *The African Origin of Christianity,* Vol. 1: *A Biblical and Historical Account.* London: Karis Press, 1991.

Brightman, Frank E. *Liturgies Eastern and Western,* Vol 1: *Eastern Liturgies.* Oxford: Clarendon Press, 1896.

Brown, Peter. *The Cult of the Saints.* Chicago: University of Chicago Press, 1981.

Bruce, F. F. *The Acts of the Apostles.* Grand Rapids: Eerdmans, 1968.

Budge, E. A. Wallis. *The Book of the Saints of the Ethiopian Church: A Translation of the Ethiopic Synaxarium.* 4 vols. Cambridge: Cambridge University Press, 1928.

———. *Coptic Texts.* 5 vols. 1910–1914. Reprint, New York: AMS Press, 1977.

Bujo, Bénézet. *Foundations of an African Ethic: Beyond the Universal Claims of Western Morality.* New York: Crossroads, 2003.

Burmester, O. H. E. (Khs-). *The Egyptian or Coptic Church: A Detailed Description of Her Liturgical Services and the Rites and Ceremonies Observed in the Administration of Her Sacraments.* Cairo: Société d'archéologie copte, 1967.

———. "On the Date and Authorship of the Arabic Synaxarium of the Coptic Church." *Journal of Theological Studies* 39 (1938): 249-53.

Burton-Christie, Douglas. *The Word in the Desert: Scripture and the Quest for Holiness in Early Christian Monasticism.* New York and Oxford: Oxford University Press, 1993.

Callahan, Allen Dwight. "The Acts of Mark: Tradition, Transmission, and Translation of the Arabic Version." In *The Apocryphal Acts of the Apostles: Harvard Divinity School Studies*, edited by François Bovon et al., pp. 62-85. Cambridge Mass.: Harvard University Center for the Study of World Religions, 1999.

———. "The Acts of Saint Mark: An Introduction and Translation." *Coptic Church Review* 14 (1993): 2-10.

Cannuyer, Christian. *Coptic Egypt: The Christians of the Nile.* Discoveries. New York: Harry N. Abrams, 2001.

Chadwick, Henry. *Early Christian Thought and the Classical Tradition: Studies in Justin, Clement, and Origen* (New York: Oxford University Press, 1966).

———, ed. *Alexandrian Christianity.* Philadelphia: Westminster Press, 1954.

Cheneau, Paul. *Les Saints d'Egypte.* 2 vols. Jerusalem: Couvente des RR. PP. Franciscains, 1923.

Conte, Ronald L., Jr. "The Martyrdoms of James and Mark." BiblicalChronology.com,

Conzelmann, Hans. *Acts of the Apostles.* Hermeneia. Philadelphia: Fortress Press, 1987.

Coptic Synaxarium. 4 vols. Hinsdale, Ill.: St. Mark and St. Bishoy Coptic Orthodox Church, and Chicago: St. George Coptic Orthodox Church, 1987–1992.

Cox, James L., and Gerrie ter Haar, eds. *Uniquely African? African Christian Identity from Cultural and Historical Perspectives.* Trenton, N.J.: Africa World Press, 2003.

Coxe, Arthur Clevland, trans. *Fathers of the Second Century: Hermas, Tatian, Athenagoras, Theophilus, and Clement of Alexandria.* ANF 2. Reprint, Peabody, Mass.: Hendrickson, 1999.

Crouzel, Henri. *Origen.* Translated by A. S. Worrall. San Francisco: Harper and Row, 1989.

Crum, W. E. *Eusebius and Coptic Church Histories.* London: Harisson and Sons, 1902. See *Proceedings of the Society of Biblical Archaeology* 24 (1902): 68-84.

Cyril of Alexandria. *On the Unity of Christ.* Translated by John A. McGuckin. Crestwood, N.Y.: St. Vladimir's Seminary Press, 1995.

Davis, Stephen J. *The Early Coptic Papacy: The Egyptian Church and Its Leadership in Late Antiquity.* New York and Cairo: American University in Cairo Press, 2004.

Delehaye, Hippolyte. "Les martyrs d'Egypte." *Analecta Bollandiana* 40 (1922): 5-154; 299-364.

Denzinger, Heinrich. *Ritus Orientalium: Coptorum, Syrorum et Armenorum, in administrandis sacramentis.* 1863–64. 2 vols. in one. Reprint, Graz, Austria: Akademische Druck- u. Verlagsanstalt, 1961.

Di Berardino, Angelo, and Basil Studer, eds. *History of Theology,* Vol. 1: *The Patristic Period.* Translated by Matthew J. O'Connell. Collegeville, Minn.: Liturgical Press, 1996.

Dickson, Kwesi. *Theology in Africa.* Maryknoll, N.Y.: Orbis, 1984.

Dionysius of Alexandria. *Letters and Treatises.* Translated by C. L. Feltoe. Translations of Christian Literature. Series 1. New York: Macmillan, 1918.

Donahue, John R., and Daniel J. Harrington. *The Gospel of Mark.* Sacra Pagina 2. Collegeville, Minn.: Liturgical Press, 2002.

Ehrman, Bart D. *Lost Christianities: The Battles for Scripture and the Faiths We Never Knew.* New York: Oxford University Press, 2003.

Ela, Jean-Marc. *My Faith as an African.* Translated by John Pairman Brown and Susan Perry. Maryknoll, N.Y: Orbis, 1986.

Elliott, J. K., ed. *The Apocryphal Jesus: Legends of the Early Church.* New York: Oxford University Press, 1996.

Farag, Farag Rofail. "A Comparison of Sawirus Ibn al-Muqaffa's Literary Technique in His Two Works, the *History of the Patriarchs* and the *Book of the Councils* 1 & 2." *Annual of the Leeds University Oriental Society* 7 (1969–1973): 50-53.

———. "The Technique of Research of a Tenth-Century Christian Arab Writer: Sawirus Ibn al-Muqaffa." *Le Muséon* 86 (1973): 37-66.

Fitzmyer, Joseph A. *The Acts of the Apostles*. Anchor Bible 31. New York: Doubleday, 1998.

Forget, Jacobus. *Synaxarium Alexandrinum*. 2 vols. in 6. Corpus Scriptorum Christianorum Orientalium, vols. 47-49, 67, 78, 90. Louvain: Peeters, 1905–32.

Frankfurter, David, ed. *Pilgrimage and Holy Space in Late Antique Egypt*. Leiden: Brill, 1998.

Frend, W. H. C. *Martyrdom and Persecution in the Early Church*. London: Blackwell, 1965.

Galván, María Elena González, and Filipe Miguel Oliveira Resende. *An African Journey Through Mark's Gospel*. Nairobi: Paulines Publications Africa, 2000.

Gerhards, Albert, and Heinzgerd Brakmann, eds. *Die koptische Kirche: Einführung in das ägyptische Christentum*. Stuttgart: Kohlhammer, 1994.

Girgis, Samir Fawzy. *A Chronology of Saint Mark*. Cairo: St. John the Beloved Publishing House, 2002.

Goehring, James E. *Ascetics, Society, and the Desert: Studies in Early Egyptian Monasticism*. Studies in Antiquity and Christianity. Harrisburg, Penn.: Trinity Press International, 1999.

———, and Janet A. Timbie, eds. *The World of Early Egyptian Christianity: Language, Literature, and Social Context*. CUA Studies in Early Christianity. Washington, D.C.: Catholic University of America Press, 2007.

Grant, Robert M. *Eusebius as Church Historian*. Oxford: Clarendon Press, 1980.

Griggs, C. Wilfred. *Early Egyptian Christianity from its Origins to 451 C.E.* Leiden: Brill, 1993.

Grillmeier, Aloys, with Theresia Hainthaler. *Christ in Christian Tradition*, Vol. 2, *From the Council of Chalcedon (451) to Gregory the Great (590–604)*, Part Four, *The Church of Alexandria with Nubia and Ethiopia After 451*. Translated by O. C. Dean. Louisville, Ky.: Westminster John Knox, 1996.

Grossmann, Peter. *Christliche Architektur in Ägypten*. Erste Abteilung: Nahe und der Mittlere Osten. Handbuch der Orientalistik 62. Leiden: Brill, 2002.

Groves, C. P. *The Planting of Christianity in Africa*. 4 vols. London: Lutterworth, 1948–58.

Habashi, Youssef. *Dalil al-Sinaksar al-Kubti*. Cairo: n.p., 1894.

Habib, Rauf. *The Ancient Coptic Churches of Cairo*. Cairo: Mahabba Bookshop, 1979.

Haile, Getatchew. "A New Ethiopic Version of the Acts of St. Mark" *Analecta Bollandiana* 99 (1981): 117-34.

Hanna, Fr. M. *The Coptic Offices for the Coptic Orthodox Church*. 1st edition, 1984. Coptic-Arabic-English. 2nd edition in 4 volumes. Los Angeles: n.p, 1991-96.

Hansberry, William Leo, and E. Harper Johnson. "Africa's Golden Past, Part 2: Historical Facts Challenge Notion That Christianity Is the Religion of the West." *Ebony*, January 1965, 86-92.

Hardy, E. R. *Christian Egypt, Church and People*. New York: Oxford University Press, 1952.

Harnack, Adolf von. *The Mission and Expansion of Christianity in the First Three Centuries*. 2 vols. New York: G. P. Putnam, 1908.

Hass, Christopher. *Alexandria in Late Antiquity*. Baltimore: Johns Hopkins University Press, 1997.

Hastings, Adrian. *African Christianity: An Essay in Interpretation*. London: Geoffrey Chapman, 1976.

Haubai, P. "The Legend of St. Mark: Coptic Fragments." *Studia Aegyptica* 12. Budapest: University of Budapest, 1989.

Heijer, Johannes den. "History of the Patriarchs of Alexandria." In *Coptic Encyclopedia*, edited by Aziz S. Atiya, 4:1238-41. 8 vols. New York: Maxwell Macmillan International, 1991.

———. "Mawhub ibn Mansur ibn Mufarrig et l'histoire des patriarches d'Alexandrie: notes sur une étude en cours." In *Actes du deuxième Congrès international d'études arabes chrétiennes*, edited by Khalil Samir. Orientalia Christiana Analecta 226. Rome: Pont. Institutum Studiorum Orientalium, 1986.

———. *Mawhub ibn Mansur ibn Mufarrig et l'historiographie copte-arabe: étude sur la composition de l'Histoire des Patriarches d'Alexandrie*. Louvain: Peeters, 1989.

———. "Sawirus Ibn al-Muqaffa', Mawhub ibn Mansur ibn Mufarrig et la genèse de l'Histoire des Patriarches d'Alexandrie." *Bibliotheca Orientalis* 41 (1984): 336-47.

Heisey, Nancy R. *Origen, the Egyptian: A Literary and Historical Consideration of the Egyptian Background in Origen's Writings on Martyrdom*. Nairobi, Kenya: Paulines Publications Africa, 2000.

Hoek, Annewies van den. "The 'Catechetical' School of Early Christian Alexandria and Its Philonic Heritage." *Harvard Theological Review* 90, no. 1 (1997): 59-87.

Holmes, B. T. "Luke's Description of John Mark." *Journal of Biblical Literature* 54 (1968): 63-72.

Jackson, John Glover. *The African Origin of Christianity*. Chicago: L. & P., 1981.

Johnson, David W. *Coptic Sources of the History of the Patriarchs of Alexandria*. Ph.D. diss., The Catholic University of America. Washington, D.C., 1973.

———. "Further Remarks on the Arabic History of the Patriarchs of Alexandria." *Oriens Christianus* 61 (1977): 103-16.

Johnson, John H. *The Black Biblical Heritage: Four Thousand Years of Black Biblical History*. Rev. ed. Nashville: Winston-Derek, 1993.

Kalu, Ogbu U., ed. *African Christianity: An African Story*. Perspectives on Christianity 5.3. Pretoria: Department of Church History, University of Pretoria, 2005.

Kamil, Jill, *Christianity in the Land of the Pharaohs: The Coptic Orthodox Church*. New York: Routledge, 2002.

Kamil, Murad. *Coptic Egypt*. Cairo: Scribe Egyptien, 1968.

Kamil, Saleh Nakla. *Tarikh Al Qidis, Mar Morqos-al-Bashir* [History of St. Mark the Evangelist]. Cairo: n.p., 1952.

Kammerer, Winifred. *A Coptic Bibliography*. Ann Arbor: University of Michigan Press, 1950.

Kannengiesser, Charles. *Handbook of Patristic Exegesis: The Bible in Ancient Christianity*. 2 vols. Boston: Brill, 2004.

Kato, Byang H. *Theological Pitfalls in Africa*. Kisumi, Kenya: Evangel, 1975.

Kirwen, Michael C. *African Cultural Knowledge: Themes and Embedded Beliefs*. Nairobi: Maryknoll Institute of African Studies, 2005.

Krause, Martin, ed. *Ägypten in spätantik-christlicher Zeit. Einführung in die koptische Kultur.* Wiesbaden: L. Riechert, 1998.

Layton, Richard A. *Didymus the Blind and His Circle in Late-Antique Alexandria: Virtue and Narrative in Biblical Scholarship*. Urbana.: University of Illinois Press, 2004.

Le Quien, Michel, et al., ed. *Oriens Christianus, in quatuor patriarchatus digestus; quo exhibentur ecclesiae, patriarchae, caeterique praesules totius Orientis*. 3 vols. Paris: Ex Typographia Regia., 1740.

Lee, G. M. "Eusebius on St. Mark." In *Studia Patristica* 12:425-27. Texte und Untersuchungen zur Geschichte der altchristlichen Literatur 115. Berlin: Akademie-Verlag, 1973.

Lemm, Oscar von, "Koptische apokryphe Apostelacten." *Bulletin de l'Académie impériale des sciences de St. Pétersbourg* 1 (1890): 509–57.

Lilla, Salvatore R. C. *Clement of Alexandria: A Study in Christian Platonism and Gnosticism.* Oxford: Oxford University Press, 1971.

The Lives of the Holy Apostles. Translated by Isaac E. Lambertsen and Holy Apostles Convent. Buena Vista, Colo.: Holy Apostles Convent, 1988.

Lubac, Henri de. *Medieval Exegesis: The Four Senses of Scripture.* 3 vols. Translated by Mark Sebanc et al. Grand Rapids: Eerdmans, 1998–2009.

Magesa, Laurenti. *Anatomy of Inculturation: Transforming the Church in Africa.* Nairobi: Paulines Africa, 2004.

Majawa, Clement Chinkambako Abenguni. *Integrated Approach to African Christian Theology of Inculturation.* Nairobi: Creations Enterprises, 2005.

Malaty, Fr. Tadros Y. *The Gospel According to St. Mark.* Translated by George Botros. Revised by Samy Anis and Dr. Nora El-Agamy. Orange, Calif.: Coptic Orthodox Christian Center, 2003.

———. *Introduction to the Coptic Orthodox Church.* Revised by Samy Anis and Dr. Nora El-Agamy. Alexandria: St. Mark's Coptic Orthodox Church, 1996.

———. *The School of Alexandria.* 2 vols. Jersey City, N.J.: St. Mark's Coptic Orthodox Church, 1995.

Manus, Ukachukwu Chris. *Christ, the African King: New Testament Christology.* Frankfurt-am-Main, Germany: Peter Lang, 1993.

Mana, Kä. *Christians and Churches of Africa: Envisioning the Future: Salvation in Jesus Christ and the Building of a New African Society.* Theological Reflections from the South. Akropong-Akuapem, Ghana: Regnum Africa, 2002; Maryknoll, N.Y: Orbis, 2004.

Martin, M. M. "Une Lecture de l'Histoire des Patriarches d'Alexandrie." *Proche Orient Chrétien* 35 (1985): 15-36.

Margerie, Bertrand de. *An Introduction to the History of Exegesis.* 3 vols. Petersham, Mass.: St. Bede's, 1991–1995.

"Martyrdom of Mark the Evangelist." In *Theological Texts from Coptic Papyri*, edited by W. E. Crum. Anecdota Oxoniensia. Semitic series 12. Oxford: Clarendon Press, 1913.

"The Martyrdom of Saint Mark the Evangelist in Alexandria." In *The Con-*

tendings of the Apostles, Being the Histories of the Lives and Martyrdoms and Deaths of the Twelve Apostle and Evangelists; The Ethiopic Texts Now First Edited from Manuscripts in the British Museum, with an English Translation, 2:309-18. Edited and translated by E. A. Wallis Budge. 2 vols. London: Henry Frowde, 1899–1901.

"*Martyrium Marci.*" In *New Testament Apocrypha,* edited by W. Schneemelcher, 2:461-464. Translated by R. McL. Wilson. 6th ed. Louisville: Westminster/John Knox Press, 1989.

Martyrium Marci. Coptic Manuscripts 9450, 9439. Vienna Austria National Library. Vienna, Austria.

———. Variously *The Martyrdom of Mark* or *Acts of Mark* or *Passio Marci.* PG 115: 163-170; cf. *Acta Sanctorum* 9:344-49.

"Martyrologium Romanum" (April 25 Calendar); cf. *Acta Sanctorum,* 9:344-349.

Masri, Iris Habib el-. *The Story of the Copts.* Cairo: Middle East Council of Churches, 1978.

Mbiti, John S. *Bible and Theology in African Christianity.* Nairobi: Oxford University Press, 1986.

McCray, Walter Arthur. *The Black Presence in the Bible: Discovering the Black and African Identity of Biblical Persons and Nations.* Chicago: Black Light Fellowship, 1990.

McGuckin, John A., trans. *On the Unity of Christ* by Cyril of Alexandria. Crestwood, N.Y.: St. Vladimir's Seminary Press, 1995.

McKenzie, Judith. *The Architecture of Alexandria and Egypt, 300 B.C. to A.D. 700.* New Haven, Conn.: Yale University Press, 2007.

———. "Glimpsing Alexandria from Archaeological Evidence." *Journal of Roman Archaeology* 106 (2003): 35-61.

Meinardus, Otto F. A. *Two Thousand Years of Coptic Christianity.* Cairo: American University of Cairo Press, 1999.

Mofokeng, Takatso Alfred. *The Crucified Among the Crossbearers: Towards a Black Christology.* Kampen: Kok, 1983.

Momigliano, Arnaldo, ed. *The Conflict Between Paganism and Christianity in the Fourth Century.* Oxford: Clarendon Press, 1963.

Mudimbe, V. Y. *The Idea of Africa.* Bloomington: Indiana University Press, 1994.

Mugambi, J. N. K. *The African Heritage and Contemporary Christianity.* Nairobi: Longman Kenya, 1989.

Neale, John Mason. *The Patriarchate of Alexandria.* 2 vols. London: Joseph Masters, 1847.

Nicoliello, Dominic A. *Our Ancestors in the Faith.* Nairobi: Paulines Publications Africa, 1995.

Nkansah-Obrempong, James. "The Contemporary Theological Situation in Africa: An Overview." *Evangelical Review of Theology* 31, no. 2 (2007): 140-49

Noshy, Ibrahim. *The Coptic Church: Christianity in Egypt.* Washington, D.C.: Coptic Diocese, 1955.

Nyamiti, Charles. *Christ Our Ancestor: Christology from an African Perspective.* Mambo Occasional Papers. Missio Pastoral 11. Gweru, Zimbabwe: Mambo, 1984.

Oden, Thomas C. *How African Shaped the Christian Mind.* Downers Grove, Ill.: InterVarsity Press, 2008.

———, and Christopher A. Hall, eds. Ancient Christian Commentary on Scripture. 29 vols. Downers Grove, Ill.: InterVarsity Press, 1998–2010.

O'Leary, De Lacy. *The Saints of Egypt in the Coptic Calendar.* New York: SPCK, 1937.

Orlandi, Tito. "Hagiography." In *Coptic Encyclopedia,* 4:1191-97, edited by Aziz S. Atiya. 8 vols. New York: Maxwell Macmillan International, 1991.

———. "La patrologia copta." In *Complementi interdisciplinari di patrologia,* edited by Antonio Quacquarelli, pp. 457-502. Rome: Città Nuova, 1989.

———, ed. *Storia della Chiesa di Alessandria.* Testo copto, traduzione [latina] e commento di Tito Orlandi. 2 vols. Testi e documenti per lo studio dell' Antichità 17, 31. Milan and Varese: Editoriale Cisalpino, 1968–1970.

Osborn, Eric. *Clement of Alexandria* (Cambridge: Cambridge University Press, 2005).

Oshitelu, G. A. *The African Fathers of the Early Church.* Ibadan, Nigeria: Sefer, 2002.

Partrick, Theodore Hall. *Traditional Egyptian Christianity: A History of the Coptic Orthodox Church.* Greensboro, N.C.: Fisher Park Press, 1996.

"Passio S. Petri" [The Martyrdom of Peter of Alexandria]. In *Passions des saints Ecaterine et Pierre d'Alexandrie, Barbara et Anysia.* Edited by Joseph-Eugène Viteau. Paris: Boullion, 1897. See below, Tim Vivian, for an English translation.

Pearson, Birger A. *Gnosticism and Christianity in Roman and Coptic Egypt.*

Studies in Antiquity and Christianity. New York: T & T Clark, 2004.

———. *Gnosticism, Judaism, and Egyptian Christianity.* Philadelphia: Fortress Press, 1990.

———, and James E. Goehring, eds. *The Roots of Egyptian Christianity.* Studies in Antiquity and Christianity. Minneapolis: Fortress Press, 1986.

Pericoli-Ridolfini, F. "Le origini della Chiesa d'Allesandia d'Egitto" *Accademia Nazionale del Lincci* 1, no. 17 (1962): 317-33.

Pobee, John S. *Toward an African Theology.* Nashville: Abingdon, 1979.

Riad, Henri, Youssef Hanna Shehatta and Youssef al-Gheriani. *Alexandria: An Archeological Guide to the City.* 2nd ed. Alexandria: Regional Authority for Tourism, 1996.

Riad, Zaher. *The Church of Alexandria in Africa.* Cairo: Coptic Orthodox Patriarchate, 1962.

———. *The Doctrine of St. Mark in Africa.* Cairo: Coptic Orthodox Patriarchate, 1968.

Roberts, C. H. *Manuscript, Society and Belief in Early Christian Egypt.* Oxford: Oxford University Press, 1977.

Robinson, James M., ed. *The Nag Hammadi Library in English.* 4th rev. ed. Leiden: Brill, 1996.

Russell, Norman. *Cyril of Alexandria.* New York: Routledge, 2000.

Samuel, Bishop Habib Badie. *Ancient Coptic Churches and Monasteries in the Delta, Sinai, and Cairo.* Cairo: Institute of Coptic Studies, Amba Reweis Abbasiya, 1996.

Sanneh, Lamin. *Translating the Message: The Missionary Impact on Culture.* 2nd ed. Maryknoll, N.Y.: Orbis, 2009.

———. *Whose Religion Is Christianity? The Gospel Beyond the West.* Grand Rapids: Eerdmans, 2003.

———, and Joel A. Carpenter, eds. *The Changing Face of Christianity: Africa, the West, and the World.* New York: Oxford University Press, 2005.

Sawirus Ibn al-Mukaffa'. *History of the Patriarchs of the Egyptian Church.* Vol. 2, Part 1. Edited, translated and annotated by Yassa 'Abd al-Masih and O. H. E. (Khs-) Burmester. Cairo: Le Caire, 1943.

———. Sévère ibn el Mokaffée. *Homélie sur Saint Marc, apôtre et évangéliste. Texte arabe et traduction et notes.* Translated by J.-J. L. Bargès. 1877. Reprint, Paris, 1952.

———. *History of the Patriarchs of the Coptic Church of Alexandria.* Patrologia Orientalis 1:101-24 and 381-518. Arabic text edited and translated by

B. T. Evetts. Paris: Firmin-Didot, 1906, 1948; Cairo: Society of Coptic Archeology, 1943–59.

Schenkel, Wolfgang. *Kultmythos und Märtyrerlegende: Zur Kontinuität des ägyptischen Denkens.* Göttinger Orientforschungen 4.5. Wiesbaden: Harrassowitz, 1977.

Scobie, Edward. "African Popes." In *African Presence in Early Europe,* edited by Ivan Van Sertima, pp. 96-107. New Brunswick: Transaction Books, 1985.

Selwyn, E. G. *The First Epistle of Peter.* London: Macmillan, 1964.

Senghor, Léopold Sédar. *Liberté,* Vol. 3, *Négritude et civilisation de l'nniversel.* Paris: Éditions du Seuil 1977. Cf. idem, "Negritude and the Civilization of the Universal" in *African Presence in the Americas,* edited by Carlos Moore, pp. 21-32. Trenton, N.J.: Africa World Press, 1995.

Shaw, Mark. *The Kingdom of God in Africa: A Short History of African Christianity.* Grand Rapids: Baker, 1996.

Shenouda III, H. H. Pope. *Beholder of God: Mark the Evangelist: Saint and Martyr,* trans. Samir F. Mikhail and Maged S. Mikhail from the 4th ed. Santa Monica, Calif.: St. Peter and St. Paul Coptic Orthodox Church, 1995.

Simonetti, Manlio. *Biblical Interpretation in the Early Church: An Historical Introduction to Patristic Exegesis.* Edinburgh: T & T Clark, 1994.

Smith, Morton. *The Secret Gospel: The Discovery and Interpretation of the Secret Gospel According to Mark.* London: Victor Gollancz, 1974.

Sylvanus, Nina. "The Fabric of Africanity: Tracing the Global Threads of Authenticity." *Anthropological Theory* 7, no. 2 (2007): 201-16.

Telfer, W. "Episcopal Succession in Egypt." *Journal of Ecclesiastical History* 3 (1952): 1-13.

Thompson, Peter. "Negritude and a New Africa: An Update." *Research in African Literatures* 3, no. 4 (Winter 2002): 143-53.

Tiénou, Tite. *The Theological Task of the Church in Africa.* Achimota, Ghana: Africa Christian Press, 1990.

Tkaczow, Barbara. "Archaeological Sources for the Earliest Churches in Alexandria." In *Coptic Studies,* ed. W. Godlewski, pp. 431-436. Acts of the Third International Congress of Coptic Studies, Warsaw, 20–25 August 1984. Warsaw: PWN 1990.

———. *Topography of Ancient Alexandria (An Archaeological Map).* Travaux du Centre d'archéologie méditerranéenne de l'Académie polonaise de sciences

32. Warsaw: Zakład Archeologii Śródziemnomorskiej, Polskiej Akadmii Nauk, 1993.

Trevijano, R. "The Early Christian Church of Alexandria." In *Studia Patristica* 12:471-77. Texte und Untersuchungen zur Geschichte der altchristlichen Literatur 115. Berlin: Akademie-Verlag, 1973.

Verstraelen, Frans J. *History of Christianity in Africa in the Context of African History: A Comparative Assessment of Four Recent Historiographical Contributions*. Gweru, Zimbabwe: Mambo Press, 2002.

Vivian, Tim. *St. Peter of Alexandria, Bishop and Martyr*. Philadelphia: Fortress, 1988. Includes translation of "Life and Martyrdom of Peter of Alexandria."

White, L. Michael. *Building God's House in the Roman World: Architectural Adaptations Among Pagans, Jews, and Christians*. Baltimore: Johns Hopkins University Press, 1990.

Wilhite, David E. *Tertullian the African: An Anthropological Reading of Tertullian's Context and Identities*. New York: Walter de Gruyter, 2007.

Wilken, Robert Louis. *Judaism and the Early Christian Mind: A Study of Cyril of Alexandria's Exegesis and Theology*. New Haven, Conn.: Yale University Press, 1971.

Witherington, Ben, III. *The Gospel of Mark: A Socio-Rhetorical Commentary*. Grand Rapids: Eerdmans, 2001.

Wüstenfeld, H. F. *Al-Sinaksari; Synaxarium das ist Heiligen-Kalender der Coptischen Christen aus dem Arabischen Übersetzung*. Gotha, Germany: n.p., 1879.

Young, Francis M. *Biblical Exegesis and the Formation of Christian Culture*. Peabody, Mass.: Hendrickson, 1997.

Young, Josiah Ulysses, III. *A Pan-African Theology: Providence and the Legacies of the Ancestors*. Trenton, N.J.: Africa World Press, 1992.

Author Index

Subject Index

Scripture Index